Ready Set Life

Ready, Set, Life

A Story Of Redemption
And The Lessons Learned

James Gwinnett

For Freddie

Boring legal stuff
I, James Gwinnett, assert the moral right to be identified as the author of this book. All opinions, ill-considered or otherwise, expressed are mine*. Complain all you want, I'm sticking to 'em.

And some other stuff about all rights being reserved, and not reproducing any part of the book, blah, blah, blah.

* Unless I'm quoting someone else. Obviously.

Cover design
Mark Guatieri, Brand51 – www.brand51.co.uk

Photo credits
Front cover: George Bishop – www.ghbphotos.com
Back Cover: Leo Francis – www.leofrancis.co.uk

Contents

Introduction ……………………………………………... 1
1: Under The Influence ………………………………..12
2: The Ultimate Accolade …………………………….31
3: Knowing Thyself …………………………………...49
4: Changing Thyself …………………………………..66
5: Penny Was A Friend Of Mine …………………….83
6: A Journey Of A Thousand Miles ………………….96
7: What Are You Running From? ……………………110
8: Hitting The Wall …………………………………..128
9: Yes, Staff ………………………………………….. 146
10: Well, Why Not? ………………………………….. 162
11: Setting Up C.A.M.P.P. ……………………………174
12: Slipping Into Something More Uncomfortable ……..187
13: I Love Your Socks ………………………………..202
14: Finding the Funny ………………………………..221
15: Getting Busy Living ……………………………...243
16: King Of the Cotswolds …………………………..256
17: To Quit, Or Not To Quit …………………………265
18: One Steppe At A Time …………………………...276
19: The Eternal Student ……………………………...291
20: Performing At Your Peak ………………………..311
21: Finding Your Iceberg …………………………….327
22: And One More Thing ……………………………341
23: Ready, Freddie? ………………………………….353
Acknowledgements ………………………………….364
References…………………………………………….368

Introduction

Dee human world, eet's a mess.
- **Sebastian the Crab**

Take A Look Around was a single released at the turn of the 21st century by nu-metal rockers Limp Bizkit. It featured on their piss-takingly-titled third album, *Chocolate Starfish and the Hot Dog Flavored Water*, and also the soundtrack to the second film in the *Mission: Impossible* franchise, featuring Tom Cruise jumping off things.

If you're not a fan of the shouty, baggy trousers- and backwards cap-wearing bad boys, you're not alone; music franchise NME named nu-metal 'the worst genre of all time' and its critics range from … well everyone from every other genre. But the line 'Now I know why you wanna hate me,' wasn't Fred Durst complaining about people's disdain for the music (albeit not mine because I have to admit that the band's angry cursing, thrashing chords, slick drums grooves and DJ thrown in for good measure appealed to my surly teenagerishness).

No, Durst's reason for you wanting to hate him was

simply 'because hate is all the world has even seen lately.' If you do indeed take a look around, you'll see that he wasn't wrong when he also sang/rapped about 'all the tension in the world today'.

The use of a Disney quote is, however, arguably more relatable and, in a bid to appeal to a wider audience of readers than just nu-metal fans, of whom there are few–not forgetting my young son, Freddie, to whom this book is dedicated–*The Little Mermaid* is where we kicked things off.

Here's the rub, though. Sebastian, the Jamaican crab, crooned that dee human world was a mess in the late 80s and Fred Durst added his two cents' worth only a decade later. But if things were fucked then, imagine how bad they are now.

Actually, don't. It's early 2024 and you won't believe the sinister panoply of what has happened on this crazy rock we call Earth since I sat down to write this book, much of which is ongoing.

To paraphrase Charles Dickens, it really is the worst of times and to demonstrate my point, I'll give you some examples:

1. Thankfully, we're not exactly on the verge of World War 3 and complete and utter nuclear annihilation … yet. But it might not be as far off as we'd hope. Because, when the tyrannical dictator of the world's largest country fabricates claims of genocide in order to wage war against a neighbouring nation and embarks 'on a path of evil,' as the leader of the invaded country put it, and NATO is fearful of 'all out war' and the head of the British Army warns that civilians might need to fight the aforementioned

dictatorial power in a future war, well, you start fearing for your safety.

2. And when a psychopathic neonatal nurse, entrusted with the lives and welfare of young children in the intensive care unit of the Countess of Chester Hospital, is found guilty of murdering seven infants, through lethal insulin injections and physical assaults, and attempting to murder seven others in what was described by The Sunday Times as a 'litany of horror', you start fearing for your children's safety too. Lucy Letby was sentenced to 14 consecutive life sentences and will rot in jail, whilst hopefully being continually subjected to laundry room beatings à la *The Shawshank Redemption*– more on which later–at the hands of her fellow inmates. Though, quite frankly, that'll be letting her off too lightly. The mind boggles as to how a human being can be such a fucking monster.

Wow, nuclear war and the killing of infants; that's quite a start, isn't it? I promise you, though, this book isn't intended as a scaremongering exercise, entreating you to build underground bunkers and stock up on spam–the edible kind, not the kind you get in your email junk–so let's dial things down a bit. To the climate. You know, that relatively minor issue, compared to, well, nuclear war and the killing of infants. Because:

3. In what can only be described as an incomprehensible act of vandalism, the UK's most photographed tree, at Sycamore Gap, made famous in the 1991 film *Robin Hood: Prince of Thieves*, was set upon with a chainsaw and cut down in the middle of the night. Having visited the location two months

prior, after ceremonially watching Kevin Costner shoot flaming arrows and catapult himself over ramparts the night before, the tree—hundreds of years old, in a dramatic dip in Hadrian's Wall, with the majestic Northumberland countryside stretched out behind it—had an almost mystical beauty to it. It's not like tearing down historic statues of slave-traders, although I disagree with such actions, but that's probably for another time. Rather, in a world of mounting problems surrounding our climate, senseless destruction of nature has to be up there amongst the most sordid of crimes. No-one gained anything. We all lost something. In short, I hate humans.

4. And on the other side of the world, Japan is releasing a million metric tons of 'treated' radioactive water into the Pacific as part of its plans to decommission a nuclear power plant. Oh, and around 10 million tonnes of plastic enter our oceans each year. Sebastian was advocating for a 'life under the sea', but perhaps it's not that much 'better, down where it's wetter'.

Otherwise, 'identity' seems to be the buzzword of the 21st century. For 2.5 million years, humankind, in its various shapes and sizes, was either male or female. It wasn't a choice; it was biology. You were one or the other. There was no in between; there were no alternatives. It was simple. Now, not so much. It's far from simple and, seemingly, you *do* have a choice.

5. Take the example of Alan Baker, who isn't quite as much of a monster as Lucy Letby, but isn't far off, holding the questionable accolade of being the UK's

longest-serving transgender prisoner. He–and if you're offended because you think that calling *him* a man is 'misgendering' *him*, or some such woke bollocks, well, with respect, I suggest you bite me– served 30 years in prison for kidnap, torture and attempted murder, during which time he decided he wanted to be called Sarah. On his release he attended a Pride rally, where he encouraged people to punch women who don't agree that men who choose to be women are, in fact, women. You know, like *actual* women. With women bits. (Incidentally, Baker castrated himself with a razor blade one night in prison.) On being recalled to prison for breaking the terms of his parole, he defended his actions, saying, 'It wasn't my finest hour.' No shit, but I suppose it's an improvement on kidnap, torture and attempted murder. Anyway, fortunately the powers that be saw sense in the circumstances, reincarcerating him in a high-security *men's* prison.

Sense, though, is increasingly hard to come by. There's enough for another book on this subject alone, but a couple of internet nuggets jumped out at me in terms of making me want to hold my head in my hands in exasperation and exclaim, 'That's it. I give up. The world has officially gone mad.' Firstly:

6. Reports have circulated of children identifying as animals and meowing in school lessons instead of responding in English. If that wasn't bad enough, the kids that have a shred of common sense and want the Jellicles to stop being complete dickheads so they can actually learn something, have been reprimanded for questioning their classmates'

5

identity. Yep, you read that right; the teachers sided with the 'cats'. Force 'em to eat Whiskas and piss in a litter tray, is what I say. Then we'll see whether they *really* want to meow in class.

Utter nonsense, right? But this one really takes the biscuit:

7. There's a girl in the US who identifies as a dog. She (or *it*, I lose track) sleeps in a crate, eats dog food, has 'handlers' who take her on walks and does training for treats. And yet, an article on the Daily Star website[1]–you know, the really high-brow, reputable news source–recounts how all of this makes her feel 'more human' and that she describes herself as a 'digital creator'. So, aside from the fact that she is about as much a dog as I am a pineapple, she's admitting she's not a dog, isn't she? What's more worrying, though, is the credence being given to her nonsense, both by the site describing her as an 'online star' when 'fucking imbecile' would be more accurate, and the staggering 11,700 followers she has amassed on Instagram. On which note, if you're one of those followers, we can't be friends. But the most moronic part of all, the cherry on the top, if you will, is her name. Something that sounds vaguely canine-esque? Luna? Willow? Nope. It's Meow. Like I said, a fucking imbecile.

I find myself saying that word more and more regularly; 'imbecile'–along with 'moron' and 'prat', both of which are just offensive enough without being too offensive, but get your point across nicely when said with enough emphasis– to describe more and more people. And, though I'm sure many people will be taken by the next story's hint of cutesy-wootsy, 'imbecile' was my first thought when I read it:

8. A woman took a bobble from a hat to a local animal rescue centre because she thought it was a hedgehog. Yes, you read that right. Apparently, she'd cared for it by putting it in a box and trying to give it cat food, but 'it hadn't moved or even pooed all night'. Which allows me to say, 'No shit. Literally.' A volunteer said, 'Our hearts melted.' Fine, but I bet their eyes rolled as well.

So, that's the state of humanity and, whether you prefer the Limp Bizkit or Disney analogy, we collectively have a lot to answer for. In short, pretty much everything is fucked.

Not a great time to bring a child into the world, then.

***

Except, this is exactly the situation I find myself in.

Yet, it is with nothing short of pure excitement and indescribable joy that my wife Krista and I embark on the bafflingly complicated, eye-bloodyingly tiring, no doubt excruciatingly maddening and soul-destroying, but deeply fulfilling and life-affirming quest of raising a tiny human.

And we do so with the knowledge that we won't get it all right. Far from it. In fact, I have no doubt we'll mess things up constantly, flying by the seat of our pants as we undoubtedly rely almost entirely on parental instinct to claw our way through the little lad's formative years in a messy blur of excrement, piss and vomit, like an inebriated student after a trip to Brick Lane; 'parental instinct' being the phrase that parents have adopted to make themselves feel better about the fact they have no clue what they're doing.

This is despite all the reams of literature on the subject, some of which I actually read, believe it or not.

Indeed, in preparing (like all dads-to-be; in vain, obviously) to be a father, I picked up a copy of *Dummy*, by Matt Coyne. The 'parenting book for real people' hilariously relates—sometimes in graphic detail—the harsh realities of being a parent. Amid the perils of believing the tripe that seems to make up my social media feed, such as, in Coyne's words, 'perfect parents' spending 'their mornings weaving their children's clothes out of hemp and dandelions, their afternoon making rice pudding out of breast milk ... never unkempt, never tired, never frustrated and always fucking baking,'[2] Coyne gives a warts and all account of the first year of parenthood.

With that in mind, obviously all we can really hope for is that our good decisions outweigh the bad and that, with as much love and attention as we can muster, he—yes, I'm assigning him a gender already; deal with it, snowflakes—turns out to be a courteous young man, well-rounded and, above all, happy.

Krista will be the world's most amazing mother; it will come entirely naturally to her. But I have already started having those imposter syndrome-type thoughts of whether I'm cut out to be a dad and how I educate Freddie on what's going on in the world, help him navigate it, and, where necessary, protect him from it.

This got me thinking about my own experiences, the people I've met, conversations I've had, things I've heard, books I've read, podcasts I've listened to and more.

In between nappy changes, whilst sleep deprived on paternity leave—an extended paternity leave, thanks to the generosity of my employer; I'm not creative enough to thrash out an entire book out in two weeks ... on which note, the fact that men are afforded only two weeks statutory pat leave is an absolute joke. It's unfair on the men to have to go back to work and spend time away from their newborns and partners, and it's unfair on the women to have to shoulder raising a child all on their own after such a cruelly short time. Anyway, with the sleep deprivation, if any sentences are gibberish, you know why … sorry, where was I? Ah yes, between nappy changes, I started jotting some of those thoughts down.

Are they useful to a newborn? Absolutely not, obviously. Newborns have an even smaller brain capacity than Sloth from *The Goonies* and are too busy either crapping or crying, or a combination of the two, to worry about the state of humanity. And who knows what problems the world will face when Freddie is old enough to recognise them?

Maybe World War 3 will have finally happened and we'll be living in a post-apocalyptic dystopia, *Mad Max*-style, fighting for our lives in a radioactive wasteland that is bereft of natural resources.

Or maybe the polar ice caps will have finally melted and we'll be living in a flooded dystopia, *Waterworld*-style, fighting for our lives in a marine wasteland that is bereft of natural resources.

Or maybe the machines will have finally become self-aware and triggered a nuclear war to bring humankind to extinction, *The Terminator*-style, or started farming humans to harvest their bioelectricity, *The Matrix*-style, and the surviving resistance will be living in fear in a technological wasteland that is bereft of natural resources as they're hunted by cyborgs or sentinels.

Jeez, what is it with these futuristic films being so bleak?

In the meantime, maybe, just maybe, someone else (perhaps even you, dear reader) will find these ramblings useful.

A note though, a disclosure if you like. I'm not a CEO. I don't drive a supercharged Range Rover with a shotgun holder and a whisky cabinet in the back. I don't fly around in helicopters. I don't wear a bejewelled watch that weighs more than my head. I don't have a rags to riches tale of making my first million by the time I was 12 despite there being no food on the table in my formative years. I'm not even a millionaire and I can't promise you reading this book will make *you* a millionaire. To borrow from Chuck Palahnuik, which I'll do again in the next chapter, '[I am] not a beautiful and unique snowflake. [I am] the same decaying organic matter as everyone else.'[3]

Nor do I know everything; far from it.

But I do know a thing or two about a thing or two. Because I've done some shit, been through some shit, and otherwise made a shit load of shit decisions. Thankfully, I've learned some shit along the way.

The result is, as you may have guessed, a book; a book that is cynical about the state of the world, part advicey, part ranty, part cultural criticism, but also one that seeks to explore how we might make the best of things. It's part autobiographical, if you'll indulge me the slightly narcissistic endeavour of telling you about some of my life, but it also leans on the experiences and knowledge of an array of incredible interviewees, all of whom are experts in their fields, to get their insights into how we can survive life.

I speak to the founder of a charity, a classics teacher, a former heroin addict, a former special forces soldier, a psychological therapist, a personal trainer, a former England rugby sevens captain, a polar explorer, a life coach, a family therapist and more. We cover topics ranging from mental fitness to identity, Stoicism to Māori *mana*, psychology, philosophy, anthropology, adventure and a myriad of other weird and wonderful subjects. I make cultural references as broad as *Fight Club* and *Great Expectations*. I include practical suggestions to implement change. It's at times silly, at times sad, but at all times aimed at encouraging a mindset of positivity, despite everything going on around us.

It might even be called a 'self-help book'. Either way, if it's in any way useful, well, you're welcome.

Are you sitting comfortably? Then I'll begin.

Chapter 1:
Under The Influence

I want you to hit me as hard as you can.
- **Tyler Durden**

It's not appropriate for my newborn but he won't be reading this for probably 20 years, if at all, whereas you are, so bugger it ... if you're young and don't realise that *Fight Club* was a book before Brad Pitt sauntered around in a pink teapot dressing gown, showing off his flawless abs, put this book down and read that one first. If you must, watch the film instead; it's one of those rare films that does genuine justice to the book, probably on my 'top five favourite films' list. Actually, do both, they're epic. Then come back and resume this book.

Chuck Palahnuik's exploration of the darker sides of the human mind, and the impact of the world around us on it, sees his nameless protagonist concoct–spoiler alert–an alter ego, 'a projection ... a disassociative personality disorder. A psychogenic fugue state.'[4] Tyler Durden is the Narrator's hallucination, awake while the Narrator is sleeping to overcome the mundane meaninglessness of his life.

Tyler is everything the Narrator isn't. He's 'funny and charming and independent and men look up to him and expect him to change their world. Tyler is capable and free.'[5] Refusing to conform to societal norms, he lives in a shithole of a house that's due to be torn down, splices pornography into family films in his work as a projectionist and, whilst working as a waiter in a hotel, sabotages the food with an assortment of bodily fluids. It's the Narrator's subconscious desire to feel more alive that sparks the ensuing chaos, starting with the iconic scene in which Tyler announces, 'I want you to hit me as hard as you can.'[6]

From the pair fronting a series of underground fight clubs, where emasculated men can feel more alive, the chaos soon spirals into Project Mayhem, Tyler's plan to wreak complete havoc and bring civilised society crashing to its knees. Vandalism escalates to terrorism and blowing up skyscrapers.

Obviously, I'm not advocating for terrorism–it's probably safer if we don't get into comparisons to Osama Bin Laden and 9/11–vandalism or even underground fight clubs, even though I practise Brazilian jiu jitsu, more on which in Chapter 19. We need an element of conformity and structure in our lives, otherwise everything goes to shit. Rather, the anti-hero Tyler represents a liberation from society's suffocating influences, such as the cynical consumerism and materialism that we are all perpetually subjected to.

What particularly fascinates me is how the book seems even more relevant now–nigh on three decades later–than it was when Palahnuik penned it. Because more has arguably happened in those 30-ish years, certainly in terms of the detriment of humankind, than in the previous 2.5 million, during which, 'For countless generations [humans] did not stand out from the myriad other organisms that populated the planet,'[7] writes Yuval Noah Harari in *Sapiens: A Brief History of Humankind*.

If you need tangible proof of those happenings, your 'iPhone's processor is estimated to run at about 2490 MHz … This means that the iPhone in your pocket has more than 100,000 times the processing power of the computer that landed man on the moon [in 1969].'[8] Provided you're not one of the people of questionably sound mind that believes NASA made up the fact that mankind took a giant leap on the moon, that computer had enough power to launch three astronauts out of the earth's atmosphere at seven miles per second, fly them 240,000 miles into space, land them on a rock travelling at 2,300 mph, and get them home again. And we now carry around a piece of equipment that's 100,000 times faster *in our pockets*.

Objectively, life has never been better. We're living like kings, able to tap our phones–the ones that have 100,000 times more power than NASA's computers did in 1969–and have food arrive on our doorsteps, or taxis, or escorts (if that's your thing), or your laundry, or fucking anything for that matter. After all, 'There's an app for that.'

Yet, these exponential improvements in technology haven't served to make us healthier and happier. Rather, in 0.001% of the time we've been on the planet, we've done more damage to our bodies and minds than in the rest of our existence. Subjectively, life has never been worse and I believe young people in particular face more challenges than ever before. Among them:

- We're getting fatter and fatter. Obesity is at an all-time high and rising; a quarter of British adults are obese, according to the Health Survey for England, and the World Obesity Atlas 2023 predicts that half of the world's population (4 billion, out of a current population of 8 billion) will be overweight or obese by 2035, representing 'an increase from 38% of the world's population in 2020 (2.6 billion).'[9] This will 'cost the global economy over US$4 trillion of potential income in 2035, nearly 3% of current global gross domestic product (GDP).'

- We're getting more and more miserable. Forget COVID-19; in what is frequently described as a mental health 'epidemic', mental ill health is also at an all-time high and rising. According to the World Health Organisation, 'two of the most common mental health conditions, depression and anxiety, cost the global economy US$1 trillion each year.'[10] Consequently, suicide is one of the biggest killers in the world; more than 700,000 die by suicide each year globally, and there are many more who attempt suicide. In the UK alone around 6,000 people take their own lives each year, a figure which has stagnated for years, and suicide is the biggest killer of people under the age of 35 and men under the age of 45.

- And if you needed any more convincing, you're in the minority; according to a recent YouGov poll, 75% of UK adults think the world is 'somewhat worse' or 'much worse' than it was in 2010.[11]

How? The answer, in my humble opinion, is simple; influence.

***

Think for a moment about the phrase 'under the influence'. Last time I checked–eight years ago, more on which later– hurling your guts up outside the local kebab shop after strawpedoing too many Reefs isn't a good thing.

Even before the advent of social media, Palahnuik's recognition that 'We are the middle children of history, raised by television to believe that someday we'll be millionaires and movie stars and rock stars'[12] was a damning indictment of the various pushes and pulls of modern society. That said, I can get on board with aspiring to be a rock star. I learned to play the drums fairly young and am forever grateful to my parents for somehow never telling me to cease the senseless thumping. This led to a few musical claims to fame, namely supporting Biffy Clyro in the glamorous setting of The Forum, a music venue in Tunbridge Wells that has the debatable prestige of having previously been a public toilet, and also curtain raising for the Fun Lovin' Criminals in a gig at university. As one does. On another occasion I got to batter the shit out of a pair of orchestral cymbals on stage at The Barbican. Which was fun.

Forgive me if I digress occasionally. Where was I? Ah yes, the pushes and pulls of modern society, particularly for young people.

Journalist Aasmah Mir, in her column in The Sunday Times, wrote: 'Have you made a success of your life? The top answers to a recent poll … were predictable – yes, if you own your home, have savings or a pension. Further down looked familiar too – owning a new car, having a second home, travelling first class.'

Which is all bollocks, isn't it? It shows how misplaced we are in our views of what's important. How under the influence we are of society's expectations. But this shallow pursuit of fame, fortune and success has risen like a virus through our ranks to such an extent that one in five children aged 11-16 now want a career as a social media influencer[13]. Nope, not a movie star or a rock star, or a fighter pilot, or even an astronaut, but one of those dickheads that makes 'content' for a living, trying to persuade the rest of us to care about what they put in their green, tastes-like-a-fucking-pond-because-we've-been-led-to-believe-that-algae-is-good-for-us smoothies or convince us to ditch a flat white, in favour of a decaf soya frappu-latte, served upside down in a flower pot at 83.2°C, probably because it'll help our bowel movements or some such nonsense.

The trouble is, though, that we *do* care.

More than half the planet (almost 5 billion people and rising, myself included) uses social media. And not just one platform; 'on a global perspective, the average individual boasts 8.4 social media accounts'[14]–a figure that, as a 40-year-old, I struggle to get my head around; I couldn't *name* eight social media platforms, let alone enough to make that figure the *average*. And despite us all being busier than ever, 'the average person globally spends a significant portion of their day—about 145 minutes—on social media.' That's more than two hours, every day, even though trust that platforms will 'protect [users'] information and provide a safe environment for them to create and engage with content' is declining and 'trust is falling across several key areas, including privacy, safety, and ad relevance,'[15] across *every single* social media platform.

Meanwhile, young people arguably have it worst because they are the first generation—I'm technically a Millennial, just, so I'm looking at you, Gen Zers—who have had to cope with the inordinate levels of stimuli from all angles at all times of the day. It's no surprise, then, that anxiety is particularly rife amongst young adults, with a three-fold increase in a decade, according to Cambridge University Press research published in 2018[16]. That was *before* the COVID-19 pandemic, which saw anxiety, loneliness and depression skyrocket further amid the closures of schools and universities. If you are of the Gen Z persuasion, you'll invariably know what I'm talking about because, by all accounts, attending university during this time was tantamount to serving hard time, albeit without *The Shawshank Redemption*-style beatings that Lucy Letby is hopefully being subjected to.

Counterintuitively, we're using social media more, despite trusting it less. We know we're being subjected to content that's potentially harmful but the algorithms are programmed to feed us with more and more of the same to keep us hooked. And there's still increasing demand for it. Businesses are projected to spend over $300 billion globally on social media advertising by 2024[17], a rise of almost a third in two years, meaning that our feeds will continue to be inundated with more and more crap. 50 million people globally now call themselves influencers and the size of the influencer marketing market is growing, by almost a third from 2022 to 2023[18].

It's clear then; like taking drugs, drinking alcohol, smoking cigarettes, watching porn or gambling, use of social media has become a societal addiction. And it has led to all sorts of shit that, quite frankly, we could do without. Such as:

- People in gyms, who take photos of themselves in the mirror, whilst flexing their right triceps or looking over their shoulder and tensing their arse, looking instead like they should be on a catwalk.

- People who stop walking in the middle of the pavement to check their phone, meaning you clatter into the back of them and then, because it's the British thing to do, you feel like you have to apologise.

- Flossing, planking, neknominations and anything, absolutely anything else that remotely resembles a 'social media trend' (apart from the Ice Bucket Challenge, which raised awareness of Amyotrophic Lateral Sclerosis and a truckload of money for research projects).

- The Kardashians. The Jenners. Jake Paul. Logan Paul. Dylan Mulvaney. I could go on.

- Gender reveals.

- Keyboard warriors and social media trolls; in an interview with the Daily Telegraph following one of his players being subjected to online abuse, Alex Sanderson, director of rugby at Sale Sharks, commented that social media 'is the worst part of the world we live in.'

- Inane videos that people watch in public—often on trains—without headphones.

- The people who watch these inane videos in public—

often on trains–without headphones.

- Crocs, although this has been a blight on society for the last two decades and is a personal pet peeve rather than a result of social media influence. If you work on a hospital ward or you're younger than 12; fine. But anyone else, and I mean A.N.Y.O.N.E. else; not fine.

A documentary that aired on the BBC in late 2023, The TikTok Effect, highlighted this precise issue, that social media is changing how we act, behave and treat each other, fuelling a need to be relevant, whilst blurring the line between what is socially acceptable and what is not, and rendering people oblivious to the potential consequences because the likes and views make them think it's ok.

Interviewed in the documentary is Jeff Allen, Co-Founder of The Integrity Institute, who says, 'As [a trend] gets more harmful, these [videos] tend to get more engagement. These algorithmically-ranked systems are all floating bad content to the top. If you see a video [in which] someone's doing something very dangerous in it, and they're getting a lot of views, [you think], "Cool, maybe I'll do something dangerous." Someone's doing something that's very disruptive and damaging to their community; "Maybe I'll disrupt my community too and maybe I'll get a lot of views if I do that."'

Other trends are proving incredibly damaging and disruptive, not just to individual users, but to communities and society, including amateur sleuths turning up at crime scenes and posting what they 'believe' to have happened, children rebelling against teachers because they think it's cool, and copycatting of violence, all escalated because of the potential eyeballs and engagement.

Then there are the crazes that go beyond the realms of stupidity, which remind me of a phrase my parents used to admonish me with. The conversation would go something along the lines of ten-year-old me exclaiming, 'It's not my fault; so-and-so told me to do it.' My parents' retort would be, 'Well, if they told you to jump off a bridge, would you do it?'

Unfortunately, the social media equivalents of metaphorically jumping off a bridge include people not metaphorically eating laundry detergent, setting themselves on fire and even snorting condoms. Yup, you read that right, snorting condoms. Sucking them up through your nose and trying to regurgitate them out of your mouth. Now that COVID-19 has kindly gone on its merry way, at least to the point that we've resumed our lives, we need a new slogan in the UK to save emergency resources from these cretins. I propose: 'Protect the NHS; if your visit to A&E is in any way related to social media, you're not getting treated. Kindly fuck off.'

Of course, social media isn't an addiction for all 5 billion global users but the analogy is important; we know it's moronic, but we do it anyway. While we're scrolling, we're thinking, 'just another couple of minutes,' which turns into 145. In some cases, we know it's potentially harmful, but we do it anyway.

***

The earliest examples of marketing we have are ancient Egyptian adverts written on papyrus but our *need* to be influenced dates back far longer. For the 2.5 million years I mentioned earlier–6 million if you count our chimpanzee ancestors–we've conformed, through our innate existence as a tribal species. For a bit of sciencey mumbo jumbo, 'The newborn brain contains more than 100 billion brain cells. But in the beginning, the cells are detached and cannot communicate with each other. Immediately after birth, connections begin to form between the neurons at the incredible rate of over 1 million per second. These connections, called synapses–tiny gaps across which nerve cells can send impulses or messages–are formed with every interaction and every sensation the baby experiences.'[19]

In other words, we are being continually influenced from the day we're born, by the language, accents and mannerisms of our parents, and by what we see and hear in the world around us. It is also in our nature to want to be part of the tribe; to fit in. It explains why, as a five-year-old, I sobbed as my mum dressed me in a Superman outfit for a school fancy dress day. Which sounds odd, right? What five-year-old wouldn't want to wear a Superman outfit, complete with flowing red cape and vibrant S 'shield' that my mum, as she loves to remind me, had painstakingly stitched together? Surely I'd be the envy of all my five-year-old school chums? Not, as my mum eventually worked out, if I thought they were all wearing the regular school uniform and I'd be the odd one out, like some weird cosplay fanatic who has turned up to the wrong convention. As if my mum would randomly dress me in a Superman costume and pack me off to school to be mercilessly bullied by my peers. The things that go through the minds of five-year-olds.

Anyway, the point is we're bound by our societal conformities and *need* to be influenced, not just on the clothes we wear, but the smoothies and coffees we drink, the food we eat, who we date, the products we buy, our daily rituals and much, much more. Conformity is part of being liked, part of acceptance by our peers. Rather than being the five-year-old me that should have wished he could go to school in a Superman costume, we're all desperate to be the other five-year-old teachers' pets who are politely wearing their school uniforms, while not wanting to upset the apple cart.

Indeed, 'Ninety-nine-point-nine percent of all decisions are shaped by others,'[20] as Wharton School professor Jonah Berger explains. A range of social experiments have demonstrated that most of the time, 'We underestimate how much social influence affects our behavior because we don't realize it is happening,'[21] and this *indirect* influence is not an inherently bad thing. There's a reason people born in Liverpool don't speak with a Jamaican accent.

The trouble comes when we crave additional *direct* influences, choosing to subject ourselves to multiple social stimuli that are designed using complex algorithms to be addictive. Countless studies have shown the correlation between the dopamine hit we get when we receive a 'like' and the feeling of being 'under the influence'.

Even if you take the date of circa 3000 BC, back when Egyptian adverts were being written on papyrus, rather than when Facebook emerged–2006, which I remember because it was my final year of university and I resisted the urge to sign up because I knew it would ruin all chances of achieving anything remotely resembling a degree–that accounts for around a gazillionth of the time we've been on the planet. As for the advent of the internet and social media, we simply haven't been able to adapt to the fast-paced changes of the last few years and young people in particular face the unprecedented challenge of syphoning through all this.

It's the same for the obesity issue, which can also be attributed to 2.5 million years of evolution, or relative lack of it in terms of our mental growth. Harari continues in his odyssey through the history of humankind: 'our eating habits, our conflicts and our sexuality are all a result of the way our hunter-gatherer minds interact with our current post-industrial environment, with its mega-cities, airplanes, telephones and computers … Today we may be living in high-rise apartments with over-stuffed refrigerators, but our DNA still thinks we are in the savannah.'[22]

Well, Toto, I've a feeling we're not in the savannah anymore.

Harari also states that our species has 'cast off its intimate symbiosis with nature and sprinted towards greed and alienation.'[23] For young and susceptible audiences– though none of us are exempt–this greed ranges from a desire for meaningless crap to snorting condoms for likes. It brings out the worst in us, such as dawn queues outside supermarkets for a hydration drink–launched by the aforementioned Logan Paul–and subsequent listings on eBay for as much as £10,000. I mean for fuck's sake, people, it's just coconut water. Actually, it's diluted coconut water. What's wrong with you?

Matthew Syed eloquently protested, also in The Sunday Times, that these 'Platforms [are] commercially designed to strangle empathy, nuance, metaphor, allegory and complex thought'. It goes without saying that there shouldn't be a lot of complex thought needed to decide whether or not to snort a condom. Syed continued, '[these platforms are] an artificial world of memes, soundbites and reductionist spats ... [that are] about virality.' In another commentary, Syed wrote, '... collective online behaviour is now consistently psychopathic.' (Worryingly, as discussed in the Introduction, psychopaths seem to rule the world.)

Addiction is often referred to as an illness, so virality–which shares its etymology with the Latin *virus*, meaning 'poison'–is appropriate. Society is being poisoned and if you think that sounds extreme, let me refer you back to the condom snorting. Or the fact that we feel a compulsion to reach for our phones as soon as we wake, searing our retinas with blue light before natural light to check what god-awful news has happened in the hours since we turned in, or what someone who once came third on *Love Island* has had for breakfast. (A show which, incidentally, represents everything that is wrong with humanity.)

Like any drug, social media provides a quick fix, temporarily tiding us over until the next craving, whether it's the latest product 'drop'–a word I abhor–resulting in people queuing overnight to buy a pair of trainers whose price has been marked up to twice their worth, or a new design for life. Palahnuik also outlines, 'A lot of young people try to impress the world and buy too many things [but] ... Then you're trapped in your lovely nest, and the things you used to own, now they own you.'[24] And your lovely nest suddenly isn't as lovely anymore because you've just seen a post from an up-and-coming furniture designer that they've done a collab with their local recycling centre in a bid to improve their green credentials and repurposed a used bin bag into a bedside lamp and you absolutely have to have it because you want to be seen doing your bit for the transition to net

25

zero and it arrives and you spend half an hour staging a photo of the lamp in the background while you read the latest Booker Prize winner and post the image on social media and get 42 likes which you're really disappointed about and then it turns out the furniture designer is exposed for child labour in its Taiwan factory and you get accused of greenwashing so have to delete the post and ... breathe ... you get the picture.

The result is we're living in a constant state of unfulfillment. We're unsatisfied with our current lot in life because social media paints a picture of the lot we could have in the future. We're chasing the next goal, and then the next, and then the next, all the while setting ourselves the goal of being happy tomorrow. But, as the 'majestic, brave and hot-tempered' chief of Asterix's tribe, Chief Vitalstatistix, whose only fear is that 'the sky may fall on his head tomorrow,' says: 'Tomorrow never comes.'[25] You never actually experience it, just as you'll never experience happiness if you're constantly pursuing it.

By telling ourselves we'll find happiness in the future, we're telling ourselves we're not happy now. And the present is the only time that matters. Of course, we all have goals but in achieving them we should learn to appreciate the accomplishment before moving on. Allow yourself to feel joy *in the moment*.

To do so, it's important to make a distinction between the quick fixes and worthwhile goals that will bring meaning to your life. As opposed to the meaning of life. On which note, Monty Python had a good take on things back in the day, albeit 'nothing very special. Try and be nice to people, avoid eating fat, read a good book every now and then, get some walking in, and try and live together in peace and harmony with people of all creeds and nations.'[26]

Living in peace and harmony is something we'll cover in the next chapter. For the time-being, we could all do with adopting a little bit more of a Tyler Durden approach to life–the anomaly-to-the-destructive-desire-to-fill-our-lives-with-meaningless-crap Tyler, rather than the Osama-esque, let's-blow-up-some-skyscrapers Tyler–and make more of a conscious effort to shun goals that are shallow and materialistic, such as wanting to be an influencer because of the fame and supposed riches that comes with the career. If you can really call it a career. Which you can't.

So, here's your first piece of advice, dear reader who is looking to make his or her way in the world: be more Tyler Durden (but less Osama Bin Laden).

And your first task: purge your social media. I'm not suggesting that we all bin off social media entirely–although it'd be interesting to see Mark Zuckerberg's reaction to Facebook's share price plummeting if we all come off the social metaverse, or whatever he calls it these days– because that's entirely unrealistic and there are situations where social media can be a force for good. Plus, I'm not immune to the irony of preaching about the pitfalls, when I'm one of the 5 billion users. But the next time you feel inclined to spend 145 minutes scrolling through one (or more) of your 8.4 feeds, pay careful attention to how each of the posts makes you feel. If the people you follow interest you or inspire you, they can stay. For example, I follow Chris Hemsworth on Instagram. Not because he's beautiful and I have a man crush on him (although I do), and I aspire to be him, with his model-hot wife and penchant for surfing, but because he employs various rituals that help him lead a healthier life. I take tips from his routine and believe I feel better as a result. But I don't worry that my abs aren't as defined as his, because he's a film star with a net worth of around $130 million, who has far more resources than me to dedicate to the practice of sculpting himself to look like a real-life Thor. But if any posts cause you to feel like you fall short, like something is unattainable, like you can't afford something, like you're missing something, like you don't have enough or that you're not enough, unfollow them. Instantly. Ditch the accounts that leave you comparing yourself to others, wishing you had something you don't have, or, it goes without saying, prompt you to do something that will leave you with a condom stuck in an orifice and an NHS nurse that has heeded my advice and is telling you that you're not getting treated, kindly fuck off.

If you're tempted by a purchase, a subscription or an action, ask yourself the following sequence of questions:

- Do I *need* it, or do I just *want* it?

    Without getting too deep into hierarchies of needs and the psychological factors that drive human behaviour, if it feeds you, clothes you, provides you with shelter or helps you sleep better, you should have a fairly easy decision on your hands. Unless it's a wagyu tomahawk steak, in which case the lines are blurred. Can you live without it? Well, it's food, so technically no. But, as someone that's eaten steak in Argentina and paid a fraction of the price of wagyu beef for the privilege, I can't imagine the Japanese version is really worth all the fuss, and the associated price-tag. Although, if I had a spare thousand pounds, I'd consider it as a one-off. Anyway, what was my point? I'm sure it wasn't specifically about wagyu steak, even though that seems like something I'd make a point about …

- If I want it, *why* do I want it?

    Now I remember. Something has piqued my interest but it's not essential to my survival. So, the question I have to ask myself is *why* I want it? In the case of the wagyu steak, it'd be because it presumably tastes delish delosh and I'd love to experience the flavour and succulence of the meat and create a memory that will last a lifetime, something that I can look back on and reminisce about with the loved one I shared it–the memory, not the food: 'Joey doesn't share food'[27]–with. But if there's an ulterior motive of wanting it simply to take a photo of it to post on my social media channels so that I can make my friends jealous, then I need to have a long, hard think about whether it's fulfilling anything other than vanity, because I'll undoubtedly be annoyed when I don't get as many likes on Instagram as I'd hoped for.

- Will it improve my life *in the long-term*?

    Well, the steak won't. But if ice baths and intermittent fasting–à la Chris Hemsworth–can boost my immune system, improve my focus and help me sleep better, I'm all for them. Anything I can do that helps me give more to my relationships, be more engaged with those around me, train harder and more frequently, and ultimately be healthier, even to the extent of extending my life, sign me up. In contrast, anything that only provides merely a fix, anything that will make me feel inadequate once the short-term joy of it has subsided, has to go. Toodles.

Otherwise, there's this amazing thing called common sense,

but I fear that getting too deep into how it seems to be dying off could be opening Pandora's box. In short, another question you could ask yourself is, 'Is there a chance this purchase, subscription or action could land me in hospital with a nurse telling me to fuck off?' If the answer's yes, DON'T DO IT.

While you're taking a leaf out of Tyler's book, take one out of Syed's, who also wrote, 'let's ignore the haters, the doommongers, the thugs, the keyboard warriors, the rancorous, the sour and the wider panoply of individuals whose serial negativity gains ever more traction in a world distorted by algorithms. Let us always remember they are a tiny minority; a twisted and bitter minority. And, it seems to me, a rather unhappy minority at that.'

And another out of Max Erhmann's. A line in his famous poem, Desiderata, reads, 'If you compare yourself with others, you may become vain or bitter.' In hindsight, the poem was written almost 100 years ago, so I should really have led with that rather than references to *Fight Club*.

Balls.

Chapter 2:
The Ultimate Accolade

What we do in life echoes in eternity.
- **Maximus Decimus Meridius**

Given this book is part advicey, part ranty, part silly and only part autobiographical–and I have the memory of a goldfish with amnesia that has gone 12 rounds with Mike Tyson–I can whistle through most of my childhood fairly quickly.

One memory–which is less a memory because I was a toddler, but which my Best Man, Ollie, kindly regaled all of our friends with at Krista's and my wedding, thanks to my mother betraying me and furnishing him with the story, so more accurately an unexpected revelation–surrounds the arrival of my younger brother, Simon. My grandmother, charged with my care for a few days while my mum recovered from a c-section, bought me a toy to keep me entertained. Not an Action Man or a super manly lumberjack figurine that would encourage me to become the strapping individual that I have become–or so I like to think–but a little baby doll. It's the thought that counts, Grandma.

A few days later, when I was no longer the undivided centre of Mum's attention, Simon not-so-subtly informed everyone that he was hungry and Mum lifted up her shirt to give him his dinner. Naturally, as an impressionable young man, I did the same with Dolly. What can I say? Dolly was obviously peckish too and I was an equally caring and doting mother. Quite where that story puts me on the current scale of transgenderish wokery is up to you.

In another memory-cum-revelation, Mum recounts the time she picked me up from school and I had clearly been crying. For someone who went on to play rugby for two decades, you'd think that I wouldn't mind a bit of mess. But, as my teacher explained, my tears were on account of art class, in which we'd done papier-mâché, and I'd gotten upset at the idea of having to stick my hands in a bowl of horrible white goo. I was obviously a sensitive little soul.

Otherwise, I didn't grow up diving into swimming pools of money, Scrooge McDuck-style, whilst being waited on by a butler called Jeeves, but I never wanted for much. My parents were as loving as a young boy could hope them to be, Mum affectionately taking charge of everything at home with devoted attention–including our history homework assignments–and Dad working extremely hard to put us through public school. The opportunities afforded to me as a result were nothing short of fantastic, including a rugby tour to South Africa one summer, during which I lost a pint-downing challenge to a guy who could open his throat but brushed off my hangover with a swim in the Indian Ocean the next morning. Not the toughest of upbringings, I will fully admit, though it *was* tough playing rugby against immense Saffa school boys, who didn't mind whether they won or lost the game, as long as they'd rendered a couple of their opposition unconscious. The fact we couldn't afford to go on summer holiday as a family that year, thanks to my gallivanting, is only something I truly appreciated several years later.

Skip forward a couple more years, A-levels done and dusted and university place secured, and I was very fortunate to do the rather stereotypical middle-class thing of taking a gap yah. Rather than finding myself on a backpacking tour of south-east Asia, or building a hospital in a remote, unpronounceable African village, I opted to head to New Zealand, to teach P.E. and build on my rugby experience, this time playing against immense Māori men, who didn't mind whether they won or lost the game, as long as they'd rendered a couple of their opposition unconscious.

From a relatively sheltered corner of Kent, to pretty much as far as it's possible to travel to the other side of the world, *Aotearoa*, the Māori-language name for New Zealand which translates as 'the land of the long white cloud', gave me so much more than rugby experience. I have the country to thank for my first love, life-long friends, a summer spent at a friend's beach house learning to wakeboard, a winter spent in Queenstown learning to snowboard, and an eye-opening glimpse into Māori culture that has stayed a part of me ever since. To this day I wear a piece of *pounamu* jade on a bracelet. No, not punani.

I am not in the slightest bit religious. I attend church with my family at Christmas because I like donning my appalling reindeer jumper with a light-up nose and belting out a hearty rendition of *Oh Come, All Ye Faithful*, but I cringe at the placard-wearing, megaphone-wielding, Jesus-will-save-you-types on our high streets. I also (accidentally) attended a fairly Christian college at university and was the only one of my friendship group that wasn't approached by the bible-bashers to attend a session of reading passages from the good book and singing *Kumbaya, My Lord*; they obviously thought I was already past redemption.

All that said, Māori culture and spirituality are captivating, particularly the focus on displaying qualities such as strong leadership, kindness, strength of character and humility. A Māori proverb that reinforces humility as a desirable trait states: *Kāore te kumara e kōrero mō tōna ake reka* (The kumara [sweet potato] does not say how sweet he is). Even the word *māori* means 'normal' or 'ordinary' to differentiate people from gods.

These values serve as integral parts of *mana*.

To attempt to translate the word would be to do it a disservice; Māoris see *mana* as a life force. As James Kerr writes in *Legacy*, which tracks the success of the All Blacks, New Zealand's all-conquering rugby team, '*mana* is perhaps the ultimate accolade, the underlying spiritual goal of human existence.'[28] While the word has earned itself a more common, contemporary place in wider Kiwi culture, the premise remains the same.

***

On returning to Blighty, I toddled off to Durham University to study Classics, which in hindsight has absolutely zero use as we approach the day that Skynet takes over and we're consigned to underground bunkers as cyborg Arnold Schwarzeneggers stalk the earth. In the event, maybe Neo will fly in and save us all. Or maybe it'll be John Wick. Who knows, they both said, 'Guns. Lots of guns,'[29] which will at least be helpful in fighting off the Terminators. Maybe I'm jumbling my cult films there but, back to the degree, and it involved five hours of lectures a week, most of which I was too hungover to attend.

In between rugby games, gigs—as the drummer in a jazz quartet—and drinking, a lot of drinking, I occasionally crawled into a lecture, if only to breathe alcohol fumes onto my poor fellow students. Among the few things that stuck with me, having taken what I had from the Māoris about *mana*, was the ancient concept of Stoicism. (I can remember thinking about the links, even though they were coincidental, what with the millennium and a half and 10,000 miles separating them. I mean, it was epic that the Polynesians canoed thousands of miles across the Pacific to settle in New Zealand in the 13th or 14th centuries, but for anyone to do so from Rome would have really been something. As such, the Roman Empire didn't have much sway down under, as far as I'm aware.)

I'd love to be able to say that I'm therefore an authority on the subject, even the vaguest smidgeon of one, but that was 20 years ago and, well, let me take you back to the goldfish analogy. If only my degree had been in rugby, playing jazz and drinking.

Fortunately, I know someone who *is* an authority on the subject. My good friend Ben Harrison, a fellow Durham alumnus, my roommate in first year, in fact, actually *studied* Classics and, would you believe it, even put it to good use. He's now imparting his wisdomness to the next generation as a Latin teacher, much to the amusement of his children.

I asked Ben to kindly remind me of what my aching brain was struggling to recall about Stoicism. The conversation went something like this:

Me: Hello mate, how are you? How's the family?

Ben: Really good thanks, what about yourself?

Me: Excellent, we have some news; Krista and I have had a baby boy.

Ben: That's wonderful, congratulations.

Me: Thanks mate. Actually, it gave me cause for pause and got me thinking—no 'about time' quips, thanks very much—about life … and the world … and bringing life into the world. And I had a wacky idea to write a book. A sort of advice-to-my-son-type-thingamajigabob. One idea was to base a chapter around the concept of Stoicism and how my son could be a good person and live a good life according to certain values, etc.

Ben: That's a great idea. If only you'd *studied* Classics, rather than rugby and drinking at Durham.

Me: Touché. But that's where you come in, old buddy, old chum, old mate, old pal. If you'd be so kind as to remind me of what I should have been studying.

***

Stoicism was founded by the philosopher Zeno in around 300 BC, though links can be made to Socrates, the so-called 'Founder of Western Philosophy', who died a century earlier. A Disney film about Socrates—this book is intended for my young son, so I make no apology for crowbarring in as many Disney references as possible, however tenuous—would undoubtedly feature an evil queen with magic powers talking to herself in the mirror.

'Mirror, Mirror on the wall,' the queen would ask, 'who is the wisest of them all?'

'Socrates, O Queen,' the mirror would exclaim, 'is

the wisest of them all because he, according to Plato, has the humility to recognise that he is not wise and does not claim to know what he does not know. He is, in fact, ignorant but, in knowing this, is wiser than all the other fucking morons out there that are snorting condoms and doing other dumb-arse shit that they've seen on social media.' Or words to that effect.

And the queen would respond, 'Yes, I saw that doing the rounds. What absolute muppets. At least that puts my problem of Socrates being wiser than me and Snow White being fairer than me into perspective.'*

---

*Side note:

Magic mirror aside, this prophetic scenario isn't too far from Plato's version of events; in his *Apology*, he recounts how Socrates' friend Chaerephon 'went to Delphi and boldly ... asked the oracle to tell him whether there was anyone wiser than [Socrates] was, and the Pythian prophetess answered that there was no man wiser.' Apparently, the oracle's fortune tellings were held in slightly higher regard than the tarot card-reading, tea leaf-swirling, Mystic Meg-type quacks of today. It is unconfirmed whether Chaerephon won the lottery that weekend with numbers 3, 6, 14, 23, 27 and 42, and the bonus ball 5, drawn by Guinevere.

Depending on which ancient historian's writings you peruse, Zeno was a merchant who visited Athens by chance after a shipwreck and stumbled upon a bookseller who happened to have an account of Socrates' teachings. Don't let the truth get in the way of a good story, is what I say.

In these teachings, as catalogued by Plato and others, Socrates discussed how to lead a good life. It was a tricky concept to get even his incredibly wise brain around because it involved differentiating between short-term pleasure and a pursuit of happiness that had greater longevity. In fact, 'happiness' didn't quite cut it because it didn't guarantee fulfilment and didn't factor in the need to live according to certain virtues and moral principles. So, these super-duper clever chaps, living a very long time ago, coined a new phrase.

Eudaimonia (εὐδαιμονία in Greek) is translated by my very, very dusty Greek lexicon, which has somehow survived multiple trips to charity shops over almost two decades, as 'prosperity, good fortune, wealth, weal, happiness'[30] and this raises a couple of points:

1. I have no idea what weal is.
2. Lumping prosperity, good fortune, wealth, weal—whatever weal is—and happiness into the same translation leaves things about as clear as mud as to what the word actually means and explains Socrates' dilemma.

Shedding some light, then, Ben tells me its meaning goes deeper, into an almost spiritual—don't worry, though, Ben and I aren't going to have you lighting candles and chanting any time soon—state of wellbeing that is judged at the end of someone's life, when you can weigh up everything they've done and achieved. Indeed, it was a teaching of Aristotle's in his *Nicomachean Ethics*, that *eudaimonia* takes 'a complete life. For one swallow does not make a summer, nor does one day; and so too one day, or a short time, does not make a man blessed and happy.'[31]

Take the mythical Greek king Oedipus, for example. After surviving being left to die on a mountainside as a baby, he ascended to the throne of Thebes and married the widowed queen in the process. But, the revelation, years later, that he had killed his father and shacked up with his mother was such a dramatic *peripeteia* (περιπέτεια; reversal of fortune) that he couldn't claim to have lived a life of particularly good fortune.

Or imagine I were to give you a million pounds. You'd be happy (at least I should hope you'd be happy, you ungrateful swine), but you wouldn't feel fulfilled. You wouldn't feel like you'd earned it.

On top of this, Socrates (although he never actually wrote anything), Plato, Aristotle and other notable ancient authors noted the importance of a range of virtues, such as humility, wisdom and self-control (σωφροσύνη, *sophrosyne*, which was very important to the Greeks), in achieving *eudaimonia*.

When Zeno picked up the mantle after his semi-believable, chance encounter with the bookseller, he designed a philosophy based around the idea that everything that happens in nature—indeed the universe—does so in accordance with divine reason. By being wise enough to accept this, we can live in harmony with the world and people around us: 'the concept of life lived according to nature.'[32] Ten points if you remember my reference to living in harmony from *Monty Python's The Meaning of Life* in the previous chapter.

Amongst the finer details of Zeno's school of thought was the system of dividing the world into the ideals of physics, logic and ethics, though Ben says it's fine to discard physics and logic, since many Stoic writers did the same. Stoic ethics, then, focus on developing the self-discipline to overcome any negative emotions that arise as a result of life's circumstances, since it's beyond our power to control the eventualities that we face. Zeno preached that the likes of anger, distress and lust are therefore irrational and show moral weakness. In contrast, the 'wise man' (σοφός, sophos) is free of such 'passions' (πάθη, pathē*) and can stick out his thumb and hitch a ride along the *eudaimonia* highway.

> ***Side note / lesson in etymology:**
>
> *Pathē* also gave us 'pathetic', originally meaning 'capable of feeling, impassioned'. Surely at some point, Zeno berated one of his students for getting upset about something by shouting, 'Stop being so fucking pathetic,' even if it didn't mean quite the same that it does these days.

All of which, one could argue, could be neatly summarised as: 'Shit happens; deal with it.' But that probably wouldn't have taken off.

Whistling through several centuries in a sentence, among other proponents of Stoicism were Cato the Elder, Cato the Younger, Seneca, Epictetus and Marcus Aurelius, who served as Roman emperor from 161 AD to 180 AD.

According to Ben, Cato the Elder [234-149 BC], 'was well known for his conservatism and opposition to anything Greek. He believed Hellenic culture was a threat and introduced stringent regulation against luxury. His rambling writings on farming, rituals and recipes, De Agri Cultura, is the oldest surviving Latin prose.'

But it's his great-grandson, Cato the Younger [95-46 BC], who is a particularly interesting case, since, Ben says, 'he staunchly defended the preservation of traditional Roman values and systems at a time when they were in decline, and this put him at odds with the most influential leaders of the day, notably Julius Caesar. In the civil war of the late Roman Republic [49-45 BC], Cato sided with [Caesar's political enemy] Pompey, more out of pragmatism than ideology because he hated Caesar more. When Pompey's side was defeated in Africa, having discussed with his friends his Stoic belief that a truly free man would never become a slave, Cato chose to take his own life, rather than beg for or receive Caesar's pardon. Apparently, though, Caesar regretted not having the opportunity to pardon him.'

Plutarch's account of Cato's suicide is rather dramatically embellished:

'Cato drew his sword from its sheath and stabbed himself below the breast. His thrust, however, was somewhat feeble ... [and] he did not at once dispatch himself ... His servants heard the noise and cried out, and his son at once ran in, together with his friends ... [A] physician went to him and tried to replace his bowels, which remained uninjured, and to sew up the wound. Accordingly, when Cato recovered and became aware of this, he pushed the physician away, tore his bowels with his hands, rent the wound still more, and so died.'[33]

You can't fault the man's commitment to the cause.

'After his death,' Ben continues, 'Cato was seen as a martyr and a symbol of the republican cause, though some ancient and modern sources criticise Cato for being too stubborn and uncompromising. The argument goes that had he been more flexible in understanding the ambition of Caesar and Pompey, etc, and supporting their reforms, then they would not have gone as far as they did in making the changes that ultimately brought down the Republic and resulted in the rule of the emperors. Taking this further, it could be said that Cato contributed to the downfall of the very system he was hell bent on preserving. But if he had compromised, then he wouldn't have been Cato.'

We digress.

As for Marcus Aurelius, if his name rings a bell, it might be because of Ridley Scott's *Gladiator*, the opening scenes of which depict General Maximus Decimus Meridius (Russell Crowe), Rome's 'commander of the armies of the north,'[34] leading the emperor's army against marauding Germanic Tribes. When the ageing Aurelius (Richard Harris) tells his son Commodus that he's not worthy of succeeding him as emperor—'Your faults as a son is my failure as a father'[35]—Commodus smothers him with a pillow and Maximus, Aurelius' choice as regent, is forced to flee.

If you'd like a quick history lesson—or even if you wouldn't, since I'm including it anyway, though you could skip this paragraph, I suppose—Aurelius did fight a series of wars against Germanic tribes, including a campaign from 177 AD to 180 AD, the year of his death. However, Ridley Scott's writers veered away from historical accuracy, since Commodus ruled jointly with his father for three years prior to his death and Maximus is a fictional character but, again, why let the truth get in the way of a good story? Especially such a damned bloody good one. I mean, brutal fight scenes, epic revenge speeches, Oliver Stone, hints of incest and a cracker of a soundtrack. What's not to like?

Back to Marcus Aurelius and his *Meditations* provides us with one of the most comprehensive texts on Stoicism, even though it was never intended for publication.

Throughout the many private notes written to himself, most likely whilst also planning military campaigns against 'ze Germans'*, the theme of living a good life stands out. Amongst a range of different virtues or ethics, anyone that can practise, 'self-mastery, immune to any passing whim; good cheer in all circumstances, including illness; a nice balance of character, both gentle and dignified; an uncomplaining energy for what needs to be done,'[36] as well as, 'Strength of character – and endurance or sobriety as the case may be,'[37] will be well on the way to *eudaimonia*. He also picked up on Zeno's preachings of moral weakness, 'because it is clearly some sort of pain and involuntary spasm which drives the angry man to abandon reason, whereas the lust-led offender has given in to pleasure and seems somehow more abandoned and less manly in his wrongdoing.'[38]

> ***Side note:**
>
> For absolute clarity, because I'm not a racist or a xenophobe and because some people get overly upset about the smallest things, this is a reference to Guy Ritchie's *Snatch*, which was coincidentally released in the same year as *Gladiator*, 2000. If you're offended by the reference and also agreed with the BBC dropping *Little Britain* and the 'Don't mention the war' episode of *Fawlty Towers* because you've got the sense of humour of a saucepan, then you probably shouldn't be reading this book. Right, now get back to reading about Stoicism 'before ze Germans get here.'

Indeed, possessing the virtues of being in control, being good natured, approaching things with vigour, and showing resilience, 'signifies the man of full and indomitable spirit.'[39]

Another area to which Aurelius pays a great deal of attention is the pursuit of fame and fortune and how we should have 'no vain taste for so-called honours,'[40] since 'fame [is] unclear. To put it shortly ... all things of the mind are dreams and delusion ... the only lasting fame is oblivion.'[41] I think he'd be turning in his grave if he had even the vaguest notion of what we covered off in Chapter 1. Maybe there should be a modernised iteration of Charles Dickens' *A Christmas Carol*, in which the Ghost of Stoic Past comes back to haunt a particularly narcissistic influencer, who then recognises the error of his ways and deletes all his social media accounts in order to live a life of virtue and seek *eudaimonia*.

There are also a couple of poignant references to Stoicism in *Gladiator*, if you have a keen enough ear to pick them out. Before taking on the barbarian hordes of the north, Maximus rallies his troops with a stirring speech from atop his trusty steed, featuring the line, 'What we do in life echoes in eternity.'[42] This idea of being aware of our actions, and the impact they have on people and the planet picks up neatly on Marcus Aurelius' claim that, 'Nothing is so conducive to greatness of mind as the ability to subject each element of our experience in life to methodical and truthful examination, always at the same time using this scrutiny as a means to reflect on the nature of the universe.'[43]

Later, when about to face off against Commodus, Maximus states, 'I knew a man who once said, "Death smiles at us all. All a man can do is smile back."'[44] He admits he's quoting the murdered emperor and, although it's not a direct Marcus Aurelius quote, this sentence along similar lines from Book 2 of *Meditations* provides a beautiful link between the two sentiments:

> 'You may leave this life at any moment: have this possibility in your mind in all that you do or say or think.'[45]

Quite clearly no-one can be as wise (or ignorant) as Socrates, as dignified as Marcus Aurelius, as courageous as Maximus Decimus Meridius, or as humble as a sweet potato, but the roots of *mana* and Stoicism lie in at least trying to demonstrate the range of virtues that would have made these people proud. Fast forward to the present day and Maximus' two Stoic references could do with being routinely shouted from tannoys, to encourage us to take a little more pride in everything we do. Life is short enough without us all being dickheads to each other and ruining the planet in the process.

***

Much of Stoic philosophy was based around self-discipline and the ritual of honing body and mind, something which, as we discovered in Chapter 1 with the obesity and suicide statistics, many of us could do more of. Whilst showing restraint against the irrational 'passions', emphasis was also placed on not pursuing pleasure (ἡδονή, *hēdonē*, from which we get hedonism) for the mere sake of it. Deriving pleasure as a result of practising your virtues was all gravy, however, so fill your philanthropic boots, people.

Seneca, a Stoic predecessor of Marcus Aurelius, wrote in his *De Vita Beata* ('On The Happy Life') that 'pleasure is low, slavish, weakly, perishable; its haunts and homes are the brothel and the tavern … you will find pleasure skulking out of sight, seeking for shady nooks at the public baths, hot chambers, and places which dread the visits of the aedile, soft, effeminate, reeking of wine and perfumes, pale or perhaps painted and made up with cosmetics.'[46]* Sounds like Old Compton Street in London's Soho on a Friday night.

> ***Side note:**
>
> In contrast, Seneca also wrote, 'You will meet virtue in the temple, the marketplace, the senate house, manning the walls, covered with dust, sunburnt, horny-handed'[47]. However, Seneca was the emperor Nero's tutor and, given that Nero's life turned into little else than a series of excesses in sport and music, intertwined with orgies and murder, we might wonder how effective Seneca's tutoring was.

That's not to say we have to be pious perfectionists all of the time, abstaining from any sort of pleasure or renouncing anything that brings us joy. Nor do we need to be emotionless robots, always neutral to things going on around us. For example, I don't drink and I don't smoke, but I bloody love an almond croissant and Ben (having been my roommate at university) will happily testify to me being able to put away two footlong Meatball Marinara Subways in one sitting. I just don't do so every day. We all get angry. We all get upset. I'm as guilty as anyone of swearing at BMW-drivers who cut me up.

Rather than assuming the rigidity of a Shaolin monk, then, rising at 4am to do one-fingered handstands or break bricks with our foreheads, keeping a check on unhealthy habits by making small adjustments can make big differences. Whether it's mastering actions like binge eating or tempering our reactions to twats in BMWs, putting this into practice can be as simple as recognising the behaviours we'd like to improve whilst riding the rollercoaster of life.

Recognition, or more accurately metacognition, is something I'll come onto later in the book as we explore the importance of developing self-awareness to build what I call 'mental fitness'. We'll also touch on the link between endurance and mental fitness. I can tell you're excited.

For the time being, Stoicism is essentially a here and now philosophy, since 'each of us lives only in the present moment, a mere fragment of time: the rest is life past or uncertain future.'[48] By taking time to explore our actions and reactions, particularly noting the emotions that arise as we experience them, we can implement more positive behaviours.*

> ***Side note:**
>
> Much of modern Cognitive Behavioural Therapy (CBT) is rooted in the idea that an event can be interpreted in different ways; in the simplest of terms, positively or negatively. While CBT is largely used reactively to cure mental health issues, such as anxiety and depression, whereas Stoicism is based on proactive principles, the founder, Aaron T. Beck, credits 'Stoicism as the main philosophical inspiration for [his] ... approach.'[49]

In doing so, we can build self-discipline, which teaches our brain to endure a measure of hardship. Similarly, a treat now and then as a reward reminds us of the effort we've put in up to this point.

With that, here's your second piece of advice: be more Maximus Decimus Meridius. Be less Shaolin monk.

Putting it into action, try and abstain from almond croissants (or whatever your vice is) during the week in the knowledge that you can finally visit that new bohemian coffee shop you've been desperate to try out that doesn't have chairs, only bean bags, on a Saturday morning to enjoy one as a treat with a nice cup of Ecuadorian coffee that has a complex mix of sweet caramel and acidic fruits in the tasting notes. One. We're not talking the equivalent of doing Dry January and then going out and getting absolutely hammered on 1st February.

Don't seek fame; show humility, like a sweet potato. Though if fame finds you because you're an absolute legend and can give a cracking, pre-battle motivational speech–like Maximus–so be it. Accept that you'll face challenges, but that it's how you respond to them that's important. Take notice of how those challenges make you feel. Don't give credence to your negative thoughts until you've been able to assess them. Show the strength of character to forgive yourself if you get angry irrationally. Learn from these experiences to hopefully make better, more rational decisions in the future, maybe not flipping a BMW driver the bird next time round. Treat yourself to the occasional almond croissant. Everything in moderation, and all that.

Live in the here and now.

Oh, and don't let the truth get in the way of a good story.

Chapter 3:
Knowing Thyself

Who am I?
- **Derek Zoolander**

Derek Zoolander (Ben Stiller) is the three-time male model of the year. Attending the Male Model of the Year Awards in New York, he's a shoo-in for the award for the fourth year in a row. Until his rival, Hansel (Owen Wilson), is announced as the winner. But Derek's already on his way up to the stage to accept the award and give his acceptance speech: 'A lot of people said winning this award four years in a row couldn't happen.' It's all he knows. It's his identity. When Lenny Kravitz interrupts him to tell him of his mistake, he runs out into the street and confronts his reflection in a puddle. 'Who am I?' he asks, if not the male model of the year. 'I don't know', the reflection responds.

Not highbrow enough for you? Want some more Socrates? Yeah you do. Coming right up after a quick skinny dip into the super exciting start of my career.

***

Though it may come as a surprise, I did in fact manage to scrape myself a degree, even if Ben has to occasionally remind me what it was in. Classics apparently. On which note, I would like to take this opportunity to officially apologise to Professor Peter Heslin, whose Advanced Latin lectures were early on a Thursday morning. Unfortunately, Wednesday was 'sports day' ... followed by drinking evening.

After a year honing my rugby skills and fitness in New Zealand, where I felt small despite my 6ft5, 100kg frame, it was a novelty to once again be playing with and against people my size. Making up the numbers of the university 1st XV as a fresher, my Wednesdays were devoted to epic coach journeys up and down the country to take on the likes of Nottingham, Loughborough, Cardiff, Bath and Birmingham in the then BUSA (British Universities Sports Association), now BUCS (British Universities and Colleges Sport) Super Rugby league. Of course, this meant epic coach journeys back, involving four-packs of Carlsberg Special Brew and a bottle of port ... each ... cries of 'naked bus', which doesn't require much of an explanation, and the occasional pack of butter, about which I refuse to provide an explanation. Just to clarify, I wasn't forced to apply it anywhere. Those poor coach drivers.

And my poor head on Thursday mornings when we went around the room translating out loud a passage of Cicero, or Ovid, or I can't really remember. If some of the other university initiation stories are to be believed, I got off fairly lightly–avoiding drinking piss or vomit out of the captain's shoe, for example. But possibly not lightly enough, given it was a weekly ritual for Prof. Heslin to ask me, simply,

'James? No? Not today?'

Two years and many failed translations later, I was shaking the hand of author Bill Bryson as he handed out plastic tubes disguised in ribbon as diplomas. In his *Notes from a Small Island*, in which he recounts the quaintness and quirkiness of Great Britain, he bids readers, 'If you have never been to Durham, go at once. Take my car. It's wonderful.' I like to think that's the sole reason he was chosen as Chancellor of the university.

The graduates' instructions for the graduation process were along the lines of, 'Step up onto the podium, shake Mr Bryson's hand, and then fuck off, quickly, because we've got about 5,000 other students to get through. Under no circumstances, hold up the line.' Ok. But what if your mother has tracked down a first edition copy of *Notes from a Small Island*, which you've handed into the university office a few weeks beforehand with a request for Mr Bryson to sign it as a memento, and when it's returned to you, there's a tidily scrawled note saying, 'Dear James, I hope you've had a wonderful time at Durham. If you ever want to go back, "Take my car!" All very best wishes, Bill Bryson,' and you want to thank him? What then?

Needless to say, I held up the line, much to the bemusement of my fellow students. In hindsight, though, not for long enough, because I should really have asked Bill, 'What the hell do I do now?'

Seriously, what the hell do you do after majoring in Latin and Ancient Greek? Apart from something commendable and useful to society such as becoming a teacher, like Ben?

You head for the City of London, of course, where

thousands of soulless organisations are eagerly waiting for you to join a relentless rat race that will sap the very fibre of your being. In recruitment, where I fell, stories abounded of starters having their chairs taken away and hands sellotaped to their phones if they didn't make enough calls, such was the pressure to bolster the fat cats' pay cheques. It's these types of damaging attitudes and behaviours that have given recruitment its 'burn and churn' reputation. Fortunately, despite having little to no clue what I was doing, specifically in the prime brokerage and securities lending space–like I said, no clue; something to do with hedge funds?–I was reasonably good at doing it and avoided such punishments.

2006, when I first graced the working world with my presence, was the City's heyday. Reports did the rounds of investment bankers securing multi-million-pound bonuses by brokering massive tax saving deals for the Saudis, raising capital from the Qataris and a smorgasbord of other probably borderline legal* activities. I was young but I didn't mind being a minnow in an ocean because I was finally earning a salary, and a reasonably decent one. I was living the dream in a questionable pinstripe suit and Infernos in Clapham, London's most infamous nightclub, was my oyster. The investment banking market was booming.

---

*Side note:

In February 2020, 'in the UK's first trial of bank executives for misconduct during the 2008 Financial Crisis',[50] three Barclays top dogs appeared in court facing charges brought against them by the Serious Fraud Office (SFO), for 'conspiracy to commit fraud in relation to allegedly misleading investors and the markets over capital raising arrangements agreed with Qatar

---

> Holding LLC and Challenger Universal Ltd in June and October 2008.' One of them, randomly, was my godfather. But it's probably best if we don't go down that particular rabbit hole. They were all acquitted, after all. But the SFO obviously thought it was all a little bit shifty, didn't it?

And then it wasn't.

In September 2008, I remember standing in the middle of Canary Wharf, handing out my business card to despondent bankers—or, more accurately, former bankers—as they left the Lehman Brothers building in their droves in the wake of the financial services firm's bankruptcy. Not that my vague attempt at ruthlessness did much to stem the flow of the Credit Crunch. In a crashing market, the recruitment sector took a monumental nosedive as organisations, financial and otherwise, axed their hiring spend. Little old James, who was last in the door, was first out of it. Bugger.

After a stint in SAP recruitment, which befuddled me even more than prime brokerage—something to do with enterprise software?—I started questioning my place in the melting pot of careers. Recruitment ticked all the right boxes; it's essentially building and brokering relationships and selling opportunities. I'm a confident communicator, presentable and, I like to think, trustworthy. I wouldn't go so far as to say that I could sell sand to an Arab, but I could definitely sell sand to … someone who really needs sand. But recruitment didn't seem to want me, so I came to the eminently sensible conclusion that I needed to put a bit more thought into my chosen profession than simply, 'That one'll do,' and opted to put myself through a course of psychometric testing.

After joining some dots, colouring some things in and

guessing the odd one out from a circle with a square in it, a square with a triangle in it and a triangle with a circle in it, I was delighted to be presented with a graph that showed pretty good results across whatever the various skill sets or personality traits that psychometric testing tests. Numerical, good. Verbal, excellent. Logical, good. Critical thinking, good. Boredom threshold, poor. Hang on. What the fuck? Poor? How very dare you?

As the nice lady who ran through my results with me–who I didn't actually swear at–kindly and patiently explained, my low boredom threshold indicated that I lost interest in things easily. 'So,' she illuminated, 'you'd be better off working in a role that interests you. What interests you?'

It was a damned good question. Did prime brokerage interest me? No. Did SAP interest me? Nope.

***

Right, I promised you Socrates.

'Know thyself' (Γνῶθι σαυτόν, *gnōthi sauton*) is often attributed to Socrates, but erroneously, since it was one of the Delphic Maxims, a series of moral codes inscribed on a column in the Temple of Apollo in Delphi*. These were originally authored by Greece's Seven Sages, a group of statesmen who lived in the late 7th century and early 6th century BC, a century before Socrates was a twinkle in his parents' eyes.

*****Side note:**

Another of the Delphic Maxims was 'Nothing too much'–and you thought I was joking when I said 'Everything in moderation' in

> the previous chapter.

If you thought it was a Socratesism, blame Plato. His *Phaedrus* in particular catalogues Socrates' disdain for understanding various natural and mythical phenomena: 'I have no leisure for such enquiries; shall I tell you why? I must first know myself, as the Delphian inscription says; to be curious about that which is not my concern, while I am still in ignorance of my own self, would be ridiculous ... I want to know not about this, but about myself.'[51]

Furthermore, in *Charmides*, Plato recounts a conversation in which Socrates explores the link between knowing yourself and *sophrosyne* (σωφροσύνη), translated as 'soundness of mind ... self-control, temperance.'[52] As a more vocal proponent than a stone column of seeking to learn more about ourselves, how we think, how we act, the virtues we practise and the emotions we feel, Socrates' mantra was picked up in the Stoic reasoning that by doing all of the above, we could achieve *eudaimonia*.

But it wasn't just Socrates and his fellow Greekians that had the idea that we should dedicate time and energy to getting to the bottom of who we are; iterations have worked their way into literature throughout history, such as in Alexander Pope's *An Essay on Man*, the second Epistle of which begins:

Know then thyself, presume not God to scan;

The proper study of mankind is man.

Around the world, sacred tribal practices also involve physical journeys of self-discovery through self-discipline:

- The *okugake* is an endurance-based pilgrimage of self-discovery undertaken by Japan's Yamabushi warrior monks. A hike along the sacred Ōmine Okugakemichi route is punctuated by *misogi*, the practice of cleansing the whole body in a river or waterfall and meditating at spiritual places called *nabiki*.

- Aboriginal adolescents in Australia undertake the ritual of going Walkabout and living in the bush for as long as six months to better understand nature and themselves before they become adults. The boys must sustain themselves by hunting for food and foraging, enduring the harsh and hostile landscape of the Australian outback, and surviving all manner of poisonous species of insect and snake.

Similar ideals permeate societies and religions around the globe, from Christianity to Islam, from Hindu to Māori ... yup, we're heading back to the land of the long white cloud because the Māori are fiercely proud of their culture and heritage, such that they have a special phrase for their belief in the importance of identity. But, like *mana* in the previous chapter, attempting to translate the phrase comes with complications, since it means different things to different people.

Taha wairua is a spiritual wellbeing that, for some, denotes a connection to the universe, while for others, it comprises knowing where you have come from, who you are and where you are going. Stick 'What is taha wairua?' into Google and the first link it returns—an article written by the New Zealand Ministry of Social Development—leads with 'Know yourself'. (I'm beginning to wonder if some unknown ancient philosopher, perhaps a young Athenian who was eavesdropping on one of Socrates' conversations, or another customer of Zeno's bookseller mate, did in fact make that 10,000-mile journey down under.)

***

In February 2022, Vanessa Sweet, from Hamilton in the north island of New Zealand, received the news that her brain cancer had returned for a third time and further metastasised to her pericardium (heart sac), spine and diaphragm. Having lost her partner and soulmate to a sudden heart attack five years prior, the impact on her and their four children, the youngest of whom were eight-year-old Nikau and seven-year-old Nivarna, was devastating.

Where many take participation in sport for granted, especially in New Zealand where sport is pretty much a religion, some don't have such clear-cut opportunities. Ness is brave beyond belief, fighting the good fight but 'having to come to grips that there may not be a happy ending.' Getting her young children to and from activities outside of the family home is therefore a serious challenge.

Help for the family has come in the form of sponsorship from The WaterBoy, a charity that works to break down barriers to give young New Zealand children the opportunity to participate in sport. It has given Nikau and Nivarna access to sport and the young pair are now thriving amid the tragic situation surrounding their mother, Nikau picking up a rugby ball and Nivarna taking to karate like a young Bruce Lee. 'It is a gift,' Ness says, 'because if they shine, I'm happy. When I watch my children play their individual sports … I don't feel like I have cancer anymore.'

Once upon a time, The WaterBoy's founder, Thomas 'Nabbsie' Nabbs, and I played rugby together. I was lucky to have him as a teammate since he is from a strong sporting pedigree; his mother is in the New Zealand Sports Hall of Fame for winning two Netball World Cups with the Silver Ferns in 1979 and 1987. But his drive isn't purely to boost sporting numbers amongst young Kiwis.

'Every child should have dreams,' Nabbsie says, 'of what they one day want to become and achieve, heroes they one day want to emulate. Unfortunately, some don't get to formulate those dreams due to limited experiences. Sport has the power to quite literally change the course of children's lives. Sport gives us mental and physical health benefits, leadership skills, social skills, and helps us express ourselves. It gives young people purpose.'

Sitting deeper at the heart of The WaterBoy's mission–and indeed Māori ideology–is the idea that who we are doesn't start with the present. It starts with the past. You are who you are because of everything that has come before you. Your *whakapapa* (heritage) is based on hundreds of years of history and the strength of your genealogy that has got you to this point. It is a powerful notion when you consider how, in the words of Oasis, 'We, the people, fight for our existence.'[53] As a human race, we have survived wars, natural disasters, plagues, pandemics and, if *Independence Day* is to be believed, the occasional alien invasion.

Nabbsie resonates strongly with his *whakapapa* through his two Māori grandmothers–it gives him a sense of identity. But the simple question, 'Whereabouts are you from?' can be difficult to answer for many who are from broken homes, if their parents are absent or in jail, and if they're being bumped around from foster home to foster home. But, 'If we can get people into sport, I think that actually becomes a part of their identity. That said, in some ways I couldn't actually give a shit about the sport itself. It could be music, art, drama, learning a new language, whatever; the point is, it gives you a chance for growth.'

Unfortunately, 'growth' isn't in enough young people's vocabulary, which is why, amongst The WaterBoy's initiatives, its *Taku Wairua** programme focuses on personal development. The mounting problem is that, amid too much screen time and the influences discussed in Chapter 1, children are not sampling the same variety of opportunities that they used to. They are not being exposed to the values of sport, such as sportsmanship, and the teachings of winning or losing a hard-fought game. Losing, and learning to overcome adversity, breeds resilience.

---

*Side note:

In the Māori language, *tōku*–meaning 'my'–is used to refer to someone or thing of higher status, e.g. *tōku papa* (my father). When the person or thing is of equal status, *taku* is used, e.g. *taku wahine* (my wife). Taku is also used when the possessor has control of the relationship, so, even though some may deem our spirit to be higher than us, *taku wairua* it is.

With that in mind I make no apologies for some more social media bashing. Because if one in five children wants to be an influencer, that's 20% of the next generation that are aspiring to be self-absorbed arseholes. Fortunately, 19.9% are going to be disappointed but they're setting their sights at the wrong targets and living a poorer–or at least unhealthier–life as a result. In contrast, if 20% *aspire* to be professional athletes, they're likely to be getting out in nature regularly, exercising, eating healthily and living their best lives. They'll develop the attributes that Nabbsie listed a moment ago, even if they don't *become* professional athletes, more on which in Chapter 20.

Nor are children finding the strengths that enable them to develop self-esteem and take pride in their achievements. Nabbsie continues, 'What we're really trying to do is make people proud of themselves. Pride is one of the strongest emotions for thriving as humans, because it helps us be our authentic selves. If we're not proud of who we are, we don't have an identity. If we do, we have the ability to form and shape our identity, based on the knowledge of what has come before.' Through the example of the Māoris, who are descended from ancient adventurers who crossed the Pacific in canoes, navigating by the stars and whale hoots alone, we can all be proud of something. We can all find an identity.

***

My response to being put on the spot by the question that accompanied my psychometric results was along the lines of, 'Er [*shrug of the shoulders*], I dunno. Sport.' To which the ever-so-patient lady then prompted me, 'Right, sports events, sports marketing, sports PR, sporting rights, sports this, sports that. Off you go.' To say it was enlightening does it a disservice.

Putting it into action wasn't easy, though. It was a leap of faith. I had no idea if I was going to find a job in a new sector, in which I had zero experience. I had to drop right back down the career ladder, starting again on a salary that could barely sustain a ferret. But I didn't care; I was no longer committed to chasing the suited City dream. The only thing I had to prove was that I could cut it in a completely different career and the only person I had to prove it to was myself. 20 applications to PR agencies and an internship that involved a lot of laminating and making cups of tea later, I was armed with a Blackberry–remember those?–and driving around Europe in the back of a Range Rover, as the press officer of a month-long charity cycling tour arranged by Rugby World Cup-winner, Lawrence Dallaglio, visiting the 6 Nations Rugby Championship stadia to coincide with the tournament's matches.

Having watched Dallaglio and his England teammates conquer all before them a few years prior, including attending a game in Wellington, New Zealand, in which England beat the legendary All Blacks on New Zealand soil for the first time in 30 years, this was a young rugby fan's dream come true. Although it had its moments, such as the night we arrived into Paris.

As my team back in the UK and I arranged media interviews that aimed to promote Lawrence's charity whilst getting his insights on the Championship, I was the point man on the ground who had the task of ensuring old Lozza was on the phone at the right time and saying the right things. An almost insurmountable task, given the guy's old school approach to going 'on tour' and his propensity for a night out. When he wasn't on a bike, he was either pissed or hungover. For the morning after our Paris arrival, we had a live interview lined up with talkSPORT Radio for Lawrence to talk about the weekend's upcoming fixtures and update listeners as to his cycling antics. As Lozza disappeared into the Parisian night to go on the razz, I reminded him of his commitment to be live on the radio at 9am.

At 8:45am the next morning, I was in the hotel lobby, armed with my BlackBerry. No sign of Lol. Still fairly new to the PR gig, I needed to ensure I got the big man on the phone to avoid copping flak from my bosses for the interview not taking place. I had to make some executive decisions.

Decision 1: ask the hotel receptionist to phone his room. I rattled off my best A Level French: 'Excusez-moi, Monsieur, est-ce que vous pouvez appeler la chambre de Monsieur Dallaglio?' The phone rang, and it rang, and it rang, and it rang, and just as I thought the sun was going to implode and suck all life from the galaxy into a black hole, a voice that sounded like the owner had eaten a roll of sandpaper answered: '[A load of indistinguishable phlegmy noises], HELLO?'

8:50am. Phlegmy McPhlegmface had to be live on the radio in ten minutes. Whilst worrying that I was about to lose my job, I mustered my politest and chirpiest voice: 'Morning, Lawrence, it's James. Just wanted to make sure you're ok for your chat with talkSPORT?'

'Oh fuck,' came the hoarse reply. 'Alright, give me five minutes.'

Five minutes later, no sign of Sandpapervoiceman. 8:55am.

Decision 2: go up to his room. I got in the lift and hit the button. The doors opened on an upper floor and as I was walking down the corridor, my BlackBerry rang. 'Hi, it's the producer at talkSPORT here. We're ready for Lawrence. Is he there?' 8:58am.

'Yes, he's right here with me', I semi-lied, whilst knocking on the door to his room. 8:59am.

The galaxy now on the brink of collapse under its own gravity, such was the eternity that it took for him to cross his room, the door finally opened to reveal the sight of the enormous frame of Lozza in just a towel. I passed over the phone and meekly said, 'It's talkSPORT.' He took it, put his hand over the receiver, called me a cunt and slammed the door in my face. 9:00am. Heart now going like a machine gun in my chest, I still had to ensure that he was saying the right things, so had the preposterous situation of trying to listen to the interview with my ear to the door. Inside the room, I could vaguely hear his gruff tones talking about England's chances and updating the DJ as to his whereabouts on the cycling tour. I finally breathed a sigh of relief. A few minutes later, the door opened, a phone came flying out at me and the door was promptly slammed in my face once more. What do they say about never meeting your heroes?

Then I was launching a sports TV channel, playing touch rugby on the hallowed turf of Twickenham Stadium, shooting hoops with NBA stars at the O2 Arena, kicking a ball around on the pitch at Wembley with a Ballon d'Or-winner, baby-sitting the Rugby World Cup trophy overnight, ahead of a 4am photoshoot (with another Rugby World Cup-winner) and definitely not filling it with beer in my living room, meeting Olympians, rubbing shoulders with World Champions, and much more.

One of my favourite memories of that time was attending a rugby game at Twickenham with some friends, after enjoying a ticket to a corporate box at the week's previous match, courtesy of an England Rugby sponsor. Walking through the stadium's fan village, a great booming voice that could well have belonged to a Kiwi cousin of the giant from *Jack and the Beanstalk* called out, 'Oi, James. How are ya mate?' Hoping that the owner of the voice didn't 'smell the blood of an Englishman', I turned to see the fridge-sized frame of Zinzan Brooke bounding up to me. One of the most iconic figures in the history of rugby proceeded to grab my hand between his sizeable paws and shake it amiably, whilst we exchanged a few pleasantries about the upcoming fixture, much to the bemusement of my friends, whose jaws had made thumping sounds on the pavement. I simply told them, 'Oh, we go way back.' As in a whole week. Zinny had been in the box the previous week and I'd plied him with free beer.

But now I'm just one of those annoying name-droppers, so I'll come to the point.

Was sports PR my calling? Probably not. Was I changing the world? Probably not. Did it interest me? Fucking right it did. Did it feel like something that I could be proud of? Damn diggity.

So, what's my advice?

Maybe the rat race is your cup of tea. And that's fine. Bully to you if you're on a six-figure salary, working for an investment bank trading complex financial derivatives with someone in Timbuktu, because the Nigerian currency has just tanked and you're getting a deal, a steal, the sale of the fucking century against the dollar, and the bonus will be enough to buy a turbocharged Porsche 911. Maybe you're brokering deals with the Qataris. In which case, maybe you've absolutely nailed it, but just be wary that the Serious Fraud Office may come knocking in 12 years' time.

If so, why are you reading this book, and not ordering another pina colada on the deck of your 500 ft yacht?

If not, be more The WaterBoy.

Open yourself up to experiences that will improve

you as a person, rather than slowly sucking out your essence, like a *Ghostbusters* proton pack. If you can find something that makes you tick; if you can give yourself a reason to get out of bed in the morning; if you can 'know thyself' enough to remove yourself from the constraints of a soul-sapping, mundane 9-to-5 that gives you absolutely no fulfilment and take a leap of faith, then you're onto a winner. You don't have to find your calling. Just a sense of who you are and something that helps you grow; that builds your self-esteem; that makes you proud; that gives you an identity.

If you're yet to find your place in the world, think about everything that has come before and the significance of your being here, whatever that looks like.

If you're reading this book *while* ordering another pina colada on the deck of your 500 ft yacht, carry on, sailor.

Chapter 4:
Changing Thyself

As human beings, our greatness lies not so much in being able to remake the world as in being able to remake ourselves.
- **Mahatma Gandhi**

If you'd asked me in the five-or-so-years before 9th February 2013, 'Who are you?', I wouldn't have put much thought into an answer. At least not in terms of the existentialist, what's-the-point-of-it-all dilemma of our existence. I'd have probably said, 'Er [*another shrug of the shoulders*], I'm a rugby player.'

In my late 20s I was playing at a high enough level to get a bit of money in my back pocket for my troubles and to take it very seriously. I had a structured routine that revolved around matches at weekends, with my fitness training, weights sessions and team drills all geared towards being as fit, strong and generally ready as possible come kick-off at 3pm on Saturday afternoons. I was disciplined, trained hard, ate the right things, was fit and healthy and, having bulked up to around 17 stone, in my own mind, fairly invincible.

For anyone that doesn't 'get' rugby, I don't blame you. The 'ruffians sport played by gentlemen'–a quote often attributed to Oscar Wilde–has become increasingly brutal in recent years as players have grown bigger and broader. A study published in the BMJ Sport & Exercise Medicine, in 2015, found that, 'In 1955 mean (±SD) player body mass was 84.8 kg (±8.2); in 2015, it was 105.4 kg (±12.1), an increase of 24.3%.'[54] In particular, 'There has been a significant increase in the body mass of male international northern hemisphere rugby union players since the game officially turned professional in 1995,' thanks to meticulously planned diets and the growing prominence of protein supplements.

That's the professional set-up but this has also filtered down to the grassroots game and 'at times bulk seems to be prioritised over skill'. My employer in the City forbade me from attending meetings when I turned up to work sporting a black eye, which was most Monday mornings and, playing at semi-pro level, I, at various points throughout my career–if you could call it a career–tore ligaments in one ankle, broke the other, tore ligaments in a shoulder, broke the other, ruptured the MCL in my left knee, hyper-extended my right elbow, suffered fractured ribs and a severely bruised sternum, and was concussed on several occasions. Concussions are particularly on the radar of World Rugby (the sport's governing body), such that a change in the laws has lowered the height of the tackle to reduce the risk of impacts. Much to the chagrin of the rugby-playing community, but that's a debate for another time.

But, and it's a big but, rugby gets a bad rap. Despite

shouts from sidelines of 'Smash him,' it is a wonderful game. I love it and I will have no problem encouraging Freddie to take it up, should he show an interest. Or even if he doesn't show an interest, quite frankly. In fact, he was dressed in an England rugby onesie about four and a half minutes after he made his screaming presence known to the world and I'll be watching him like a hawk for his first step so I can thrust a rugby ball in his hands and do tackling drills with him in the garden. But I resent the accusation that I'll be a pushy parent.

Because no other sport comes close in terms of the camaraderie developed between teammates. A determination to put your body on the line for your teammates epitomises the do or die attitude of going through 80 bruising minutes on the pitch and it gives rise to the lifelong friendships off it; there aren't many sports in which opponents pummel each other for an hour and a half, then dust themselves off, shake hands and challenge each other to a boat race.

This weekly routine gave me purpose and an identity. I was a rugby player; a big, strong, macho rugby player and out to prove, if you were my opposite man on a Saturday afternoon, that I was a bigger, stronger, more macho rugby player than you. Possibly not a particularly healthy identity, in hindsight, but an identity nonetheless.

That all changed on Saturday 9th February 2013. As my long list of ailments will prove, I had been throwing myself into tackles fairly recklessly and suffered with a few injuries along the way. But the straw that broke the camel's back happened on that fateful afternoon as I found myself as the last line of defence against the opposition winger, who was hurtling down the wing towards our tryline. I lolloped across the pitch to the accompaniment of those sideline shouts of 'Smash him'. And smash him I did. Except that, where I should have neatly chopped him in half with my right shoulder, he changed direction at the last second and the mistimed tackle saw me flying full pelt, head first into his midriff. In fairness, I prevented the try.

At the time of the collision I felt an acute pain down my right arm—called a 'stinger'—and, to this day, still have a vague numb sensation in my right thumb, thanks to some kind of nerve damage. But I was able to sit up and waft away the circling, tweeting cartoon birds. The team physio came on to inspect me and, after wobbling various limbs and asking me what day it was—part of the concussion protocols—hoiked me off the field. Since then I have often wondered at how the human body is capable of pushing past the pain barrier—something I'll cover off in greater detail in subsequent chapters—because 15 minutes later, all-healing ice pack administered, I was desperate to return to the field to play more of a part in an epic home victory against the top side in the league. Fortunately, the physio convinced me that I was better off seeing out the rest of the match from the sideline. (Hannah, if on the small off chance you're reading this, I probably have you to thank for the fact I'm not writing this from a wheelchair, something for which I am grateful every day.)

That evening I attended a charity dinner-dance with my then girlfriend, Penny*, and the Sunday was spent with my best man-to-be, Ollie, larking about and playing darts in the pub. It was a full two days, more than 48 hours later, that the pain kicked in. And Christ alive, when the doctor asks you to rate your pain out of ten and you're the idiot that says 11, well, this was more like 27. Lying in bed at 2am on the

Tuesday, throbbing from head to toe, I'd had enough bumps and bruises to know there was something wrong. I woke Penny and fumbled my socks on whilst insisting I needed to take myself to hospital. After a drowsy attempt to get me to go back to bed, she drove me to A&E.

> ***Side note:**
>
> I have changed the name of Penny, more on whom later, to protect her privacy.

Unfortunately, I wasn't high up on the list of priorities for the small-hours-of-Tuesday-morning, skeleton crew of the Kent and Sussex Hospital and, in hindsight should have made more of the situation than causally strolling into the department complaining of shoulder pain. As it was, I was left sitting bolt upright in a plastic chair, dosed up on a heady, pain-killing cocktail of two paracetamol tablets. Yup, two whole tablets.

Four hours, two x-rays, and a CT scan later and the results were in. In a collision that had resembled the irresistible force paradox, I had compacted my neck so severely that I'd cracked my C6 vertebra. So, not actually the camel's back; my neck.

It was as if a nuclear reactor had started to go into meltdown in the hospital, minus the hazmat suits. I had six members of staff, probably the entire midnight roster, levering me into a stretcher and I was secured to a hospital bed with sellotape across my forehead so that I couldn't move my head. Despite having walked around for two days, gone to a dancing soirée and spent an afternoon in the pub playing darts, it seemed there was a dire concern that my head would simply fall off of its own accord, unless I was strapped in like I'd been sentenced to death by electrocution.

I think I've scrubbed much of the five days that I lay there from my memory, since I wouldn't wish the experience on my worst enemy. All that really sticks with me of waiting for my scans to be referred to a specialist in London, was being in constant pain and willing myself to not need the loo and go through the embarrassment of shitting myself and having a nurse clean me up, when I knew I was perfectly capable of walking to the bathroom. Five days of aching and mindful constipation later, the specialist confirmed that the fracture was stable and my head would most likely stay attached to my body. The 'pain team', in its wisdom, had finally realised that a bulky, 17-stone rugby player needed more than a couple of paracetamols to tide him over, and dismissed me with a bag full of so many drugs that I had to take special drugs to stop the rest of the drugs from corroding my stomach. It's a wonder I didn't end up hooked on morphine.

So, on 9th February 2013 I was a rugby player. And then I wasn't. That was that. That identity was ripped out from underneath me. I went from being big, strong, macho, fit and healthy to having to wear a rigid neck brace 24/7, being signed off work for three months and being subjected to watching the wretchedness that is daytime television. Bear in mind this was before 'Netflix and chill'.

When it turned out I wasn't invincible, I didn't like the new version of me; weak and frail. I couldn't handle being incapacitated, dependent on statutory sick pay, which for anyone that hasn't ever had to endure it, covers approximately the cost of a Tesco Meal Deal each week, and not much else. With the loss of exercise came a loss of discipline. The void left by a lack of routine, on which I had depended so completely, had to be filled with something. The highs of a hard-earned win on a rugby pitch had to be replaced. The boredom needed to be balanced out.

In an attempt to derive some measure of pleasure in the early stages of those three fateful months, I found myself wandering to the fridge one afternoon. You know, the looking-in-the-fridge-for-answers-type situation, even though you're not sure of the question. Am I hungry? Not particularly. Thirsty? Not really. But now that I'm here, a beer would be a lovely treat, given the circumstances of having just survived the pomposity of Tim Wonnacott in the latest episode of *Bargain Hunt*. Tssshhhck. Aaahhhh, that's good. Now, when is the next *Friends* rerun on? I could do with a giggle.

After a week or so of struggling to cope with this new version of myself, which started as a beer–as a treat, remember–and turned into two, three and four, I plucked up the courage to venture into the outside world. My feet took over and I found myself–as if it was a perfectly natural thing to do–wandering into the local Wetherspoons, ordering a Carlsberg (the cheapest lager on offer) and parking myself at the next table along from a charismatic gentleman in a raincoat and flat cap, despite it being sunny outside, who was having an intimate conversation with his pint. As I left the pub, leaving raincoat-and-flat-cap-guy–I like to think his name was Alfred, since he had an air of elderly sophistication to him, despite being in a Wetherspoons at 3 o'clock in the afternoon–caressing his ale, I remember thinking, 'At least I'm not like him.'

I wanted to keep my four-pint gentle buzz going and reasoned that the most economical way of doing so, considering my rapidly deteriorating, statutory financial situation, was to buy a bottle of spirits. Just a half one, mind. Only an alcoholic would buy a 75cl bottle. I can just treat myself to a cheeky G&T before Penny gets home.

After that final digestif, I hid the remainder of the bottle in my rugby bag, which I reasoned was a perfectly natural thing to do. A week or so later, on my pilgrimage back and forth to Wetherspoons, I bought a 75cl bottle. My enjoyment of a once-weekly, post-rugby match booze up with the boys had now turned into something that was habitual, solitary and secretive. The shoe was firmly on the other foot. My judgement of Alfred, who was perfectly within his right to enjoy a quiet, solitary pint and talk to it in the process, or could even have been waiting for someone–I didn't stay long enough to find out–was the hypocritical equivalent of Greta Thunberg throwing an empty plastic bottle out of the window of a moving supercharged Range Rover. Alfred, I'm sorry.

This continued until I returned to work, three months after my injury, and resumed something that more vaguely resembled a routine. But the seed of addiction had been well and truly sown. It had become my new identity.

***

Someone who knows a few things about identity and addiction is Michael Maisey, who I met on my subsequent journey through sobriety.

Michael grew up on the Ivybridge Estate in Isleworth, the son of a heroin addict father and a mother who struggled with alcoholism. During a traumatic childhood, he was the victim of physical and sexual abuse, and was exposed to drugs and violence as part of the estate's gang culture. Drug use and crime of escalating severity followed, such that he was confined to Feltham Young Offender Institute three times in his teens. After being convicted of armed robbery—even though the gun was fake—at the tender age of just 15, he was subsequently sentenced to stints in prison for assault and attempted murder. After a suicide attempt in prison, whilst on detox from heroin addiction, it was the early stages of sobriety for his mother that set him on his own path to recovery.

In a remarkable story of redemption, Michael is—at the time of writing—now 15 years sober. He is a loving husband and devoted father to three daughters who have never seen him drink or take drugs. He is a businessman, a mentor to young offenders and addicts, a TEDx speaker, and the host of transformational retreats that advocate the power of change.

The identity that Michael carved out for himself on that Isleworth estate is fascinating, since 'None of us are born evil.' As Michael recounts, 'I experienced pretty much every form of torture and each one made me feel worse, more threatened, more desperate to protect myself. If all you know is that the people closest to you hurt you and you can't trust them, you have to be on guard. If you're led to believe that the world isn't a friendly place, you have to find a way to survive.'

Michael's means of survival was to create an adapted version of himself; a defence mechanism. 'Crime, violence, drugs and addiction,' he recounts, 'were part and parcel of everyday life.' Being 'angry and unpredictable' was his version of safety. In some ways, he's the narrator from *Fight Club*, concocting an alter ego to help him deal with his version of life.

'In hindsight, having done years of therapy and self-development, and getting sober,' he calls the persona he developed the 'security guard', whose job it was to protect the scared little boy that Michael had suppressed. The security guard kept the little boy safe from trauma, abuse and violence.

After his survived suicide attempt came the 'epiphany that maybe this isn't who I am, maybe there's more here. From that rock bottom, there was only one way and that was up.' That up was hearing that his mother was three months sober. Michael describes how having 'his first healthy role model, someone who he could finally rely on,' was the start of a journey of self-development.

It was an arduous journey and one during which Michael, for the first time in his life, had to show vulnerability and let people in. Everything that he had been desperately trying to protect himself against had to be rewritten to force the security guard into retirement.

Albert Einstein once said: 'I think the most important question facing humanity is, "Is the universe a friendly place?" … For if we decide that the universe is an unfriendly place, then we will use our technology, our scientific discoveries and our natural resources to achieve safety … But if we decide that the universe is a friendly place, then we will use our technology, our scientific discoveries and our natural resources to create tools and models for understanding that universe.' By that reckoning, if we see the world as friendly, when we experience adversity, we grow stronger from it. It doesn't break us because we believe that the world has thrown us a road bump for a reason. If we think the world is unfriendly, we've got to fight every day. But you can't fight every day because the world's relentless. The world will eventually win.

Put yourself in Michael's shoes. Wouldn't such mistreatment lead you to believe the world was unfriendly and prompt you to use your resources to achieve safety? When I spoke to The WaterBoy's Thomas Nabbs in Chapter 3, he said something similar about the young Kiwis he works with: 'Whatever habits you develop, they become part of your identity.'

The security guard wasn't who Michael was. Believe me, when you meet him, he is softly spoken and compassionate. 15 years on from his first days of sobriety, he is no longer the scared little boy from a broken home, nor is he the angry, unpredictable teenager. He is a loving father and husband, an entrepreneur, a public speaker, a campaigner and more. His life is markedly different but he wouldn't have it any other way. He says, 'The boring routine is mundane to some people but, for me, that's the gold in life; that's the real stuff that I never had growing up.'

Michael points out that, 'Learning who you are requires an ability to be honest with yourself and for that you have to let yourself be vulnerable. Allowing others to see you for who you are can be scary. They might ridicule or hurt you. Or reject you.' But the realisation that you don't need to seek approval can be liberating.

I've taken a lot from my friendship with Michael. He's an inspiration to many, myself included. But, above all, the notion of an identity that isn't rigid sticks with me. You might be a rugby player one minute, or an armed robber, or a father, or a friend, or a lawyer, or a shepherd, or a butcher, or a baker, or a candlestick maker, but that doesn't define you. That's not who you are.

Michael is proof that if you're not happy with your identity, no matter how deep-rooted it may seem, you can change it. I'd like to clarify, though, referring back to the Introduction, that this doesn't mean you can suddenly decide to be a cat at any given moment. Nor should we go down the sordid rabbit hole of gender ideology. French nouns have genders. *Le fromage*. Masculine. *La merde*. Feminine. People do not. But, if we *are* going to wander down the confusing alley in which sex and gender seem to lurk in the shadows these days, waiting to pounce on you and steal your will to live, how is it that we were happy with having two sexes for 2.5 million years, but now we're wasting time with nebulous nonsense such as cis-? I mean, why do we need the word 'cisfemale', when we've already got the word 'female'? They mean the same thing. If you identify with being female because you're female, then you're just fucking female. It's insulting, quite frankly. Oh, and for clarification, if your name is Alan and you want to be called Sarah and wear a skirt, go nuts–or nutless, if you want to castrate yourself–but that doesn't make you a woman. I'm going to stick to my guns with this one because, having witnessed the Herculean efforts of my wife over nine-and-a-bit months of carrying and delivering Freddie, there are only two sexes. One can carry a child and give birth to it. The other can't. There, I said it. End of. And I've gone down the rabbit hole after all. You can go ahead and cancel me now.

Where were we? Ah yes. To demonstrate the point that you can change your *non-sexual* identity, I'm going to borrow from another of my esteemed Greek friends, Aristotle, who pointed out that, 'Happiness is an activity of soul, in accordance with perfect virtue.'[55]

Aristotle uses the word ενέργεια (*energeia*) for 'activity'. The implication is that, if we can practise *sophrosyne* ('soundness of mind ... self-control, temperance') in our virtues and the emotions we feel, and reflect this in our actions, we're pretty much buying a one-way ticket to *eudaimonia*-ville. It's the action that makes the difference, as in getting off your lazy arse and making a change, even being 'the change you want to see in the world.' Which is supposedly a Gandhisim, although Gandhi didn't actually say that. What he said was, 'If we could change ourselves, the tendencies in the world would also change. As a man changes his own nature, so does the attitude of the world change towards him. This is the divine mystery supreme. A wonderful thing it is and the source of our happiness. We need not wait to see what others do.'

It's a powerful sentiment that, quite simply, we have a choice. A choice about who we are and how the world sees us. And that by not being defined by who we ought to be we can find a source of happiness; *eudaimonia*, even.

But I want to take things one step further than Aristotle and suggest that we don't *need* an identity. Why do we have to be x, or y, or z. Why can't we simply *be*?

This is a concept that deserves some attention, since we are so intent, as a society, on being human *doings* rather than human *beings*. The horrible irony of all the technology that has been designed to make our lives easier is that it has only served to make us busier. Productivity and efficiency sit at the heart of our personal and business lives as we cram our diaries full of meetings and check our emails at all hours of the day and night, frantically trying to tick things off our to-do lists. But that only gives us longer to-do lists. Meanwhile, I referenced the phrase, 'There's an app for that', as in absolutely everything that you could possibly imagine. Even one that replaces your alarm with a phone call from a stranger. Which is just creepy.

As a result, phrases like 'work-life balance' are thrown around and burnout is at an all-time high, with 42% of the workforce reporting it.[56] Limitless distractions mean we're never really present in our daily endeavours, from conversations with loved ones to team meetings at work. I can be as guilty of it as anyone, and that's why I make a conscious effort to examine the version of me that those around me are getting. Am I being the best husband, father, friend, or colleague that I can be? Am I bringing all of myself? Am I engaged? Or am I flicking through social media while Krista is talking to me?

Krista and I have a simple rule—no screens during dinner. That means no phones at the table, whether that's at home or when eating out, and dinner in front of the TV is also a no-no. We refuse to be one of 'those couples' that sit opposite each other in restaurants, each flicking through their respective newsfeeds and not saying a word to each other throughout their meal. Dinnertime is 'us' time. Checking in, asking each other how our days were, being present in the conversation. The mundane stuff but the stuff that, as Michael puts it, is 'the gold in life'. Similarly, I want to be present for my son; the best dad I can possibly be. I can't achieve that whilst watching a reel of a Vizsla balancing a satsuma on its head (as cute as that may be).

Unfortunately, we can't float through life without occasionally being descriptive as to our circumstances or who we are. Imagine a job interview where the prospective employer asks you to tell her about yourself and you launch into: 'I'm afraid I can't do that, since I don't like to define myself in any given moment because it could lead to a case of mistaken identity with my other selves.' That said, in this day and age, maybe the interviewer would be all over that kind of hippy dippy shit, who knows?

Whether you're a circus performer who likes shaping bonsai trees, or you farm alpacas and have a side hustle making lemon curd, or you can solve a Rubik's Cube with your eyes closed, we each have our various weird and wonderful quirks that make us unique. While we talked about being part of the tribe in Chapter 1, we also have an innate need to be unique *within* the tribe. We want to conform, but we also want to stand out.

So, put some thought into how you introduce yourself, but without resigning yourself to this definition. This might even change, according to the setting. So, professionally, I'm a Director at a PR agency. I specialise in PR and digital marketing within the professional services and environmental, social and governance space (snore, I know, but I branched out of sport after a big campaign, it still interests me, and we've covered the importance of that). Personally, I'm a husband. I'm a dad. I'm a dog owner (a fox red Labrador called Harvey, if you must know). I'm a former rugby player, an ultra-runner and I've just taken up Brazilian Jiu Jitsu (more on these later). I like exercising, getting out in nature, adventure, travel, film nights with my wife, *any* night with my wife, gardening and the latest *Jack Reacher*. I love a Sunday roast, a meat feast pizza, a 1kg T-bone steak from the local farm shop as a treat on my birthday and anything, absolutely anything, that involves the words 'pulled' and 'pork', or salted' and 'caramel'. I can solve a Rubik's cube (but not with my eyes closed). But is any of that who I *am*?

'None of us are born evil.' Quite right, Michael. Nor are any of us born to be litter pickers or CEOs, accountants, insurance brokers, marketing managers, teachers, dentists, circus performers or alpaca farmers. We don't start life with an inherent love of playing tiddlywinks, painting Warhammer figurines, collecting foreign coins or dressing up as Batman. We're exposed to various experiences throughout our lives and make decisions about whether to pursue those experiences. Our decisions lead to certain eventualities and we have to learn to adapt accordingly. But none of this defines us. If Michael can go from being a heroin-addicted, three-time convicted criminal in his teens to being a successful businessman, we are all capable of change. Indeed, the non-profit that Michael runs that offers transformational retreats is called the CIP Project. Standing for? Change Is Possible.

Season 5 of *The Simpsons* features an episode called *Bart's Inner Child*, in which Homer and Marge take Bart to a seminar on account of his bad behaviour. Leading the seminar is self-help guru Brad Goodman, who says, 'You see, folks, we're all trying to please someone else. And as soon as you're not a human being, you're a human doing.' When Bart interjects and is commended for expressing his 'inner child', Springfield descends into a chaotic free-for-all, with everyone doing what they damn well please as they discover a newfound sense of freedom. As everyone else acts the rebel, Bart becomes depressed at losing his unique bad boy identity amongst all the other hell-raisers. Why? 'It's simple, Bart,' his wise-beyond-her-years sister Lisa explains. 'You've defined yourself as a rebel and in the absence of a repressive milieu, your societal niche has been co-opted … You've lost your identity. You've fallen through the cracks of our quick fix, one hour photo, instant oatmeal society.' Or in other words, he has lost a sense of who he is, as part of the bigger picture.

Lisa's solution? 'To develop a new and better identity.'

There are deeper philosophical subplots running through the episode that even Nietzsche would have been proud of, exploring the effects of society on our identity and, once again, our need to conform, but the simpler premise of continually exploring who we are is poignant. This doesn't come through quick fixes.

So, be more human being. Be less human doing. Be more present in the moment, without that moment dictating who you are. Ask yourself, 'Who am I?' without consigning yourself to a singular answer. Please yourself, not others. Take action. Adapt. Be.

And above all, learn to solve a Rubik's Cube, because it's a cool party trick.

Chapter 5:
Penny Was A Friend Of Mine

She said she loved me, but she had somewhere to go.
- **The Killers**

Addiction is a funny thing. You're powerless to stop it.

What followed my rugby injury was a three-year spiral into alcoholism and depression, or depression and alcoholism—we'd have to go deep to know which sparked the other. The extent of my drinking problem grew to the point that I could quite happily knock back an entire bottle of spirits in one sitting. That's not intended as a brag, simply a statement of how far along the curve I was. You have the brown-paper-bag, asleep-on-a-park-bench, cursing-at-strangers stereotypical alcoholic, and one step below that is the guy who can polish off a whole bottle of Jack Daniel's Tennessee Honey—or a single malt if I was spoiling myself—in an evening and get up and go to work the next day.

Addiction is a funny thing. You know what you're doing is wrong, but the back of your brain tells you to crack on regardless.

Like having a morning sharpener to start the day. Like buying a gin in a tin just to drink during the walk back from the shops. Like putting away a four-pack of beer, or a bottle of wine, on my hour-long commute back from London. On a Monday. Like making excuses not to go out, so that I could drink alone at home, or finding reasons to go out because I know it would provide a good excuse to have a drink.

Addiction is a funny thing. It skews your priorities.

My health was deteriorating. I wasn't exercising, I was putting on weight, and there'd be days when I wouldn't want to move from the sofa, despite the haunting memory of having been confined to the fucking thing for the three months after leaving the hospital. But I refused to admit to myself that there was anything wrong.

That said, most of the time I could go about my day without behaving like a complete dickhead. On the occasional day when I didn't drink, I wouldn't be desperate to do so and wouldn't be irrational and irritable. Nine times out of ten, when out with mates, I could have a couple of (alright, a few) quiet pints and call it a night. Nine times out of ten I'd come home and Penny wouldn't be faced with the unedifying spectacle of me dribbling.

But there was always that tenth time, when the devil on one shoulder would slip on a set of brass knuckles, strut over the back of my neck onto the other shoulder and beat the living shit out of the angel, whilst asking, 'Do you know what "nemesis" means?' in a gruff, Brick Toppian cockney twang, before feeding the angel to a starving pack of pigs.*

> ***Side note:**
>
> This is another reference to Guy Ritchie's *Snatch*, if you didn't pick up on it.

Such as the time I slept outside Charing Cross station, after missing the last train home. In December. To be fair though, I was the smartest dressed person sleeping outside Charing Cross that night, since I'd been at a black tie dinner.

Or the time I caught the last train home by the skin of my teeth, but then proceeded to sleep all the way down to the south coast. On realising that I was stuck there for the night, I found a bar with a late licence, carried on drinking on my own until it closed, bought a kebab, then went back to the station to sleep until the first train left in the morning.

Or the time I slept halfway down to the south coast and came to the conclusion that walking home through the night, along pitch black country lanes, would be better than sleeping until the first train back.

Or the time I got stuck into a free bar at a wedding and tried to get the bride to down a pint, in the process pouring beer all over her.

Or the time I went to a rugby lunch, and staggered home at 9pm, the evening before starting a new job.

Or the time I fell and cracked my head open, and was rushed to A&E, only for the hospital staff to throw me out because I was too drunk to treat.

Or all the times—so many times that it still scares me how many hours of my life I have lost—I drank so much I blacked out and have no fucking clue what I did.

***

I was introduced to Penny at my former rugby club, Tunbridge Wells RFC. Penny had been to school with the wife of one of my teammates and, in a move that Cilla Black would have been proud of, she was invited to come and stand on the sidelines, pretending to care about the rugby unfolding in front of her. I was club captain at the time and she did me the courtesy of pretending to care as we got chatting after the game, even though I vaguely recall part of the conversation being about my scrum cap, the padded headgear that rugby players wear to protect against the dreaded condition known as 'cauliflower ears'. I like to think she wasn't pretending to care a few hours–and a few drinks later–while we were kissing in the rain outside the town's Pitcher and Piano.

I'd moved home to live with my parents after the credit crunch and I was desperate to turn my life into something that I could once again be proud of. A solid relationship was high up on the list of priorities, having been single for a time in London, and here was a girl with whom I'd instantly hit it off, despite my evidently appalling chat. Penny was a match for my alpha male, overbearing personality, motivated in her career, caring and outgoing. She'd be a stalwart supporter of mine on the rugby sidelines for the next three years, alongside my proud father, who never missed a Tunbridge Wells RFC home game.

It was–if you believe in these things–a match made in heaven and we were comfortable with things moving quickly. I took the opportunity to escape my parents–albeit amidst their unconditional kindness and generosity at being forced to feed a bulky 25-year-old rugby player in between careers–and moved into Penny's flat in central Tunbridge

Wells, where we lived happily together for five years. She supported my career switch and my low salary, and her extremely generous parents treated us to annual, all-inclusive skiing holidays, complete with the luxury of ski-in-ski-out hotels and jacuzzis overlooking the Alps. I proposed on her birthday in the privacy of our living room, since she wasn't one for big public surprises. Life was good.

And then it wasn't.

God only knows what was going through her mind as I was sellotaped to a hospital bed. In the aftermath of my rugby injury, Penny confided in me that she couldn't bring herself to be the one to have to sit me down and have the stern conversation with me that that part of my life was over, since she didn't want me holding her accountable for the loss of rugby. I spent three months wearing that god awful neck brace, a part of me knowing the inevitable, but the other part of me refusing to accept it. Only when the consultant finally gave me the all clear to remove the brace, after I'd thankfully avoided him slicing my throat open to place a titanium cage around my spine, did he gently break the news to me that my rugby days were behind me. I remember him saying, 'I don't want to see you again', in the nicest way possible.

For the most part, Penny tolerated the ensuing rollercoaster of addiction but, as my drinking problems grew, so did my covert ability to mask them. She is an incredibly intelligent woman, but addiction is a funny thing. An addict will come up with any manner of strategies and lie through his teeth to cover up his inebriated movements, such as hiding a bottle of gin in a rugby bag, and I don't think she fully knew the extent of my issues. But our relationship deteriorated as I slowly chipped away at her patience by promising, 'It'll never happen again.' Until the next time. Even the knowledge that I was always running the risk of drinking in the last chance saloon didn't stop me from doing so.

Despite having pretended to care about my scrum cap banter, there was no pretence in how deeply we cared for each other throughout our relationship. We loved each other, no question of it. But being on the other end of my drunken antics must have been hideous, from the perspectives of seeing me deteriorate, the worry I must have caused her and also the anguish of her thinking that I was choosing booze over her. Again and again. Like I said, addiction skews your priorities.

Ultimately, there's only so much that someone can take and, in the words of The Killers, 'she had somewhere to go'[57]; somewhere that wasn't anywhere near me, especially when the final straw came when I proved that I could have quite easily done her–and others–significant harm by thinking that it was acceptable to drive through the busy centre of Tunbridge Wells, after spending the afternoon quietly drinking myself into a near-unconscious stupor.

Several months of counselling sessions, both together and separately, wasn't enough to convince her that I was capable of change–because I wasn't–and Penny called time on the relationship, cancelling the wedding. I was drunk. I was bitter. I resented her. We were due to promise to love each other 'in sickness and in health' and this was my sickness. I blamed her for ending things but now realise how hard it must have been for her to come to the decision and recognise her bravery.

Have yourself another little Disney quote, this time from wise old Rafiki after he has battered an adolescent Simba, afraid to confront his past, over the head with his staff: 'The past can hurt. But the way I see it, you can either run from it or learn from it.'[58]

I certainly didn't learn from it. Nope, what I did was run as far away as I could from anything that resembled making the right decision, convincing myself that my drinking was fine because it was Penny's unforgiving cruelty that was the reason for our relationship failing, rather than me being shit-faced most of the time and coming worryingly close to a hit and run in Tunbridge Wells town centre. I had a brief hiatus but soon returned to the booze.

Mark Twain is credited with the quote, 'We regret the things we don't do more than the things we do.' When looking back, I think regret is a waste of an emotion. That may sound emotionally stunted but dwelling on things doesn't teach you anything. There's nothing you can do about the past, apart from learn from it, as advised by Rafiki, changing where necessary to move forward. Taking action, as we explored in Chapter 4.

It's for that reason that I don't regret my actions—or lack of them in attempting to change—but what does eat at me is my inability to recognise the pain I was causing those closest to me. My family suffered a great deal of upset as I distanced myself from them, because doing so was easier than facing them and admitting I had a problem; a serious fucking problem. My mum has since said, 'We tried to support you but you shut us out.' I went through a series of unhealthy and sometimes turbulent relationships, each time laying the blame elsewhere despite being the common denominator. My friends humoured me as I went back to ordering pints during nights out, telling them that, 'This time, I won't let alcohol control me.' But as we'll discover in the next chapter, overcoming a drinking problem requires admitting you're 'powerless over alcohol'. You can never control it; it will always control you.

Since then, I've spent many a moment racking my brains as to whether there was a deep, dark psychological trauma in my childhood that could have prompted this unhealthy approach to alcohol–aside from the identity crisis I explained in the previous chapter. I can't find one. I was never abused, physically, sexually or emotionally. I was never neglected. I was lucky to benefit from complete and unwavering love from two wonderful parents. I have a group of friends so loyal that we'd cross continents to help each other out. Even the butter scenario on the post-rugby match university initiation coach journey wasn't *that* scarring. What's more, Richard Olley, a clinical hypnotherapist specialising in hypno-analysis, believes that 'one of the contributing factors [to problems with alcohol] is a subconscious lack of self-love … people who lack self-love are much more likely to become alcohol dependent because their innate instinct for self-care is reduced.'[59] But I don't agree with that either; I just think my brain is wired differently and I lack an 'off-switch'. Where most people think they've had enough after five pints, I'd think, 'This is awesome, I'll have five more.' That tenth time would come around and my cartoon Brick Top devil would take over with a vengeance.

The brief abstinence only served to draw out my cravings and, on falling off the wagon, I descended even further into the spiral. The next few months were the loneliest of my life and I did many things which I'm not proud of. Like, with a girlfriend away, seeing the opportunity to 'enjoy'–definitely not the right word–a session on the beers, whilst telling her that I was attending an Alcoholics Anonymous meeting. Which is pretty dark.

When she came home early to surprise me and saw the state I was in, I blamed her for catching me red-handed and a blow-out argument ensued. I stormed out of the flat, taking a bottle of Jack Daniel's with me, checked myself into a dingy hotel and proceeded to drink the entire bottle, doing so in the relative peace of my own pathetic company. The next morning, through the haze of a horrific hangover–I had drunk several pints *before* knocking back a whole bottle of whiskey–I saw myself clearly for the first time in three years. And I didn't like what I saw.

It was my rock bottom.

***

You may not be a fan of South Park. I appreciate it's puerile but I've dipped into a few episodes here and there and it always makes me chuckle. While many of the episodes morph into one another and I have little-to-no recollection of any specifics, one has always stuck with me. In Season 14, in the highly inappropriately named *Coon 2: Hindsight*, reporter Jack Brolin is the 'victim of a freak accident that gave him the power of extraordinary hindsight'. The emerging alter ego, Captain Hindsight, is pegged as 'the hero of the modern age' but is unquestionably the most useless–but arguably the funniest–superhero in all of the multiverses, metaverses, megaverses, miniverses and other verses.

Rather than fighting crime alongside his companions Shoulda, Coulda and Woulda, he swoops in, tells people what they've done wrong and then flies out again. For example, in the advent of a burning building with people trapped inside and the fire service unable to get to them, he declares: 'You see those windows on the right side? They should have built fire escapes on those windows for the higher floors, then people could have gotten down. And then the roof. They should have built it with a more reinforced structure, so a helicopter could have landed on it. And then you see that building to the left? They shouldn't have built that there because now you can't park any fire trucks where you really need to. Well, looks like my job here is done.'

At which point he's off to cries of, 'Thank you, Captain Hindsight.' The fire service decides it's done for the night and packs up, leaving the building (and people inside) ablaze.

Were I a South Park character, I imagine being shocked and appalled at the latest episode's creative killing off of Kenny and then feeling a pang of dismay at the consequences of my latest drunken antics. At this point, Captain Hindsight would swoop in and say something along the lines of, 'James, you see the trail of destruction you've left in your wake? And the people you've upset. You should have realised the extent of the cataclysmic chaos you were causing and done something about it. Like quitting drinking when you really needed to. Well, looks like my job here is done.' And I'd shout, 'Thanks, Captain Hindsight.'

In hindsight, I have a lot to thank Penny for. Ultimately, it was the realisation that I had driven her away that led to me making the decision, once and for all, to quit drinking. That said, not for a second would I change the course of my life that has led me to the here and now. Krista is an astonishing partner and it is testament to our relationship that she accepted me writing about an important chapter in my life that involved another woman.

***

Years after Penny ended things, when I was around three months sober, I was working my way through the Twelve Steps of the AA programme. I'll cover these in a little more detail in the next chapter but a couple deserve mention, even though it's skipping ahead. Steps 8 and 9 read as follows:

> 8. We made a list of all persons we had harmed, and became willing to make amends to them all.
>
> 9. We made direct amends to such people wherever possible, except when to do so would injure them or others.

As part of this process I needed to make amends to many people and Penny was top of the list for everything I had put her through. I didn't feel it would 'injure' her so I drafted a letter. Here's what it said:

> Dearest Penny,
>
> Please excuse the out-of-the-blue nature of this email but I've been doing a lot of soul-searching in the last few months and wanted to get in touch.
>
> I have been a deeply selfish person in recent years—I'd like to think caused mostly by my alcohol problem—and I've taken a lot of people for granted. I'm starting to come to terms with that and am trying to vaguely put right some of the wrongs I have caused to so many people. Unfortunately there's no grand gesture that can magically amend everything I've said and done but I hope that some good will come of getting some things off my chest that

desperately need to be said.

Ultimately I am truly ashamed of my actions and will, I'm sure, live with them for a long while to come. I know now that being unable to accept responsibility is why I (unfairly) resented you for ending things the way you did but it was wrong of me to have any ill-feelings towards you, which I absolutely no longer do. In hindsight, you were right to do what you did as I would have just ended up hurting you even more.

So with that I mind I want to say sorry for the pain I caused you. You deserve to be happy and I'm sorry that what I put you through didn't make you so (and should you [find] someone who's able to give you all those things, he's lucky to have you).

I can't truly understand the grief that you must have gone through time and time again and I kick myself everyday in the knowledge that I wasn't willing to do anything about it. The thought now that I repeatedly said "it'll be the last time" but actually considered alcohol more important than our relationship is absolutely maddening.

For what it's worth I'm now three months sober. I am regularly attending AA meetings and also went to a special seminar called the Allen Carr Easyway, which was a very practical way of looking at things and pretty eye-opening. Hopefully as a result I can be a better person for myself and those around me.

While I don't want anything in return for this, it would mean a great deal if you can find it in your heart to forgive me.

With love,

James

To Penny's credit, she gracefully indulged me, thanking me for the apology and saying she didn't hold any bad feelings towards me. She also clarified that as our relationship petered out, there was 'too much history, too many second chances, and the trust was gone.' I thanked her for her honesty and allowed her to get on with her life without further interruption.

Until recently, when she courteously gave me the nod of approval to write about her in a book for all the world– or, probably more accurately, three and a half people and maybe a fox rooting through a recycling bin–to see.

Chapter 6:
A Journey Of A Thousand Miles

Even Superman has a weakness. Kryptonite.
- **A guy at an AA meeting but it's Alcoholics** *Anonymous*, **so I can't tell you his name.**

When I was three years old, my mum tells me, there was an episode of Postman Pat that had me fleeing from the room in fear.

Yes, Postman Pat, that most terrifying of children's TV shows about a postman who, 'early in the morning, just as day is dawning, picks up all the post bags in his van.' And then seems to do anything but deliver them. Including in the episode *Postman Pat and the Magpie Hen*, in which he makes one delivery and then takes time out at lunch to have a nap in a field. Lazy Postman Pat.

Anyway, while he's snoozing, Mrs Thompson's hens come clucking past, one of whom is a particularly demonic, scary-looking, black menace of an individual who seemingly thinks she's a magpie. She steals Pat's van keys and a saga ensues where Pat's up a tree—because apparently hens can climb trees—finding a stash of shiny objects that the hen has been hoarding. When Pat eventually gets round to doing his job, he returns the various lost items to the residents of Greendale.

Of course, when I say scary, what I really mean is the most unscary hen-magpie hybrid you could possibly imagine, but it's easy to say that as I turn 40. 37 years ago, that thing chilled my blood. Apparently.

***

They say, 'Nobody likes a quitter.' But that's bollocks. Utter bollocks. A quitter absolutely loves a quitter if the quitter is making the correct decision to quit whatever they're quitting because whatever they're quitting is doing them harm.

The trick is recognising the appropriate time to quit, whether it's knowing when a strategy isn't working or recognising when a habit is doing harm to you and others. All of the world's most successful people have given up on one thing or another—a business, a strategy, a dream—when it hasn't been working, in their pursuit of an end goal. The trouble many of us face is getting too invested in a project or too deep into a problem and struggling to see the wood for the trees.

Three years after breaking my neck was three years too late to quit drinking but, as they also say, 'Better late than never.' As I intimated in my letter to Penny, Alcoholics Anonymous became a big part of my journey. And that word might seem fluffy and naff, but it's one I use deliberately. One of my favourite quotes is attributed to American writer Ralph Waldo Emerson: 'Life is a journey, not a destination.' It's a quote that epitomises the mentality we should adopt of not being sucked into society's judgements of our achievements. By focusing too hard on what we're *doing* and the results, we don't experience the process of *being*, as explored in Chapter 4. We become fixated on pleasing others, not ourselves. We don't get to explore our values and what's important to us. We don't learn and we don't grow.

I had tried AA the first time I 'quit' after Penny ended things and decided it wasn't for me. It was beneath me. I looked down on the other people in the room as being 'worse off' than me. They had *real* problems; *serious fucking* problems. I just enjoyed a drink or two. I wasn't 'one of them'. I wasn't like my friend Alfred, talking to my pint in Wetherspoons.

But something finally clicked in me on 26th March 2016, whilst sitting in the breakfast room of that dingy hotel, the morning after seeing away several pints and a bottle of Tennessee's finest. Staring at one of those cheap full English breakfasts that give you heart palpitations shortly after eating them, failing to stomach the rashers of bacon that were more fat than meat on the plate in front of me, I no longer wanted to be the person I had become. It was as if an inner part of myself–that I didn't believe in–floated out of my body, turned around and then gave me a good slap across the face. I can vividly remember jolting out of a bacon grease-induced reverie and thinking, 'Enough is enough.'

Call it an epiphany. Call it a light bulb moment. Call it a spiritual awakening. Call it whatever you like, I was no longer able to wreak drunken havoc and inflict misery on all that I loved. 'Whatever habits you develop, they become part of your identity', is what Nabbsie said in Chapter 3. As a result of some severely toxic habits, I identified as a raging alcoholic. I needed to kick those habits in order to change who I was as a person. And I had to rediscover the ability to like who I was for the first time in a long time.

I knew what I had to do but I was afraid to do it.

**

There are, in the broadest possible terms, two types of fear; physical and psychological.

Physical fear is the life-saving kind. It is stimulated by a threat to ward us off from danger, based on prehistoric instincts that are governed by our mammalian brain, which we'll explore further in Chapter 10. It's the 'real' fear, honed over thousands of millennia and the cumulative experiences of the species. In today's world, it stops us stepping out into moving traffic or snorting condoms (most of us). It's based on knowledge, fact and causality. If you step out into traffic, you know you are likely to be hit by a car. And that will hurt. If you snort a condom, it's likely you'll end up in A&E with a nurse telling you you're a fucking moron. Whether you do either one is governed by the level of risk, and you weigh this up against whether it's worth it for the potential outcome; getting to the other side of the road, or having an inane video to post on social media.

But the second type of fear is essentially the unknown. Psychological fears are often an overreaction, based on what we think we might know about a situation. We concoct narratives that allow us to take the path of least resistance—the one that doesn't require us to face our fears—without having properly identified whether or not there is indeed a threat, based on incomplete knowledge, data or experience. As such, these 'fake' fears are constructs that exist only in our minds. They are lies. And these lies can cripple us. Think about it; how often do we live in fear of something, only to discover that the reality isn't as bad as we imagined? Or worse, miss an opportunity, for fear of failure or judgement at its outcome?

These stories are like masks worn to protect ourselves but we have to be aware of the difference between *protect* and *prevent*. Fear can serve us—even save us—but it can also be debilitating and can prevent us from realising our full potential and being our true selves. This is something I resonate with extremely strongly when I look back at the mask I was wearing by relying on alcohol to get me through social situations, or even dull afternoons.

But, on 26th March 2016, through a combination of necessity and desire, I made a decision to stop riding the rollercoaster. I donned my humble hat, tucked my tail between my legs and found a local Alcoholics Anonymous meeting. In doing so, I forced myself to concoct a narrative that would better serve me; that AA wasn't beneath me, that I was no better or worse off than anyone else in the room, and that I too had a *real* problem; a *serious fucking* problem (henceforth called an SFP). That, yes, I was 'one of them'. While I was at it, I sought more counselling, tried hypnotherapy, attended the Allen Carr seminar I mentioned, watched webinars, scoured the internet for information on addiction and read books. I soaked up everything I could surrounding sobriety. I became addicted to recovery.

Of these, AA provided the strongest foundations of my sobriety. It is a phenomenal programme, which has helped countless millions of addicts and alcoholics achieve sobriety, myself included. From the first few months, I was able to take what I'd seen and heard, and use the learnings to develop my own approach to staying on the wagon.

The heart of the AA programme lies in being able to keep an open mind, something I hadn't been able to achieve the first time, and in following the Twelve Steps. For newcomers, the first of these read:

> 1. We admitted we were powerless over alcohol – that our lives had become unmanageable.
>
> 2. Came to believe that a Power greater than ourselves could restore us to sanity.

Which can be 'translated' along the lines of:

> 1. Admitting you've got an SFP.
>
> 2. Realising that you can't solve your SFP on your own.

For the benefit of (hopefully) the vast majority of people reading this who don't have an SFP, I'll hop, skip and jump through the nitty gritty details. In short, if you've got an SFP, half of the battle is admitting it. That requires being brutally honest with yourself, when telling my friends in the pub that I wasn't going to let alcohol control me had been like–drum roll, another Disney reference coming up–Pinocchio telling the Blue Fairy that he met two big monsters with big green eyes, that they tied him in a big sack, that they put Jiminy Cricket in a little sack, and oh shit, my nose is three feet long and has a bird nest at the end of it. It was only by surrendering to the complete lack of control, the powerlessness, that I could start to, finally, empower myself.

Scratch beneath the surface of AA and you discover this is what the whole programme is about; empowerment. It gives you the tools, through the Steps and through listening to the lived experiences of others, to manage and reframe your thoughts about your SFP.

And to overcome the other half of the problem; the fear.

For three years, I had been a fugue state, semi-present version of myself, not bringing my all to anything, and my greatest fear was therefore that I wouldn't be able to rediscover the real James. That my friends would judge me for having been an alcoholic. That they'd shun me if I gave up drinking because I'd no longer be one of the lads.

My inability to quit drinking the first time I attended AA was therefore based on the narrative that my friends would no longer be my friends if I was teetotal. It seems utterly ridiculous to write that now, because they'd have been pretty shitty friends, and it was their support that got me through the earliest and toughest stages of my sobriety.

When we face a challenge of this nature, when a battle rages between our internal narrative and the reality, it's the realisation that fear is an illusion that invariably proves the defining factor. Separating the two and making decisions based on the reality allows us to find the strength to move past the *prevent*.

The *Tao Te Ching*, written in around 400 BC by the Chinese sage Laozi, contains the famous line 'A journey of a thousand miles begins with a single step'. Taking the first step can be like setting off from Munchkinland along the yellow brick road. You don't know what the journey ahead will entail–maybe witches and flying monkeys–but sometimes you've just got to link arms with a brainless scarecrow, a heartless tin man and a cowardly lion and crack on regardless. It's true that you might be afraid of taking the first step but, if it was easy, it wouldn't be an SFP. That's the challenge.

But taking the first step is always liberating. In my case, doing so led me to the major realisation that my challenge—that I wouldn't be able to rediscover myself and my friends would think the new James was as dull as dishwater—was my own construct that existed only in my mind. My own narrative I was telling myself. A lie.

It was empowering and it didn't so much as dent my friendships; it reaffirmed them.

Because admitting you're powerless is a waste of time if you're the only one who's in the loop. Other people need to know of your intentions. So, what I perceived as my challenge was actually my support. I couldn't solve my SFP on my own. Telling my two best friends, two of the world's most wonderful humans, Ollie and Rich—who would later be Best Man and an usher at Krista's and my wedding (plus Rich is Freddie's godfather)—and hearing their supportive words gave me the confidence to tell more people, and more, and more. In truth, they were relieved; Ollie has since said, 'I think James used to miss the point of the phrase "being able to hold your drink", thinking it was about how much you can drink and still be standing, rather than how much you can drink without it affecting you. James could put away more than I could imagine, but you could see the changes pretty quickly when he was drinking.

'The worst consequence for me at the height of his drinking was just a sense of not being able to enjoy some nights out to their full, as I felt a need to stay in control and be in some sort of fit state to sort any issues, or to be a peacemaker. Most times went off without any incident—it's not like he was an aggressive drunk—but the obviousness of drunkenness did throw the odd spanner in the works.

'After the neck break, he spiralled and the main thing was more a feeling of not being able to help, or not helping enough. I remember not having a clue how to approach the situation when we were supposed to be going on a lads' trip to Barcelona; could we go and not drink? Do we go at all? Is it just a terrible idea? With the benefit of hindsight, forcing a proper conversation early on would probably have helped, but at the same time people were coming at him from all sides. And how do you approach this kind of situation that is paradoxically both shocking and unsurprising?

'It was probably at its worst when he started drinking again, with an apparent "awareness" to keep it under control. After SOS messages from his mum, it became a team effort to support James, and also to get past the bravado and get the real story about what was going on with him. It just meant worry on different levels; worries after a disappearance to go on a bender; worries about his physical health; and–probably most of all–worries about his state of mind and general mental health.'

So, it was hard for all around me because they knew that with my drinking came the risk of me pressing the self-destruct button. For me, though, the relief of confiding in friends allowed me to tell more people, so I wouldn't constantly have to dodge the question, 'Alright mate, can I get you a pint?' By admitting my SFP to myself, and subsequently all of my friends, their support in encouraging me–after some close-to-the-bone banter to start with, but that's what you get when you've played rugby for two decades–and congratulating me as I hit my 24 hour, one week and one month sober milestones was a major part of my success in those early days. The people who fuelled my fear were the key to overcoming it.

That's not to say it didn't involve some tough decisions. For example, ditching the one or two friends that tried to convince me that I was fine; that I didn't in fact have an SFP. Or former friends to be precise, since if they weren't going to support me, they had to go. And, as I'd come to learn, people who are negative towards such decisions are generally trying to justify their own SFPs. Watch out for them. They're the party starters. The ones that think you're the Archbishop of Banterbury if you fall and crack your head open and are rushed to A&E, only for the hospital staff to throw you out because you're too drunk to treat. The ones who are first to shout, 'Let's do shots,' at 6:30pm when you've only come out for a quiet catch-up. The ones that guzzle their glass of wine and barely a second has gone by before they're helping themselves to another whilst offering to top up everyone else even though you're still appreciating the vintage because 2020 was a very good year for Pomerol. The ones that insist that you have 'one for the road', even if that means you'll likely be divorced because you promised you'd be home in time to read little Johnny one of the Mr. Men books as his bedtime story. The ones that aren't healthy to be around when you're trying to quit drinking. So, actually some pretty easy decisions.

The crucial takeaway is that we can 'quit'; we can change a narrative that isn't serving us to one that can. This requires moving towards the thing we're fearful of but, when we make the effort to learn more about the situation, based on the facts and more complete knowledge, we invariably discover that the threat either didn't exist, or wasn't as bad as we'd thought. We can therefore shift a limiting belief and suddenly the illusion starts to dissolve.

I had been pretending to be somebody else for three

years and the idea of rediscovering who I was had been built up in my mind as an undertaking that filled me with trepidation. But it's only when you face your fears that you truly discover who you are.

On 26th March 2016, I put a plan in place to address my SFP and I haven't looked back. Since then I have been more, well, me. I've been more content and more confident. The reason for that is I'm no longer wearing a mask, pretending to be somebody else. I'm all in, bringing my all to everything.

***

In the early days of my sobriety, I met some inspirational, wonderful and fascinating people and learned some valuable lessons. Your SFP doesn't have to be alcohol-related–or anything to do with addiction for that matter–to also benefit from those lessons. Here were my key ones; my three Rs:

- Recognising.

    This is the admission bit. You're facing a challenge. Something is stressing you out, causing you to behave irrationally, impairing your ability to enjoy life, or you can't stop getting uncontrollably shitfaced to the point of blacking out and waking up in a wheelie bin, and the fact you have no recollection of anything past 8:30pm and the subsequent shame are eating you alive. You have an SFP. By recognising the issue, you're putting one foot on the yellow brick road and, from there, you can formulate a plan. It could be a habit you're trying to kick, a deadline you're trying to meet, a difficult client, a leaky tap or morbid fear of a magpie hen. It doesn't matter.

- Reallocating.

    This is the sharing bit. If you've got an SFP, tell someone. Actually, tell everyone. There's no shame in admitting defeat and roping in as many people as possible to help you fix things. In the case of the leaky tap, tell a plumber. The difficult client; your boss. A bad habit; every. Single. Person. You. Know. If they judge you for it or don't want you to stop because they've got their own SFP, strike them off the friend list. I make no apologies for telling you to be brutal if necessary, especially if there's a chance they could compromise your plan. You are your number one priority and anything that is going to come in the way of your plan, your focus, your relationships or your health has to go. On the other hand, cling on like a limpet to anyone who is keen to get behind you. Build an army of supporters. 'A problem well-stated is a problem half-solved', is a quote attributed to a chap called Charles Kettering who worked at General Motors a century ago. But it's still pretty apt 100 years later.

- Reframing.

    This is the flipping it to make it seem like it's no longer an SFP bit. In short, if you've got an SFP, don't think of it as a problem. Ok, that may sound overly simple but the thought process is important when approaching your plan so that it's something you can relish, rather than resent. In my case, simply thinking, 'I *get* to give up drinking', rather than, 'I *have* to give up drinking', made it seem positive. It was the tiniest change but it gave the challenge an entirely different, more productive perspective and made it seem like I was Spiderman shimmying up a New York City skyscraper, rather than Alex Honnold climbing El Capitan without ropes. I was benefitting from giving up, *gaining* my Sunday mornings–alright, most mornings–enhancing my focus at work, improving my health and fitness, reconnecting with friends and being more present for my loved ones, rather than *losing* the occasional–alright, regular–pint. And it works in most situations. I *get* to fix my leaky tap, and no longer have that incessant dripping, rather than I *have* to fix my leaky tap, which will involve phoning the plumber, haggling over a price, arranging a time for him to come, having to make idle small talk over a cup of tea, while I'm technically paying him for work that he's not doing, etc, etc. Circling back to identity, I also get to say, 'I don't drink', rather than having to say, 'I'm a recovering alcoholic', which has negative connotations.

When my anonymous friend imparted his sage counsel about Superman being weakened by kryptonite, it was transformational for me. It helped me to shed the invincible identity I'd been desperate to cling on to and adopt an approach that I didn't have to go at things alone. From there, rather than fear being an indication of what not to do, it became an indication of what to do. The mask came off and the illusion lifted.

By admitting my lack of control I was no longer fearful of quitting. I gave myself permission to ask for help. And that was ok, because I had an SFP. If you do too, be more Kryptonite guy. Not in the sense of feeling like you need to attend an AA meeting and pour your heart out necessarily–as we've covered, your SFP could be completely unrelated to addiction–but in the sense that we don't ever have to suffer through crippling fear. We can face a challenge in the knowledge that support is at hand, but we have to take the initiative and seek it out. Unfortunately, unlike Superman, it won't just swoop in and save us of its own accord, but if we know where to look, it can be liberating and empowering.

We all need help once in a while, even if it's to take a single step. 37 years ago, my greatest fear was a magpie hen; it's now not being a good father to my son. But nothing will *prevent* me from doing everything in my power to be the best dad that I can possibly be–and I'm obviously thinking I *get* to, rather than I *have* to–so I'm able to change the narrative to something that serves me. It will be a challenge but one that I am relishing. I'm thinking of the positives, not the negatives. It's the unknown but I will show up as all that I am. I'm fearful, but I'm happy to step out into traffic.

Chapter 7:
What Are You Running From?

I'm able.
- **Esmée Gummer**

Don't worry, I'm not going to go through each Step of the AA programme one by one in some never-ending diatribe of redemption, but Step 3 also deserves some attention because it's a little harder to digest, particularly with the word 'God' floating around in there. If you come a cropper at Step 1, it's simple: you don't recognise that you have an SFP. Or you're flat out denying it, asking things like, 'What's wrong with a cheeky sharpener in the morning?'

If it's Step 2 that you can't get past, you know that you have an SFP but you can't see how you're going to solve it. The yellow brick road lies ahead of you but you haven't moved from unwilling to willing to set off from Munchkinland. You know the challenge but you haven't identified the support.

Step 3's a bit trickier to navigate because it can be

off-putting if you're, like me, as religious as a block of cheese. It was a stumbling block for me the first time I attempted to sober up as I failed to get my head around how a reference to God wasn't going to have me on my knees in silent contemplation or, at the other end of the spectrum, shouting 'Hallelujah, praise Jesus' at the top of my lungs, whilst shaking a tambourine. It reads:

> 3. Made a decision to turn our will and our lives over to the care of God as we understood Him.

That's daunting, right? That implies giving up all your worldly possessions and going to live in a monastery where you'll spend the rest of your life wearing a hessian sack tied up with a rope and sporting a very dodgy haircut. But the trick is to not get too bogged down by the religious undertones.

In simple terms, the 'decision' is exactly that. It isn't a flaky, half-arsed, 'I'll try and do better.' It's a whole-hearted guarantee that it really will 'never happen again'. And those last four words—'as we understood Him'—aren't a commitment to God per se; they're a commitment to whatever your interpretation is of Him. If your interpretation of Him is that there is no God, that's fine. That doesn't mean you can't find something to hang your hat on. Your Higher Power.

To get over an SFP, you have to acknowledge that you need help; that you can't go it alone by simply gritting your teeth and thinking, 'I've got this.' Because, unfortunately, you don't got this. At least not through willpower alone. When you accept Step 3, you can begin to explore the notion of fulfilling something other than your SFP. You can make a promise to think about someone other than yourself for a change. That's not to say you necessarily mean to be a selfish prick when you have an SFP; you just *are* a selfish prick.

If that needs any clarification, reread Chapter 5. But it doesn't have to be a full-blown, bottle-of-whisky-a-day alcohol addiction. Not addressing *any* SFP is selfish.

Take being overweight; it's selfish. Yup, I went there. Add fat-shaming to the list of reasons why I should be cancelled. There are, of course, exceptions such as disability and medical conditions but, otherwise, chowing down on a Hot Wings Bucket Deal or eating a pack of Hobnobs every day puts your health at risk, which has ramifications for your family. And the NHS, come to think of it. If you struggle to go for walks in the countryside or kick a ball around, you're not bringing all of yourself for your children. You're depriving them of access to the benefits of physical exercise and, by your poor example, you're setting them up to be unhealthy in the future.

Your Higher Power, then, doesn't have to be the dread-inducing, Kumbaya-singing, bible-bashing you might think it does. You don't need to pick up a copy of the Good Book, light candles, burn incense and get up at 4am every day to discipline yourself through self-flagellation–though if that's your thing, don't let me stop you. But it does need to be something powerful enough to drive you, something to give your life meaning, whether that's devoting yourself to a relationship, committing to being a better parent, or a dedication to be more present for those around you. Mine, I would come to realise, was rediscovering my health and fitness.

***

For as long as Esmée Gummer can remember, she was

captivated by movement. She has a crystal clear memory of announcing to her mother: 'Mum, I know what I want to be when I'm older. I want to be a dancer.' She spent her teenage years in pursuit of that dream and, aged 18, was due to start dance college. However, in a sad twist of fate, Esmée had a bad reaction to the anaesthetic administered to her during a routine operation on a hernia and suffered seizures which left her with an SFP; paralysis from the waist down. She was told she may never walk again.

In the weeks and months that followed, she faced the trauma of being confined to a hospital ward and the agony of reteaching herself all the things that many of us take for granted. From learning to walk without feeling the floor because her feet were still numb, to the strain of using parallel bars and making herself unwell due to wanting to push too hard, it was a long journey of rehabilitation back to fitness.

Along the way Esmée had good days and bad days, physically and mentally, and learned better than most the connection between the two. She recalls, 'The mental side [of my rehabilitation] was a lot harder than the physical because you know what to expect physically. If you can't walk, you can't walk. But, with the mental side, I never knew how I was going to feel each day, whether in rehab or in physio or at 2 o'clock in the morning if I couldn't sleep. I never knew what emotions I was going to get.'

After a while, the negative thoughts of 'I can't do this' started to take over and she hit a plateau in her recovery. She recalls one of the physiotherapists, who was 'hard as nails', approaching the side of her bed and instructing her, 'Well, come on then, stand up.' Despite Esmée's protests that she couldn't, the physio insisted. Es was sick after attempting to get to her feet but the tough love helped her overcome the fear of trying. It reinforced her willingness to put the work in.

'It was the first time I'd met that physio,' Es says, 'and I found her horrendous. I thought she was evil. But it was a version of good cop, bad cop; a tactic to make sure I was trying, when it seemed like I was giving up. She didn't change the physiology of the issue, she just changed my mindset. She made me want it ten times more. She made me want to prove I could do it.'

And prove it she did. 'The physio was very hard on me but had a massive impact, since I left the hospital a few weeks later. I wasn't completely back to walking again—I left in a wheelchair—but her tough love made all the difference.' One of the doctors too had a profound effect on her outlook: 'When I left the hospital, I remember the doctor saying to me, "If you hadn't wanted to walk, you wouldn't have." And that has stuck with me because he was right. I could have decided that my legs were numb and that I was just going to lie there. I could have made myself immobile out of choice—or lack of it.'

Not that it was all rosy after that; she experienced the darkest few months of her life after leaving hospital. Stuck at home, unable to fulfil her childhood dream, despite being on the road to recovery, she 'was in a really bad place, so resentful of my friends at dance college that it made me sick. I haven't felt jealousy like it, before or since. Some days I wouldn't move from the sofa.'

Help came in the form of being offered disability allowance and Esmée 'started filling out the form'. But she couldn't bring herself to complete it. 'I thought, "I'm able, I'm just not able right now. I'm not strong in my legs yet,"' she explains.

Movement was still her dream so, whilst working a nine-to-five office job–still in a wheelchair–she started taking her Level 2 Fitness Instructor qualification online as she continued with her rehab. The minute she was able to complete the physical part of the test, demonstrating the exercises, she quit the job. Since then she has become a renowned personal trainer and TV presenter. She has completed various marathons, even ultramarathons, climbed Mount Kilimanjaro and was, for a time, the Head of Exercise Wellness at Virgin Active. In 2024, because running a marathon is seemingly not hard enough, she completed the London Marathon whilst interviewing other runners.

I could wax lyrical about how inspirational she is but, rather than gushing embarrassingly–for both me and Es–I want to focus on her motivations and the outlook that the doctor prompted in her, even though she didn't realise it at the time.

'I thought I took my fitness qualifications because of the link to dance and my love of movement,' she says, 'but now I understand that I took them because I wanted to help people. Having gone through the highs and lows of such an arduous rehabilitation, I couldn't bear the thought of someone else thinking they couldn't do whatever they wanted to do. I wanted to help people challenge a negative "I can't do that" way of thinking and show people what they are capable of achieving.' In simple terms, she has a passion for wanting other people to feel good.

Don't believe her? In a bid to inspire people who

struggle to find the motivation to work out, she partnered with a mental health charity during the COVID-19 lockdowns and filmed herself completing 30 different exercises in 30 days to demonstrate the variety of ways that people can exercise. As she elaborates, 'You don't hate exercise, you either hate *what* you're doing or *why* you're doing it.'

The 'what' is self-explanatory. Some people like to run, others prefer football, rugby, rowing, racquet sports, martial arts, lifting weights, yoga or walking the dog. Whatever your bag, any form of exercise is a good form of exercise. The 'why' is more complicated.

In Chapter 1 we looked at how social media is taking over our lives and causing us to do all manner of inane, indescribably stupid things. What it's also doing is making us more body conscious. The pressures of society and the influence of fitness models and ripped movie stars (like my man-crush Chris Hemsworth) make us want to look good, lose weight, tone up, bulk up, have a six pack or be a certain dress size, but these are goals set according to how we want to be seen by others, rather than how we want to see ourselves. They're unrealistic in the context that Chris Hemsworth has bucket loads of cash, his own fitness app and a hefty wedge of spare time each day to workout, when the rest of us mere mortals—in the sense that we're not millionaire movie stars, as opposed to not being the Mjölnir-wielding god of thunder and lightning—have limited time to spend shifting tin. And, personally, with the arrival of a bundle of joy, that spare time has become even more limited to the point that any fleeting moments I do have are mostly spent trying to catch up on sleep or bemoaning my lack of sleep.

Esmée, then—and I would come to completely align

with her way of thinking—doesn't 'believe in body goals.' It's an enlightening statement from a personal trainer of all people but it makes perfect sense when you think of the immediate results. As Es expands, 'You don't see a physical change immediately after a workout and that can make you feel like you haven't made progress, if your goal is only based on physical appearances. For example, if you go into a workout thinking, "I want to lose weight," you might sweat a bit, but you won't lose body mass. But if you work out with the intention of feeling good or improving your mood, you'll feel the benefits as soon as the endorphins kick in.'

In case you need a brief biology-mixed-with-military-references lesson, because that's the analogy I fancy, imagine your brain as a high-ranked military officer sitting in a command post. A recon team posing as goatherds has scoped out the possible location of Pain and Stress, two key enemies on the Disposition Matrix*. Content that he has sufficient intelligence for an operation, your brain / the officer orders a special task force of hormones, split into Alpha Team (endorphins) and Bravo Team (endocannabinoids, eCBs), out into the field. Under cover of night, Alpha and Bravo advance to tactically safe positions to assess the validity of the intel and verify the objectives. Alpha and Bravo confirm the targets and additionally learn that Pain and Stress are planning an assault on your compound. Now an imminent threat, Pain and Stress must be neutralised, so Alpha and Bravo locate the enemies' weapons cache and send a transmission (or a neurotransmission, in the case of your brain) back, detailing the location and requesting an immediate air strike. With the target locked on, your brain calls in a couple of MQ-9 Reaper drones for a double-tap strike on the cache, with the aim of the second strike hitting

Pain and Stress as they respond to assess the damage. There are no rescue workers in the area, so the likelihood of civilian casualties is minimal.

> ***Side note:**
> The Disposition Matrix, aka the 'Kill List', is a database of individuals identified for targeted assassination.

Or, in short, endorphins block pain when you're exercising and give you a sensation of improved wellbeing during pleasurable activities such as laughing, listening to music, sex and even eating chocolate or spicy food.* There's some more sciencey stuff debating whether it's endorphins or eCBs that produce the resulting euphoria, known as a 'runner's high', because 'endorphins cannot cross the blood-brain barrier because of their hydrophilic structure, [whereas] lipophilic eCBs easily penetrate the brain and are excellent candidates to explain exercise-brain interactions'[60]–whatever all that means–but either way, exercise makes you feel good. Bio-fucking-logical fact.

> ***Side note / note to self:**
> Must try a combination of all of the above.

Back to Es, who'd 'like to educate the world that you don't just get physical benefits from exercise, you also get mental health benefits. And if working out is a mental health decision, you're going to feel those benefits straightaway.'

Or as Phil Knight, the Founder of Nike, puts it: 'If people got out and ran a few miles every day, the world would be a better place.'[61] We'll revisit Knight later.

***

After three years of not exercising, rekindling a love of movement became a crucial part of my recovery. In the weeks after my second attempt at a first AA session, I was struggling with the concept of the Higher Power. I don't necessarily believe in fate because, in the words of Neo, 'I don't like the idea that I'm not in control of my life.'[62] My mum always says, 'Things happen for a reason', so whether it was fate or my mum's intuition or just sheer coincidence, I found myself watching the London Marathon on TV one Sunday morning shortly after. I was in awe. 40,000 people pushing themselves to their limits, taking on an undoubtedly physically and mentally tough challenge, overcoming hardship and adversity, some with incredible stories of why they were doing it, thousands in aid of charitable causes, outrageous fancy dress outfits from fruits to dinosaurs, Storm Troopers to Paddington Bear, you name it. There were even four lads tied together in the shape of a fire truck and a guy carrying a dishwasher for fuck's sake. My emotions completely and utterly got the better of me and I was a sobbing, blubbering mess as I watched people smiling and cheering whilst conquering 26.2 miles along the streets of our capital.

Overwhelmed, I knew my reaction was the start of something. I had found my elusive Higher Power. I resolved to take on the challenge the next year and the next day contacted a rugby charity for whom I'd previously done some work to secure one of their places for the 2017 event.

They say you can train for a marathon from scratch in as little as three months. I had a year. And the inclination. Arguably more inclination than many because it would now be the thing that I could devote myself to in the knowledge that it would be powerful enough to drive me. The challenge would give my life meaning.

I added a sub four-hour finish and to not walk at any point along the 26.2-mile route to my lists of goals and planned out my training regime. After three years of abusing my body, I had some work to do. Fortunately, I had some vague element of residual fitness in the deep, dark recesses of my muscle memory, so didn't have to start out with five-minute walking intervals but, having never run much more than about 10 km, and with the consideration of dragging my sizeable frame around London, I certainly wasn't going to be breezing over the finish line alongside Eliud Kipchoge.

Some days later, whilst sitting in an AA meeting, the thought struck me that the hour could have been spent on a training run. I haven't been to an AA meeting since, and I'm now—at time of writing—eight years sober. There is no doubt that I—and countless millions—have AA to thank for my sobriety, at least the introduction to it, but I have running to thank for my continued implementation of it. Because running—and I use running as my personal example, where any form of exercise or mindfulness is the same—is more than just running.

I can't get on board with the idea of sitting cross-legged, stimulating energy by touching my thumbs and pinkies together, and humming. But I also can't get on board with people who say, 'I don't like meditation.' What? You don't like relaxing? Relieving stress? Taking a few moments just to slow everything down after a tough day? What a load of bollocks. I now take a leaf out of Esmée's book in that running has nothing to do with my physical fitness. In truth, it never has. Running is my form of meditation. It's a chance to move and be with myself. And there is a form of meditation for everyone.

It's a mantra of Esmée's that, 'People should move every day. As a consequence of moving every day you'll feel happier, you'll feel proactive and you'll feel motivated. So, rather than having a physical goal, let that be the by-product of your workout and let your intention be something to do with the positive feeling that you get out of it or how it helps you. Rather than focusing on the physical, focus on the mental. After all, fitness is about mindset.' Even the great Sir Roger Bannister, who we'll meet again in the next chapter, saw 'his running as a very personal affair. It was a way of achieving mastery over himself, control over his body and mind.'[63]

A year later, on Sunday 23rd April 2017, training done and with the mindset that I was going to cross the London Marathon finish line in under four hours and having run every step of the way, I set off from the southern end of Greenwich Park just after 10am. I meandered through Charlton, hit the river, turned east and passed the historic Cutty Sark in Greenwich just after the six-mile mark feeling pretty good. The crowds were amazing, with everybody and their uncle offering words of encouragement and handing out sweets to the hordes of runners passing them. I plodded through Deptford and Rotherhithe en route to Bermondsey, where I'd planned for my family to be among the supporters. Seeing them gave me a boost and I turned right over the Thames to be met by a wall of noise whilst crossing Tower Bridge just before the half marathon marker. Dishearteningly watching the elite runners practically sprinting past me in the other direction, I turned away from the city centre and slogged through a section of the route around the Isle of Dogs where the crowds were less plentiful, struggling at the relative lack of support. My family had trudged up the Jubilee Line to make their way to Canary Wharf and I got a second wind as they waved me through mile 19-or-so. Shortly after, I turned left onto Poplar High Street in the knowledge that I was on the home straight back into the city, albeit it a six-mile home straight and further than I'd ever run before because the longest advised training run is 20 miles, which seems valid when you're training but is a shock when it comes to the real thing and you realise you've got another hour of running still to go. Plodding along the Embankment, around miles 23-25, I hit another low point as my legs increasingly turned to jelly beneath me and I was overtaken by someone dressed as a cancer charity foam coffee mug, and then a guy in a full suit. But on approach to the Houses of Parliament the energy returned and I galloped along Birdcage Walk to Buckingham Palace and rounded the corner onto the Mall. I managed to hobble over the finish line in 3 hours 55 minutes, having run every single step, just in front of someone in a full tyrannosaurus rex outfit. The guy in the suit was chatting on his mobile phone, as if he'd stepped out for a run halfway through speaking with his broker about the trades he wanted executing when the stock exchange opened in the morning and had now resumed the conversation.

After hugging some strangers, I accepted my finisher's medal, knelt down, kissed the concrete and burst into tears. The sense of accomplishment from crossing that finish line was like nothing else I'd ever experienced. It was greater than the feeling I'd had on hearing the full-time whistle after a hard-fought rugby match. Partly because of the nature of the event and the sense of joy in all those around me who had just completed the same challenge. Partly because it had been a year in the making and I'd had the discipline to stick to my training plan. And partly because I'd put my body through such abuse over the previous three years that it had seemed nigh-on impossible for me to run 26.2 miles.

In the aftermath, a counsellor who I was still seeing from time to time asked me, with a wry smile, whether I'd replaced one addiction with another? Booze for running. And, if so, what was I running from? My immediate thoughts, in all honesty, were that it was a stupid question and it didn't help that he seemed to imply that he'd somehow caught me out. Even if there was the tiniest smidgeon of truth to his suggestions, I'd pick running over booze every time and I wasn't going to pay the smarmy fucker by the hour to put paid to my discovery of my Higher Power. He could take a long walk off a short pier.

But it did get me thinking about who I'd become; my new identity. I felt like I'd been an entirely different person for the first 30 years of my life. I was no longer drunk, moronic, need-to-be-the-alpha-male, not-giving-a-shit-about-anyone-else, selfish dickhead James. He was gone. I'd retired him, like Michael had retired his security guard. In his place was someone new. A runner? Possibly, though I'm no Mo Farah. Someone who had reframed the negativity of a serious injury into something positive? You betcha. Someone who could be proud of himself? I thought so.

***

Everything's relative. Where Esmée's story of rehab is remarkable, I'd gone through a similar, albeit far less significant, less literal journey of 'getting back on my feet'. My story pales in comparison but both were based on a refusal to quit–or maybe a promise to quit, in my case.

And while I'd taken on an epic physical challenge, it was how it made me feel that was important; the benefits to my mental health that Es talked about.

My point? Be more mental. Be less physical. Before hitting the gym because you want to get ripped or because you have a dress you want to fit into or because summer's coming and you want a beach bod, focus on how you feel and why you're setting yourself these arguably empty goals. So you're now ripped. Good for you. But does it really make you *feel* any better, or do you now want to go down the rabbit hole of getting even more ripped? Why be only 9% body fat, when you can be 8%? And define 'beach body'. Where's the cut off? Are you happy that you can see a glimpse of abs when you tense really hard and the light's shining at the right angle or do have to do your 'morning's stretching exercises', 'stand in front of a chrome and acrylic Washmobile bathroom sink … and stare at [your] reflection', 'pour some Plax antiplaque formula into a stainless-steel tumbler and swish it around [your] mouth for a few seconds', 'squeeze Rembrandt onto a faux-tortoiseshell toothbrush and start brushing [your] teeth', 'inspect [your] hands and use a nailbrush', 'use a deep-pore cleanser lotion, then a herb-mint facial masque', 'use the Probright tooth polisher and next the Interlax tooth polisher (this in addition to the toothbrush) which has a speed of 4200rpm and reverses direction forty-six times per second', 'rinse again', 'wash the facial massage off with a spearmint face scrub', 'use … a water-activated gel cleanser, then a honey-almond body scrub, and on the face an exfoliating gel scrub', 'press a hot towel against [your] face for two minutes to soften abrasive bread hair', 'slather on a moisturizer … and let it soak in for a minute', 'keep it on and apply a shaving cream over it', 'wet the razor with warm water before shaving and shave in the direction the bread grows, pressing gently on the skin', 'rinse the razor', 'splash cool water on the face to remove any trace of lather', 'use an aftershave lotion with little or no alcohol', 'use an alcohol-free antibacterial toner with a water-moistened cotton ball to normalize the skin', 'splash on water before applying an emollient lotion to soften the skin and seal in the moisture', 'next apply Gel Appaisant ... which is an excellent, soothing skin lotion', 'then apply an anti-aging eye balm ... followed by a final moisturizing "protective" lotion', 'lightly blow-dry the hair to give it body and control (but without stickiness) and then add ... lotion shaping it with a Kent natural-bristle brush, and finally slick it back with a wide tooth comb', like Patrick Bateman, because you're still not entirely happy.[64]

Part of the reason we don't set ourselves mental health goals is because they aren't tangible. You can set yourself the goal of running a marathon or achieving a certain level of fitness through measurements like the time it takes you to complete the goal, the number of reps you can do or–if you're ten years old and in P.E. class–the level you can get to on the Bleep Test. In contrast, because we think we can't *see* mental fitness (a concept I'll come onto in a subsequent chapter), we ignore it. But it's a simple truth that if you focus on you and what you're getting out of a healthy routine mentally, the physical changes will come. It's simple biology. If you eat healthily and exercise, you'll experience changes in your body that will make you feel good.

And we can make mental fitness visible if we choose to. Have you ever seen those 'Please rate the cleanliness of our facilities' smiley faces in public loos? There are usually four of them, a dark green one with a beaming smile, a light green one with a neutral expression, a slightly sad pinky-orange one, and a red one that looks so livid that you wonder if it's even possible for the loo to be that filthy. I mean, has someone taken a dump on the floor or something? You tap the button of your choosing and, in all likelihood, nothing happens whatsoever because the janitor's on a cigarette break and it's not like the loos are getting cleaned any more frequently than he's paid to clean them. But it's a nice idea. And it makes us feel like we're ensuring that other people get to enjoy exemplary levels of sanitation because maybe it chivvies the cigarette-smoking janitor into action.

Well, guess what, hombre or hombrita*. You can adapt the idea to your mental fitness. There are a bajillion apps out there that track all this stuff for you or you can simply take a couple of moments each day to grade yourself on a similar scale, green to red, one to ten, you choose. Make a note of it and see how your mood shifts over time. Do it more than once a day as well to ensure that you're aware of slumps and highs at different times. Over time a pattern will emerge and you can assess what work you need to do, if any, to change or improve things.

---

*Side note:

I don't speak Spanish, in case you hadn't guessed.

It's proactive action like this that can be the difference between the slumps becoming more frequent than the highs. Imagine a car. Before setting off on a road trip, you fill it with petrol, check the tyre pressure, top up the oil and put your seatbelt on. Or at least you should. In contrast, not checking in with ourselves mentally on a regular basis is the equivalent of going to the local scrapheap, tossing over a few notes for an old banger, cutting a hole in the floor and wheeling it, Fred Flinstone-style, the wrong way down an off-ramp with HGVs coming towards you at 60 mph down the inside lane of the motorway.

Esmée rounds off our chat by encouraging us to 'strengthen our mind muscle through exercise. Focus on you and how you feel first of all. Then use fitness to shape your life.'

From there, we can achieve anything.

Chapter 8:
Hitting The Wall

It's kind of fun to do the impossible.
- **Walt Disney**

I spent a week recovering from the exertions of the London Marathon, including having to walk backwards down flights of stairs because, as I learned the painful way, you work your legs harder going downstairs than you do going upstairs. This is due to something called eccentric exercise which is to do with lengthening your muscles and not, in fact, a description of the people who attempt to play quidditch without real broomsticks. Whatever floats your boat.

Anyway, it was excruciating but, as the pain eased, I started convincing myself that it hadn't really been all that bad. According to the catchily titled *Climbing Dictionary: Mountaineering Slang, Terms, Neologisms & Lingo: An Illustrated Reference To More Than 600 Words*, the 'Fun Scale' was coined by Dr Rainer Newberry, a geology professor at the University of Alaska, Fairbanks, 'while teaching a field geology class around 1985', in an attempt to quantify the 'fun-to-suffering ratio.'

'What could a geology teacher possibly know about fun?' you might ask, and it'd be a valid question, but photos of Dr Newberry online suggest he's a wacky individual who knows how to live it large in the world of rocks. The book goes on to list the different grades, or 'Types', of fun, with arguably varying degrees of success, but I'll let you be the judge:

Type I fun is, 'True fun, enjoyable while it's happening. Good food, good sex, 5.8 hand cranks, sport climbing, powder skiing, margaritas.' Good food and good sex, definitely. Sport climbing and powder skiing, yup. Margaritas, I can see why they're included. But what in hell's name are 5.8 hand cranks? I mean, come on guys, is that just a euphemism for wanking? You get the idea though.

Type II fun is: 'Fun only in retrospect. Hateful while it's happening. Things like working out till you puke, and usually ice and alpine climbing.' It's the *Climbing Dictionary*, remember.

Type III fun is: 'Not fun at all, even after a *lot* of retrospection. As in, "What the hell was I thinking? If I ever even consider doing that again, somebody slap some sense into me."' Ironically, one blog I read on the subject listed 'writing a book' as an example of Type III fun, alongside 'Failed relationships that lacked Type I fun.'[65] Who knew?

People's outlook on a marathon varies after they cross the finish line. I think it's fair to say that no-one runs around 40,000 steps without at some point thinking, 'I could be at home in the comfort of my armchair, watching Tim Lovejoy interview a D-list celebrity on *Sunday Brunch*, while Simon Rimmer whips up an epic tarragon roast chicken,' but many love the process. They get the running bug. Others do one marathon and then vow never to do another. For many it's a ticking-it-off-the-bucket-list exercise and that's absolutely fine. Each to their own.

Personally, the marathon came in somewhere between Type I and Type II. The elation I felt at various points along the course was enough to override the tougher bits and, even though I spent a week administering ice packs to parts of my body I didn't realise I had, the pain wasn't enough to put me off another.

In fact, it was the pain that pulled me back in and the reasons for my taking part went deeper than ticking a box. I knew I had more in me and in the back of my mind was a concept I hinted at in the previous chapter: the impossible.

***

On 6th May 1954, a relatively unknown 25-year-old medical student packed his sports bag and headed out the door of his London flat. His name was Roger Bannister. He boarded a train at London Paddington and made his way to Oxford, to the running track at the Iffley Road Sports Centre*.

> ***Side note:**
>
> The track at the Iffley Road Sports Centre is now called the Sir Roger Bannister Running Track.

Bannister was due to compete for the Amateur Athletic Association, in a meet against Oxford University. He was an uncoached, amateur athlete (in case Amateur Athletic Association didn't give that away), only able to train 'between 12.30 and 1.30 … on a track in Paddington' on account of his studies 'and had a quick lunch before returning to hospital.'[66] The day before the race, he 'slipped on a highly polished hospital floor and spent the rest of the day limping.'[67] His running shoes were made of leather and he was in hospital on the morning of the race 'sharpening my spikes on a grindstone in the laboratory. Someone passing said, "You don't really think that's going to make any difference, do you?"'[68] The conditions were horrendous; the track was wet and 'a wind of gale force was blowing which would slow [Bannister] up by a second a lap.'[69] Bannister considered pulling out of the event that he had his sights on–the mile race.

Since the late eighteenth century, according to various reports, professional and amateur athletes had been racking up attempts to 'achieve the impossible' of running a mile in under four minutes. In the pre-IAAF (International Association of Athletics Federations, now known as World Athletics) era, there are various unstandardised documentations of attempts in the late 1700s and early 1800s, before the first recognised record, which dates back to 1855, when a Brit, Charles Westhall, ran 4:28 in London. A series of Brits dominated the record books for three decades, systematically knocking the odd second or two off the time until Walter George registered a time of 4:12¾.

George's record would stand for almost three decades, until the IAAF was established in 1912 and the professional era kicked in. Attempts started flooding in from around the world, including a time of 4:14.4 from an American John Paul Jones, not to be confused with the Led Zeppelin bassist. This was eclipsed in the 1920s by Paavo Nurmi but, despite nine Olympic gold medals for Finland, including in the 1,500 m (just shy of a mile) in the 1924

Olympics in Paris, the 'Flying Finn' could only inch closer to the four-minute target, clocking 4:10.4.

Respectable efforts, again chipping away at the record, were registered by France (Jules Ladoumègue; 4:09.2), New Zealand (Jack Lovelock; 4:07.6) and the US again (Glenn Cunningham; 4:06.7), before the record was back in the hands of the UK, courtesy of Sydney Wooderson shaving milliseconds off the time by clocking 4:06.4. But the sub-four-minute time was still out of reach; some said that a later effort of Cunningham's of 4:04.4, in an indoor arena on wood with no wind resistance, 'probably represented the limit of human achievement'.[70]

Then it was the turn of the Swedes. For three years the record switched back and forth between Gunder 'the Wonder' Hägg and Arne Andersson, until Hägg eventually came agonisingly close with a time of 4:01.4 in 1945.

But no-one else came close for almost a decade and the world believed that the four-minute mark couldn't be broken; that it was impossible. As John Bryant writes in *3:59.4: The Quest to Break the 4 Minute Mile*, 'There were those who feared the human body couldn't take it.'[71]

Until, on 6th May 1954, in those wet and windy conditions at Iffley Road, at just after 6pm, Roger Bannister proved the world wrong by running a time of 3:59.4. He recounted the feeling–or lack of it–after crossing the line in his autobiography: 'My effort was over and I collapsed almost unconscious, with an arm on either side of me. It was only then that real pain overtook me. I felt like an exploded flashlight with no will to live; I just went on existing in the most passive physical state without being quite unconscious. Blood surged from my muscles and seemed to fell me. It was as if all my limbs were caught in an ever-tightening vice.'[72]

He was soon on his feet again after the time was announced, completing a lap of honour in front of the 1,200-strong cheering crowd. It was arguably the most significant athletic achievement of the decade, if not all time; Harvard Business Review called it 'the Holy Grail of athletic achievement'[73].

But it wasn't a solo effort. Bannister enlisted two athletic teammates, Chris Brasher and Chris Chataway*, to compete in the event with him and to act as pacers. After a false start by Brasher and Bannister still questioning the windy conditions, the team were off at the second time of asking, with Brasher taking the lead and Bannister coasting behind him in his slipstream. Despite Bannister insisting Brasher pick up the pace, Brasher kept his head and the first two laps were recorded in 1:58. Chataway took over the pacing and guided Bannister in for the historic time.

---

*Side note:

In a tangent, but a super-duper interesting one, Chataway, as an employee of Guinness—yes, Dublin's finest ruby red stout—was one of the founding members of the Guinness Book of Records, and Bannister's record was one of the inclusions in the first edition in 1955.

By enlisting the help of Brasher and Chataway and using a 'knowledge of physiology that no other runner who flirted with breaking the 4-minute barrier had', Bannister ensured he was able to run mile splits of under a minute. 'By measuring his oxygen consumption, Bannister discovered that running consistent lap times required less oxygen than running variable times, so he focused on running steady quarter-mile splits. Through intense interval training of running 10 laps with 2-minute breaks in between, Bannister had dropped his average quarter-mile splits from 63 seconds to 59 seconds, sufficient to break the elusive barrier.'[74]

The scientific and tactical strategies that Bannister employed to achieve the feat are worthy of another book entirely–indeed, Bryant's *3:59.4* is an un-put-downable read–but that's not the bit of this more-than-one-hundred-year saga that I want to focus on. It's how quickly and frequently others then started eclipsing Bannister's time after he demonstrated that the 'impossible' wasn't, in fact, impossible.

After Bannister announced to the world that the four-minute mile wasn't beyond 'the limit of human achievement', it took just 46 days for someone else to replicate, and better, his efforts. John Landy, an Australian, knocked another second and a half off Bannister's time and since then the record has dropped a further 17 times to the current time of 3:43.13, held by Hicham El Guerrouj of Morocco. Furthermore, as of June 2022, the *The Sub-4 Alphabetic Register*[75] lists 1,755 men as having broken the four-minute barrier, including 'Nick Willis, of New Zealand, [who] has broken four minutes for a record 19th successive year, and in 2022 he has now made it 20! … Steve Scott, of the USA, is … the most prolific sub-four-minute miler in history, with 137 such times to his credit.' Even though 1,755 may seem like a comparatively meagre figure and is only a quarter of the number of people who have climbed Mt Everest– another 'impossible' feat achieved by Sir Edmund Hillary and Sherpa Tenzing Norgay as they became the first people to stand at the top of the world in 1953–it's still 1,755 more than had run the time in the previous century.

Of course, records are made to be broken and advancements in running shoe technologies have allowed the time to drop considerably in the 70 years since Bannister's efforts but it's fascinating how the mental barrier prevented the physical barrier from being broken, when it was eminently doable.

Henry Ford–you know, the guy who invented the car–arguably said it best: 'Whether you think you can, or you think you can't, you're right.'

Bannister himself wrote that the four-minute mile was 'a challenge to the human spirit', but when he thought, 'I can', he 'recalibrated expectations of what the human body is capable of achieving'[76]. The same can be said for Eliud Kipchoge's sub-two-hour marathon run in Vienna in 2019, even though his use of 41 pacers and a motorbike providing him with hydration means his time of 1:59:40 isn't recognised as the official marathon world record. Shame.

It was the idea of what the human body is capable of achieving that really got me thinking in the weeks and months after the London Marathon. After all, if I could run 26.2 miles, surely I could run further? Surely that wasn't the extent of my potential?

***

Without wanting to bite off more than I could chew too soon, I signed up to run the Paris Marathon a year after London. I have a half brother, Alex, and half sister, Victoria, who grew up in Paris, courtesy of my dad living there during his first marriage, and Alex has now run the Paris Marathon seven times. After my London efforts he roped me into joining him for the 2018 iteration and the thought of cruising through the City of Light, down the Avenue des Champs-Elysées, around the Place de la Concorde, past the Louvre, through the Bois de Vincennes, along the Seine—taking in the Eiffel Tower—towards the Bois de Boulogne, and circling round to finish on the Avenue Foch, just shy of the Arc de Triomphe, was really rather appealing. Don't mind if I do, merci beaucoup.

It was glorious—glorious weather, glorious setting, just glorious—but I got carried away. I completely buggered up my timings, coasting along with the 3 hour 20 minute marker runner for two hours and conking out at about 18 miles as a result.

Hitting the dreaded wall is not, as many believe, a mental barrier that you hit when you think you don't have enough in the tank. It's a physiological barrier when you quite literally don't have enough in the tank. Much of endurance running is based on ensuring the body has enough energy in the form of glycogen (derived from carbohydrates), which is stored in muscles and in the liver. If this is depleted the body can turn to other sources of fuel, such as fat, but this isn't broken down quickly enough to produce sufficient energy to keep you going in a long race when your glycogen is exhausted, and you *feel* exhausted. Bearing in mind we can store, on average, enough energy to cover around 18-20 miles without refuelling, ensuring you are taking on enough carbs to power you through your race is key to a wall-free marathon, as is pacing. Going out too fast will burn through your glycogen stores too quickly and you'll run out of energy sooner than you anticipate. Suffice to say, at my second marathon attempt, I didn't replicate my sub-four-hour, run-every-step efforts of London. But as Van Helsing says to Dr. John Seward, 'We learn from failure, not from success!'[77]

Meanwhile, a friend, who shall remain nameless–ahem, Alex–had suggested we take on something a little spicier. This anonymous friend–Alex, his name is Alex–was living in Corbridge, a quaint little town just outside Newcastle, at the time and stumbled upon The Wall, the route of which went almost past his front door. He suggested we enter.

Pegged as 'the UK's most iconic ultramarathon*' and 'the perfect first step into ultramarathon territory for those new to the world beyond 26.2', The Wall is an undulating 70-miler along historic stretches of what remains of Hadrian's Wall–so a sharp little double entendre as you aim to run along the Wall, without hitting the wall.

> ***Side note:**
>
> An ultramarathon is defined as anything longer than a marathon; 26.2miles or 42.2km.

It was just two months after Paris and I was nervous about taking on something more than twice the distance with so little time to prepare. What's more, Paris was only my second endurance challenge and I'd overcooked it due to lack of experience. I was worried about doing the same and hitting the wall–not Hadrian's Wall, because causing damage to World Heritage sites is frowned upon–in my first ultra.

That said, it was just what I was looking for to push myself a little further and test the Type II pain barrier. So, after an 'I'll do it if you will', figurative handshake with he-who-must-not-be-named—Alex, not Voldemort—I signed up.

Most marathons are littered with regular water stations to keep participants hydrated and you can stick a couple of energy gels in your pockets and not stress too much about a fuelling plan. It's not something to be complacent about—as my Paris debacle had taught me—but as long as you take on a few extra calories along the way, the adrenaline and support of the crowds will generally get you through the last few miles.

It's a different kettle of fish, however, when you're taking on longer distances. I'll go into some of my hows and the key components of endurance running in Chapter 11 but, touching on it fleetingly, you need more training miles under your belt, more kit, more fluids and more calories; sufficient calories to give your body enough energy to sustain it burning a very rough guideline of about 100 calories per mile.

I upped my distances, clocking up a couple of 30- and 40-mile training runs, armed myself with an Osprey running backpack, loaded it with some energy gels and a bag of Haribo, and boarded a train up north to meet Alex, have a catch up with a chum over a carb-heavy dinner and do some race planning.

Except, I'd entered. Alex 'didn't get round to it.'

So, at just before 7am the next morning, standing on the start line in front of Carlisle Castle, I was friendless and planless. Billy No-mates. Johnny No-plan. And seriously worried about how I was going to run the width of the country to Newcastle, and do so before it got dark that evening, as was the goal I had set myself for this more epic of challenges. Until the guy next to me, halfway through a groin stretch, casually introduced himself: 'Alright mate, I'm Phil. Have you got a race plan?'

In the second and a half that I had to look the guy up and down and assess the situation, I could tell he was reasonably seasoned at this ultramarathon malarkey. His kit looked like it had seen a few miles, whilst at the same time like it was perfectly moulded to his slight frame. He had a streamlined appearance, like every part of his attire had been thought through to reduce excess weight. And his shorts were short. Very short. Too short. It wasn't his first rodeo.

At this point, I think it would have been wholly justifiable for me to drop to my knees, grab at the hem of his too-short-shorts and start uselessly sobbing, whilst begging him to give me some advice. But something in the back of my brain told me to keep it together, whilst recalling the lessons I'd learned in Paris. My response was, 'Hi, I'm James. Um, no, not really, just not go out too quickly, I guess.'

I immediately panicked that he would find my amateurishness contemptible but he seemed to accept my response, kindly nodding and saying, 'Sounds like a winner.' As the starting klaxon rang out, we exchanged a few pleasantries and I admitted it was my first attempt at a serious distance, and I was just going to 'see how I go'. He seemed to welcome the approach based on the strategy–if you can call it a strategy–of listening to your body and what it needs, rather than systematically planning out the intake of every calorie in advance. It can in fact be better to 'see how you go' because your body is an incredible machine that has evolved over 2.5 million years and if it needs water, you'll feel thirsty–so you should drink. Same with food.

When you're going through the highs and lows of an ultra, sometimes it's hard to take on food and, at the opposite end of the scale to the wall, many people make the mistake of overdrinking or overeating. If you make yourself sick, that's also very hard to come back from.

After a few miles, Phil picked up his pace and left me plodding but I was perfectly happy 'seeing how I went'. While I had always enjoyed team sports and now appreciated the solitary meditation of running, ultrarunning gives you the best of both worlds. It's a solitary sport, undertaken as a community, if that makes sense. As you run, you have times when you're on your own, able to listen to the world and muddle through your thoughts, but you also strike up conversations with fellow runners, exchange stories, swap snack bars and motivate each other. And occasionally ring out each other's sweaty socks, pop each other's blisters and share a pot of anti-chafing cream. Because who cares? You're there to do whatever it takes to get over the finish line and, unless you're aiming to win the thing, which I ain't, get each other over the finish line.

So, with my Parisian pacing lesson in my back pocket and the longer northern days on my side, I kept to a steady speed, safe in the knowledge that anything under 15 hours would have me arriving into the Newcastle quayside in what remained of the evening's daylight—even though a head torch was on the list of compulsory kit, just in case.

It wasn't long until the sleepy residential streets of Carlisle were replaced by the scenic English countryside, open fields and picturesque villages. Signs of encouragement such as 'Good start! 5 miles down' accompanied the arrow signage and the occasional bit of 'off-roading' broke up the monotony of a route that was mostly on tarmac. I arrived at the first checkpoint, at mile 15, feeling chipper. It was a well catered event, so sausage rolls, sandwiches and soups were on offer as well as coffees and teas. If you've never seen the British piss-take of the Hierarchy of Needs pyramid, 'a cup of tea, a biscuit and a nice sit down' is the most important thing to man, rather than Maslow's 'Physiological needs', and I don't think I've ever had a better brew than at just after 9am on the morning of Saturday 16th June 2018, accompanied by a chocolate Hobnob, whilst perched on a plastic, fold out chair.

Hit of caffeine on board, I plodded on, shortly after passing the remnants of one of the turrets that were originally spaced out along Hadrian's Wall and manned by soldiers gazing into the distance for signs of White Walkers– or maybe that was a different wall. As the signage took a turn for the more banterous, such as '20 miles down. Does it hurt yet?' I chuckled to myself. You've got to keep a sense of humour about you for these things, as we'll discover in Chapter 14.

Checkpoint 2, at around 27 miles, was followed by a steep incline and then endless sheep fields, each separated by having to scramble over stone walls via little wooden ladder-stiles. Trudging through the Northumberland National Park–and passing a stone's throw from the Sycamore Gap tree mentioned in the Introduction, may it rest in peace–was the most beautiful but most taxing part of the run, although passing sites such as the Roman fort, Vindolanda, reminded me of the historic significance of the route and spurred me on.

I had a decent rest at the 44-mile checkpoint in Hexham and probably too decent a rest, as it took me a while to summon the energy to get going again, knowing that I still had a marathon left to go. Corbridge wasn't far from Hexham and I lumbered through the village cursing Alex, given he was probably–at that precise moment in time–sitting with his feet up in front of the TV, watching rugby; that afternoon was England's second fixture of a three-test summer tour in South Africa. The fucker. I'm not sure why we're still friends.

As if the universe knew I needed a pick-me-up, a chirpy guy called Luke emerged from one of the town's pubs and fell into step alongside me. I asked him if he'd been for a loo break but he confessed that no, he had in fact stopped in for a cheeky, mid-ultra pint of Guinness. As you do. Or as I definitely don't, but whatever butters your crumpet. We got into the 'Have you done anything like this before?' pleasantries and it turned out Luke was a runner with various ultra notches on his belt including the UTMB.

'The what?' I asked.

The world-famous Ultra-Trail du Mont-Blanc. It pits the world's greatest runners–and amateurs that can qualify by amassing points through the completion of other challenging ultras–against each other in a loop of over 100 miles around Mont-Blanc, starting and ending in Chamonix, France, crossing the Italian and Swiss borders, and taking in over 10,000 metres of elevation gain.

'You what?' I said. 100 miles? Stop it. That's insane.

It was something I pondered as Luke proceeded to figuratively drag me through the next 20 miles along the Tyne until we could see Newcastle's Tyne Bridge and the Wembley-esque white arch of the Millennium Bridge. Geordie crowds of Saturday night revellers in the bars along the north bank of the river provided a boost for the final few hundred metres and I crossed the Millennium Bridge and stumbled across the finish line.

It was just before 9pm, and I was broken. But there was still light in the sky and I had completed 70 miles in a not unrespectable time of 13:52:48, coming in the top 10% out of the starters in my first ever competitive ultra.

I gave poor Luke an engulfing, vice-like bear hug, collected my finisher's medal, was reunited with the overnight bag I'd thrown in a minibus in Carlisle and limped off to find my hotel. Then, on the recommendation of Ollie, my uni friend who would later deliver the Best Man speech I mentioned in Chapter 2, who had lived in the Toon whilst managing a local bar, I headed for the city centre to find the most filthily satisfying recovery meal I could in the infamous Bigg Market. I would later read that this 'is a haven of shocking bars full of charvers [sic] with Ben Sherman shirts and tatoos [sic] of spiders on their foreheads drinking until they beat each other to a pulp … probably the most threatening place in Newcastle.'[78] Thanks for the recommendation, Ollie, but at the time it suited me just fine. I hobbled into a kebab shop, ordered two, yes two, portions of meat and chips, with extra lashings of garlic and chili sauce, and proceeded to devour the lot. Whilst doing so, I was approached by an inebriated Geordie lass who demanded that I give up my seat for her. When I explained that no, I'd earned it because I'd run all the way from Carlisle, she gave me an odd look as if to say, 'This guy's not worth my time because he's obviously even more drunk than I am', and left me alone.

I contemplated what I'd achieved. If you'd told me two years prior that I'd be sitting in a kebab shop in central Newcastle, at 10 o'clock at night, surrounded by drunk

Geordies, with two portions of meat and chips in front of me, having just run 70 miles in under 14 hours, I'd have called you mental. Fucking mental. But I had.

There had been incredible highs and some terrible lows. It was definitely Type II fun. And from my chat with Luke, there was already a new itch that needed scratching. I'd done 70 miles, which had seemed 'impossible'. So, was it unthinkable that I could manage 100? A seed had been sown.

***

In Bannister's autobiography, he also tells of how, despite wanting to 'travel up to Oxford alone because I wanted to think quietly … I opened a carriage door, and, quite by chance, there was Franz Stampfl inside.'[79] Despite Stampfl coaching Chris Brasher and Chris Chataway, Bannister himself had insisted on going it alone but Stampfl was still a voice of reason, providing some words of encouragement at Bannister's uncertainty that that day was, in fact, *the* day. Bannister couldn't control the conditions or the weather, but 'Franz knew with certainty that a man could run a mile in under four minutes, and he knew that Roger had the talent and the will to do it … It's all in the mind, argued Franz, the mind can overcome almost anything. And what if this is the only chance you get? … tomorrow may be too late.'[80]

Sports Illustrated has named Bannister 'The Original Sportsman' but even he had doubts. So, if we're to take anything from the story, it's not that we can all run a mile in under four minutes, necessarily, otherwise more than 1,755 people would have done it. I can just about run a kilometre in under four minutes but a mile? Not on your nelly. I'm not built for speed. But endurance events—and the learnings we can take from them, which I'll cover off in a later chapter– are a different bag. I firmly believe that anyone can complete a marathon, or an ultramarathon for that matter. You just need to believe you can. Such barriers, like fear, exist only in our minds.

Henry Ford said it well. As did Franz Stampfl. Adidas did too, for that matter, in its famous strapline: 'Impossible is nothing'.

So be more Henry Ford. Be more Franz Stampfl. Believe in what's possible, not what's impossible. Don't let the mental barrier determine the physical barrier.

Chapter 9:
Yes, Staff

You better make friends with the devil, because you're about to go through hell.
- **Ant Middleton**

I once attended a wellness festival at which I didn't properly read the promotional blurb ahead of one of the sessions on breathing. The words 'warrior' and 'drumming' jumped out at me and I thought it sounded like it would be up my street. After all, we breathe every second of our lives, so there's no doubt of the importance of learning to do so in a way that can benefit our physical and mental health. There's probably even something in discovering a deeper version of yourself, activating your higher senses, etc, etc. And let's face it, drumming is ridiculously cool. But when the instructor, who was part shaman, part Amazonian tribeswoman, started chanting in what sounded like the language of James Cameron's Na'vi and told me to, 'Draw a circle of light around your breath so that you can anchor yourself to the energy of the world and feel the power in every single cell of your body, pulling the vibrations up your spinal cord and out of your third eye so you can embrace your full potential,' I became sceptical. In all honesty, she lost me at 'circle of light'.

But I did resonate with the full potential bit.

***

Along my journey of discovering what's ~~impossible~~ possible, I watched the third season of *SAS: Who Dares Wins*–the one in the Moroccan desert. For anyone that hasn't seen the Channel 4 show, four Directing Staff (DS), all of whom are absolute fucking badass former special forces operatives, take a group of 25 civilians off into a wilderness somewhere and shout at them. A lot.

The premise is a condensed version of special forces selection. The real thing is known as the most intense military recruitment process on the planet, with recruits aiming to survive a series of phases that test their physical fitness, mental aptitude, navigational skills and survival techniques, and subject them to tactics and procedures training in some of the world's harshest environments, such as living for weeks in the Belizean jungle. Those who make it through endurance and jungle training then get the joy of 'escape and evasion'. They're let loose in the countryside for three days and have to escape capture by a hunter force, whilst surviving on minimal rations, then, whether captured or not, have to return to base to undergo 'tactical questioning'. This is a savage mock interrogation interspersed with hours of enduring 'stress positions' designed to wear the candidates down and make them give up sensitive information. Usually, around five out of 200 recruits make the cut.

I'd seen the first couple of series of the show too, but never contemplated the idea of putting my name in a hat for it. But this time, at the end of the show, when a message flashed up saying, 'If you want to apply for the next series of *SAS: WDW*, apply by emailing such-and-such address', I had a little think to myself. I was as fit as the next guy, if not fitter. It looked absolutely horrible. But survivable and somehow appealing. Like Type II fun. The chances of me even being considered were minimal. But what did I have to lose?

The application forms came through and I crafted my sob story and reasons for wanting to subject myself to a televised equivalent of Dante Alighieri's journey through the nine circles of hell, short of the gluttons, heretics, sodomites and 'The deepest circle of hell … reserved for betrayers and mutineers'[81]–albeit that's Captain Jack Sparrow, rather than Dante–before sending them off into cyberspace. An automated response came back: 'Unfortunately we cannot respond to every application we receive, however one of the casting team will be in touch should you be successful in getting through to the next round.' To be honest, I thought nothing more of it.

Until a month later, when I got an email inviting me to a casting session at a school somewhere in north London, which involved a brief fitness test and a few questions on camera. I did 50 press ups in two minutes, 50 sit ups in another two minutes, shuttle runs with some weights, clocked up level 12 on the Bleep Test, answered a nice lady's questions about my reasons for being there, and went about my day. To be honest, I thought nothing more of it.

Until another email winged its way into my inbox. Asking for my DBS details. Then another asking for my clothes sizes. Then another asking me to attend a cardiopulmonary exercise test (CPET) of VO2max, which is where you put on a mask that makes you look like Bane and sit on a bike whilst hooked up to various monitors and sensors and they get you to peddle, slowing cranking up the resistance until peddling is impossible and you're heaving out of your hoop. All to tell you that you're in decent enough physical shape to go on the show. Then another email asking me to undertake a psychological assessment to check that I wasn't completely fucking mental. And to tell me I was in decent enough mental shape to go on the show. Then another checking if I had any dietary requirements. And every single one came with a caveat along the lines of, 'We understand that you might still be waiting on confirmation of your status, but we will get this to you by the end of the week. Thank you for your patience.'

I didn't hold my breath but I upped my training. By the time September rolled around I'd been running twice-weekly half marathons whilst carrying 10kg on my back, as well as hitting the gym hard. On a couple of free Saturday afternoons, I ran a half marathon into central London (I was living in Harrow at the time), did an hour-long weights session in the gym and then ran the half marathon home.

So, I felt I was ready, though it was still a surprise, genuinely, when on 7th September, seven months after my initial enquiry, another email landed, saying: 'Congratulations! You have been chosen to be a recruit on *SAS: Who Dares Wins, Series 4*. This is a huge achievement and the DS are looking forward to meeting you.'

Looking forward to meeting me? Yeah right. Looking forward to metaphorically bending me over more like. What was I saying about sodomites?

Two weeks later I was meeting my fellow recruits at our designated rendezvous–RV, if you want to use military parlance–point: outside Caffè Nero at London Heathrow's Terminal 4.

Michael (you met him in Chapter 4) was a recovering heroin addict.

Esmée (you met her in Chapter 7) had been paralysed as a teenager and told she may never walk again.

Nadine had been a victim of sexual abuse.

Mark had lost his wife to suicide.

Milo's brother had been killed in action.

Rick had been mercilessly bullied at school.

Sam had been a member of a London gang.

I had my own sob story of alcoholism and depression.

In short, we were a right sorry bunch. But, I like to think, an astonishing bunch of individuals who had come through some serious adversity and were looking to test themselves against one of the most arduous sets of challenges ever devised by man. Or at least a compacted, two-week version of one of the most arduous sets of challenges ever devised by man. I'd like to make it very clear that I by no means think a mock, televised version of selection is in any way comparable to the real thing. Soldiers that are put forward for selection are already in incredible shape and have at least two years' military experience under their belts, usually with elite units like the Royal Marines Commandos or the Parachute Regiment. But I'm a

PR consultant, so everything's relative.

Boarding an overnight flight to Santiago, Chile, I surgically inserted myself into a seat that didn't have enough leg room for Happy, Doc, Grumpy, Dopey, Bashful, or Sneezy. So Sleepy was definitely out of the question, despite some epic manspreading, much to the annoyance of the passengers to either side of me. But they were probably headed to a vineyard in the Maipo Valley wine region, so I didn't lose any sleep over it. Except I did, but you know what I mean.

On arrival, we decamped to a hotel on the outskirts of the city and were driven into the Andes for a day of acclimatisation to altitude. This involved one of the medics– himself a former paratrooper–taking us out for some 'light fizz'. No, not a Champagne aperitif but, more accurately, light phys, as in a physical session that wasn't in the slightest bit light, rather it involved endless shuttle runs up a section of a ski slope, leaving us all feeling like we were breathing through wet leather because of the lower oxygen levels at altitude. And this was just the warm-up. That night I ordered everything on the hotel room service menu in a bid to get in some of the calories that would see me through approximately eight and a half minutes of what was to come and tried desperately to get a decent night's sleep. But what's that? A mix of apprehension and jet lag. You think you're getting a wink of sleep, do you, young Jimmy Lad? Not on my Chilean watch.

The next morning our personal effects were bagged and tagged, and we were told that we were heading out on another warm-up outing. Deliriously naive after two nights of no sleep, the fact that we were mic'd up wasn't enough of a hint to me that shit was going to go down.

After two hours of being driven further and higher into the mountains along pothole-ridden tracks in a rickety old bus built before the invention of suspension, one of the group spotted a drone flying through the valley alongside us. Seconds later, an explosion rattled the windows. The bus screeched to a halt, the door opened and four masked men with machine guns came running on screaming 'Get the fuck down', amid various other obscenities. All of which was, in fact, shit going down.

We were marched off the bus, heads down, and after a few moments of kneeling in the snow, the not-so-dulcet tones of Ant Middleton invited us to 'make friends with the devil, because you're about to go through hell.' Like Dante. And yes, he actually said that. Which left me half trying to stifle a giggle and half wondering whether the DS sat at home drafting their one-liners before the show.

Home for the next 12 days was what seemed to be a remote, disused military barracks deep in the mountains. When I later found it on Google Maps and Wikipedia, because I'm a bit of a nerd like that, I discovered that the '"Refugios del Yeso", [was] a shelter built in the 50s to house workers during the construction of the [Yeso] reservoir. In the Beagle Conflict [a border dispute between Chile and Argentina in the 1970s and '80s], it used by the Chilean Army, given its strategic value (it protects the source of drinking water in the capital, and at the same time can defend the capital against the Argentine advance, artillery being necessary).'[82] You didn't think you'd be getting a miniature history lesson as part of a recount of my time on *SAS: Who Dares Wins*, did you?

In the facility's parade square, we stripped down to our underwear, were given our military fatigues and numbered armbands—I was no.14—and Ant politely informed us that we were to refer to him, Billy, Foxy and Ollie as 'Staff' at all times. 'Is that understood?'

'Yes, Staff', we bellowed in unison.

After 12 days spent simultaneously in a blurry state of sleep-deprivation and in a constant state of high-alert, I whiled away some time on the plane home attempting to catalogue the experience. I imagined a comical conversation with the border patrol officer tasked with examining my passport on my return to the UK and scribbled the following in a notebook:

'Hello Mr Gwinnett, how was your time in Chile?'

'Funny you ask actually. I was on a bus up into the Andes when there was a roadside explosion and our group was held up at gunpoint by masked men. I was made to run five km down a mountain, loaded into a military transport vehicle and taken to a desolate, disused barracks 2,500 m above sea level, where I was stripped down to my underwear, and kitted out in military fatigues. Then I was submerged in an ice-cold waterfall and almost froze to death before being beasted around the barracks' parade square. I resupplied an artillery position with important equipment, hailed pulks of kit up a snowy valley, saved myself from falling down a dangerous precipice with an ice pick, trudged a 100 kg log up an enormous hill, played murderball with a tyre, snuck in a cheeky no-defence-allowed boxing match, was beasted, abseiled face first down a vertical cliff face, almost froze to death in a random swimming pool halfway up another mountain, free fall abseiled off a bridge, built an ice shelter, was beasted, climbed another mountain, tiptoed over a ladder stretching across a 200 m drop into a ravine, flew in a helicopter up to 3,500 m to swim under the ice of a glacial lake, almost froze to death, searched for a weapons cache, was tracked by local militia with sniffer dogs, was apprehended and held at gunpoint, then was crammed into the back of a rickety old Defender with a bag over my head and driven to a remote, secret location, where I was subjected to torture in the form of increasingly excruciating stress positions and the occasional punch to the ribs, all while surviving on about three hours sleep a night and insufficient calories for a guy my size. So, a fairly typical fortnight. Run of the mill actually.'

The free fall abseiling is worthy of elaboration. Stick 'Why do you want to kill him?' into Google and the fourth result is a Channel 4 video clip on YouTube, which I'm oddly proud to say has been watched over 2 million times.

Rick and I had been paired up as oppos (short for opposite number) in the military 'buddy-buddy' system, to demonstrate the importance of looking after your squad mates. We had to do everything together; check each other's kit, eat together, and piss and shit together. No joke. If one of us needed a piss in the middle of the night, we had to wake our oppo up and take them to the loo with us. Part of this teamwork phase of the course involved a free-fall abseiling task into a gorge and the video clip shows me plummeting about 50 feet and my arse bouncing off the rockface below*.

*Side note / terrible joke:

It was the second 'rock bottom' of my life. Two drums and a cymbal fall off a cliff. Ba doom, tsh.

Not on account of Rick's failure to pull the safety

cord, I might add, but on account of the safety crew rigging the system OVER A FUCKING ROCKFACE. Thanks guys.

Otherwise, the helicopter was class. I was sat in the back with Mark (who went on to pass the course) and Ant was taking selfies of us from the front seat. Sadly, though, we don't exchange Christmas cards and I never saw the photos.

Another memory that stands out is from the infamous 'mirror room' where recruits are brought in with a bag over their head, shoved into a seat and then it's always amusing to see their gormless expressions as the bag is whipped off and two of the DS are sat across the table with menacing looks on their faces. My second mirror room experience was with Ant and Billy. After Billy had threatened to 'bounce me around the table' for being cocky, I think, we got onto the subject of drinking. It was left on the editing floor but Ant came out with a line that puzzled me: 'Never trust someone who doesn't drink.'

I was sleep deprived and not exactly firing on all cylinders at this point, so I mumbled a response about not trusting myself when I drink. But, in hindsight, maybe I should have told him that it was the stupidest thing that I'd ever heard, Staff. Or maybe not, since he and Billy probably would have then bounced me around the table.

People often ask me, 'Is the show as bad as it looks?' My answer is always the same: 'No. It's worse.' The editing team compacted 12 days into six 45-minute episodes. I was cold and wet for two weeks. I got an average of about three-to-four hours sleep a night and spent most of the small hours of each morning, whilst struggling to sleep, trying to relight the cabin's log burner for fear of freezing to death. Going without a shower or change of underwear for almost a fortnight left us honking so badly that one of the group likened us to mountain yaks. The stress positions were the most painful few hours of my life—more so than breaking my neck—and the reason I VWed (voluntarily withdrew) was that I thought I was going to do more serious damage to my already seriously damaged neck. I lost a stone. On my return to the UK I spent a day in A&E on an intravenous antibiotic drip because an infection in my hand had caused it to swell to twice its usual size. The show's doctor had told me to 'Put some ice on it.'

But, while the experience was brutal, it was also fascinating and exhilarating in equal measure. On the first day, we were ordered to get our shit together and present on the parade square within five minutes. 15 minutes later, we were scurrying out of our accommodation in various states of undress, looking like a dishevelled group of hobos, rather than a squadron of mock-elite soldiers. As a punishment for keeping the DS waiting, we had to pour the ice-cold water in our bottles over our heads and stand there freezing our tits off, teeth clattering, for ten minutes. After two weeks of refining our personal admin, when the final eight of us were given a similar order, we were outside four minutes later, waiting for a minute for the DS to emerge from their accommodation.

Few will ever come close to experiencing such a punishing and yet thrilling few days in such a spectacular setting. Pop 'El Yeso Reservoir' into Google and you'll see that it is quite possibly the most stunning reservoir on the planet, and a beautiful backdrop for another session of 'light fizz'. The camp was situated under a glacier that glistened in the sunlight at certain times of day and every now and then, when I was either soaked and chilled to the bone, carrying an enormous load up an enormous hill, dangling from something, falling off something, or being sworn at by Ant, I took a re-energising look around me at my surroundings.

And I'd do it all again in a heartbeat. All apart from the stress positions. Because it's a matter of perception. If you think to yourself, 'This is going to be worse than what that poor old fucker Dante went through', then guess what. It will be. But if you adopt the mindset that being thrust into such an environment allows you to embrace potential you never knew you had and push limits further than you thought possible, you'll come away feeling like you can arm wrestle Superman. Once the antibiotics have staved off an infection in your hand that has caused it to swell to twice its usual size.

You may have guessed by now that I love a motivational quote and there are countless that are perfect here. 'Once we accept our limits, we go beyond them', is a nice one. That's Albert Einstein again. I also like another by American philosopher and psychologist, William James: 'Beyond the very extreme of fatigue and distress, we may find amounts of ease and power we never dreamed ourselves to own; sources of strength never taxed at all because we never push through the obstruction.'

In his *Divine Comedy*, Dante finds himself struggling through the eighth circle of hell, while thieves are bound and bitten by serpents all around him. While he is mortal and has to suffer through the exertions of the journey–'The breath was from my lungs so milked away'[83]–his companion, the soul of the ancient Roman poet Virgil, is light and not limited by such exhaustions. As Dante rests, Virgil part encourages, part chastises Dante for doing so:

> "for sitting upon down,
> Or under quilt, one cometh not to fame ...
> And therefore raise thee up, o'ercome the anguish"[01]

Dante wants to impress Virgil and is inspired into action, pushing himself beyond what he previously thought he was capable of:

> Then I uprose, showing myself provided
> Better with breath than I did feel myself,
> And said: "Go on, for I am strong and bold."[85]

Finding the resilience to 'raise thee up [and] o'ercome' epitomises the mantra of the special forces and is the reason selection is so ridiculously hard. It's what struck me about the whole process; the DS weren't looking for the fittest, strongest or bravest among us, or the most charismatic leader, they were simply looking for the recruits that weren't going to give up, no matter what was thrown at us.

I've kept in touch with DS Matthew 'Ollie' Ollerton since the show and have taken a lot from getting to know him. I don't think he'll mind me saying that he also has a story of recovery–from drink, drugs and some generally self-destructive behaviours–and he's got some incredible stories and learnings from them. When I told him I was scribbling down some of my own thoughts, he was quick to offer his time to discuss, well, a range of things. (To be honest, it's hard to get him to stop talking when he starts but the nuggets he comes out with are gold dust!) So we chewed the fat about *SAS: WDW*, the mentality that goes into becoming a special forces soldier, a concept that he calls 'infinite potential' and, of all things, anthropology, more on which in the next chapter.

'Unfortunately,' he says, 'some people think it's time to throw in the towel as soon as they start feeling uncomfortable. You see it on *SAS: Who Dares Wins*. They've made it through the various recruitment tests and flown all the way out to somewhere like the Andes, but can't hack it when it comes to the real thing. Because of the level of physical discomfort.'

The special forces have a rule that helps them move past limiting beliefs: the 40% rule. It's dead simple: when you think you're done, when you think you have nothing left in the tank and you're ready to tap out, you're only 40% done.

'The mind will give out before the body,' Ollie agrees, 'but when you hear that "no" in your head, you should really see that as a great opportunity.' He admits that 'Some of the things in selection and that we ask you to do on the show are designed to be impossible tasks. They're there just to blow your mind. But, when your mind is saying it cannot be done, you've just got to keep moving a step at a time. Just do today. Just do the next second, even. Whatever it is, just keep moving forward.'

But it's different for special forces soldiers, right? They're just wired differently.

'It's true that you have to have a certain amount of military experience and base level fitness to be recommended for selection,' he says, 'but there's a misconception that special forces operatives are impervious to pain or difficult situations. We're not superhuman and unfortunately not bulletproof—that's what all the protective gear is for. What makes the special forces so good at what they do is understanding the relationship between what they're being asked to do and the mind telling them they can't do it. And then pushing through it regardless.'

So, for us average joes and janes, how do we unlock infinite potential? For Ollie, it starts with recognising your thought processes: 'If you can observe the "no", you can then do something that contradicts it. You can start pushing through what you thought were your limits. And that starts to rewrite the programme and build a limitless mindset, from the inside out.

'We don't all have to run around wearing a balaclava and wielding a laser-sighted weapon, but we all need to be able to overcome our limiting beliefs. Because the more we focus on anything, the bigger that becomes, positive or negative, and our lives reflect our thought patterns. Regardless of the task, if we can contradict the negativity of the mind, we can have positive outcomes.'

While Ollie bemoans the increasing lack of resilience shown by humanity–'I think everyone has tapped out on that, haven't they?'–there is still a glimmer of hope for us if we can adopt a special forces mindset. For many who are struggling, 'It's all down to the thoughts in your head' and realising that we have more, much more, to give than we think we do.

Dante realised it.

So, be more Dante Alighieri. Raise thee up and o'ercome.

Or be more William James. Find amounts of ease and power you never dreamed yourself to own.

Or, if you like, be more special forces. You don't

even need a balaclava or a laser-sighted weapon. You just need to recognise when a negative thought is preventing you from unlocking infinite potential and contradict it.

Chapter 10:
Well, Why Not?

Because it's there.
- **George Mallory**

After the dust had settled from The Wall, what I considered to be a reasonable achievement would occasionally come up in conversation. OK, more often than occasionally. I'd just run an ultramarathon, thank you very much, and I wanted to tell people about it. So, I crowbarred it into any conversation I could, be it with friends, family members, colleagues, complete strangers, basically, anyone that would listen. Usually along the lines of:

Friend / family member / colleague / random person who had absolutely no desire to be bored senseless about my running antics: 'Hi, how are you?'

Me: 'Great thanks. [Couple of seconds pause] I ran an ultramarathon six weeks ago.'

After they'd gotten over the combination of receiving this entirely unexpected nugget of news and the nature of it, they would–and still do–invariably give me one of three responses.

***

George Mallory was one of Himalayan mountaineering's pioneers, taking part in the early expeditions to recce and attempt to reach the summit of Mount Everest. A school teacher who served as a lieutenant in the First World War, he was a keen climber and a member of Britain's prestigious Alpine Club, which was founded in 1857–as 'the world's first mountaineering club'–and still exists to this day. When the Club teamed up with the Royal Geographical Society to put together the Mount Everest Committee in 1921, Mallory was a shoo-in for the group that would make up the first ever and two subsequent expeditions to the mountain.

After two expeditions that were predominantly focused on surveying and mapping out the Everest region, it was on the third expedition, in 1924, 30 years before Sir Edmund Hillary and Sherpa Tenzing Norgay stood atop the earth's highest peak, that Mallory disappeared into the mist, along with his climbing partner Andrew Irvine. The last sighting of the pair was by their expedition crewmate Noel Odell, at 12:50pm on 8th June as the clouds cleared and they were sighted at an elevation of just over 8,600 m–250 m below the summit–at the second of three famous 'Steps' on the north-east ridge of the mountain. It wasn't until May 1999, 75 years later, that Mallory's body was found by a dedicated search team.

The events of their passing on the mountain will remain forever shrouded in Everest mystery. Various theories have emerged over the years as to whether or not Mallory or Irvine did indeed stand atop the world, before perishing on the way back down. Quite frankly, whether or not they did doesn't matter. What matters was their approach to the pursuit of the peak. At one point, Mallory was asked by a reporter why he was attempting to climb Mount Everest. He famously replied, 'Because it's there.'

It's a subject that I also touched on with Esmée, since her reasoning for taking on the physical challenges she does is, 'Because I can.' There was a point in her life when she couldn't have dreamed of running an ultramarathon or climbing Mount Kilimanjaro, but now that she can, she's damned well going to. 'One day we will hit a point when we can't,' she continues. 'We'll have to say no, whether that's because of age, illness, circumstances, financial reasons, whatever. So, say yes, while you still can.'

It leads me onto the first of the responses to my just so happening to slip into conversation that I'd run an ultra: 'Why?'

Well, why not?

In truth, you could come up with a hundred reasons why not. They're hard. There's inevitable chafing, even if you bathe in anti-chafing cream. There are hours of training. Early mornings. Late nights. More chafing. Fatigue. Feeling lower than you've ever felt in your life. Did I mention there's chafing? But it's precisely because of these elements of hardship that people put themselves through any endurance challenge. For some they're excuses not to. For others, they're reasons to.

The second response I frequently receive is: 'Oh, I could never do that.'

What always strikes me is how quick people are to

doubt themselves. How quick they are to put themselves down in this way. It's often such an instantaneous response that it can barely have been thought through. Sometimes it's a negativity that is seemingly so mentally ingrained that the response seems to come back in a matter of milliseconds, even before the brain can have processed the information.

Well, why not?

My counter in both situations is the same. I don't mean to be an arse about it or make the other person uncomfortable, but I love delving into the subplot of this inherent unwillingness to challenge ourselves and why we approach things from a place of insecurity, rather than from a place of strength and confidence in our abilities. I have done so in detail with many people over the course of the last few years, not least with Ollie Ollerton. In fact, our chat even extended to anthropology and the survival of the species.

'When we were living as hunter gatherers,' Ollie explains, 'there was so much that could go wrong, that the tendency is now to *look* for things to go wrong. Imagine ten berries foraged by our ancestors; they didn't remember the nine tasty, juicy ones, they remembered the one that made them sick, so they didn't have it again. When we're born, our primal coding is therefore solely to survive. It's a default setting that has been programmed into us over millions of years of evolution, all centred around the survival of the species.'

This evolution with survival ingrained into us has got us to where we are today–I'll leave you to decide whether that's a good thing or a bad thing–but is prohibitive in terms of the limits we set ourselves and a lack of willingness to push ourselves out of our comfort zones.

In biological circles they–whoever 'they' are–talk about homeostasis. This is the body's state of balance, where its internal systems are all stable and regulated; you're breathing calmly, your heart rate is normal, your digestive system is working, all is well. It's a useful tool, since it determines our ability to stay alive, but the mind is very quick to panic when it senses that your body is no longer in homeostasis, and it does so well before you're in any danger of keeling over. Take the fight or flight response to danger. Adrenaline causes your heart to beat faster and your lungs to breathe more deeply, sending more blood and oxygen to your brain and muscles, but it also restricts flow of blood to the stomach, shutting down the digestive system. If you can't eat, you can't survive, so the mind doesn't like being in that state for long.

'Unfortunately,' Ollie continues, 'there's absolutely no advantage when it comes to the survival of the species in being positive. It makes the concept of pushing ourselves out of our comfort zone difficult, because we're wired to take shortcuts to conserve energy. We're wired to choose the path of least resistance. So, our minds would be more than happy for us to sit in a corner, eat food and procreate, because that will continue the species. That's why we love nothing more than scrolling through Instagram or bingeing Netflix. And they're fine, occasionally, but not where we should be setting up camp. Because our soul wants to discover more, wants to experience more, wants to do great things. But we spend so much time in that survival default mode, that it takes work to build a positive mindset. The conflict comes because your survival blueprint is stronger.'

Our biological unwillingness to push ourselves is

compounded by a mental one, also millions of negative years in the making.

'These lessons span our whole lives and we're programmed to not believe in our true potential. When faced with difficulties, we panic, we go into our shells, we complain, "Why is this happening to me?" This negativity comes from an unwillingness to put ourselves through discomfort. But when you step out of your comfort zone, you move forward and grow as a person. It's this discovery that we don't have to be constrained by our limiting beliefs that allows us to go beyond what we thought we were capable of.

'The problem is that people have become so comfortable in that space that they're terrified to step outside of it. Then they start to create their own self-imposed limitations. But the longer they stay in that comfort zone, the thicker the wall gets to break out of it. And before you know it, you're so restricted from within that you'll never do anything in your life.'

American writer Elbert Hubbard said: 'There is no failure except in no longer trying.' Failure for our ancestors meant getting eaten by a sabre-tooth tiger or trampled by a woolly mammoth. But, surely in a sabre-tooth tiger- and woolly mammoth-free society, we could do away with the excuses that come thick and fast. I'm not fit enough. I'm no good at running. I don't have the stamina. But no, these are our overriding thoughts because we're inherently scared of failure. Perhaps 'There is no failure except in not *even* trying' would be more appropriate.

Everyone knows that we can learn from failure. That's old hat. A million other books will tell you that it's only through failure that we succeed, blah, blah, blah. With examples like Walt Disney, who left his first company, Iwerks-Disney Commercial Artists, to make money elsewhere and whose second company, Laugh-O-Gram Studios, went bankrupt. And now The Walt Disney Company is worth in the region of $150 billion. Van Gogh. Albert Einstein. Bill Gates. Oprah Winfrey. Michael Jordan. There are countless others.

'Even Roger Bannister went as a favourite to the [Olympic] Games of 1952 and it was out of his 'failure' there, where he finished in fourth place, that the drive to break the four-minute mile was born.'[86]

But if it's so well documented that all these incredibly successful people were abject, pathetic, miserable failures, and with sabre-tooth tigers no longer roaming the earth, why are we so reticent to even consider testing ourselves? Why do we continue to limit ourselves with seemingly instinctive phrases like 'I could never do that' or 'I'm not cut out for that'? Why have we already found an excuse not to? Why do we justify and reinforce an innate negativity by putting ourselves down in comparison to others? Why are we not as fit, fast, clever, strong, talented or 'really, really, really, ridiculously good looking', at least as Derek Zoolander?

I put these questions and more to Caroline Outterside, a psychological therapist. Not *my* therapist, I might add, though I'd have had no reservations working with her in that capacity, rather I was lucky to be a colleague of Caroline's briefly at a mental health start-up. Caroline's quick to back-up Ollie's evolutionary notion, explaining that 'There's hardly been any change in the way our brains work in 30,000 years. For a basic understanding, it still consists of three regions called the reptile brain, the mammal brain and the human brain, that all work together but, in today's world, not as well as they could.

'The most primitive part, the reptilian or 'lizard' brainstem, governs the heartbeat and breathing rates and the urge to feed and breed. Like a lizard, there is no ability to feel emotion. This only came with the development of the limbic system structures in the central part of our brain, also known as the mammalian brain because we share these structures with mammals; we have instinctive behaviours and emotional responses. It controls the fight or flight response and conditions us to dangers. It's always on the lookout, always scanning. We need the emotion of fear for our survival and if, for example, a man with a gun popped up at my window now, I'd be very grateful for the primitive behavioural response of moving quickly.

'The most advanced part of the brain, which is still over 30,000 years old, is the prefrontal cortex which sits behind your forehead and provides our ability to reason and be rational. But, when the limbic system senses danger, it overrides the prefrontal cortex in favour of our life-saving fight or flight response. If it didn't, by the time we weighed up if the gunman was friend or foe, we would be dead.'

The automatic responses are therefore designed to protect us, but 'There is a self-fulfilling nature to the responses you get to your challenges,' Caroline continues. 'If you make a statement like, "I could never do that," you've sort of set the tone, haven't you? You've undermined yourself.'

It's Henry Ford, from Chapter 8, all over again and Caroline recalls her dad bringing her up with a similar mantra: 'There's no such thing as can't.'

***

The third response I often get is: 'You're mental'.

Which is a bizarre thing to say, when you think about it. Because it's not a compliment, is it? Which I'd argue it should be for the achievement of something like completing an ultramarathon. I'm not saying I deserve a medal–although I've got a healthy collection of them–but maybe a comment that's slightly less derogatory. Instead, 'You're mental' infers being sectioned, strapped in a straitjacket and locked in a padded cell. Men in white coats with clipboards peering at you through a glass window that's shatterproof so you can't headbutt your way through it. Randle McMurphy being lobotomised by Nurse Ratched and Chief Bromden smothering him with a pillow in an act of mercy.

These people may be joking, but the implication of being 'mental' is that it's a bad thing. But I don't want to be made to feel bad about my achievements, fuck you very much.

Ok, they never mean it as an insult per se, but let's flip it. Imagine someone were to say 'You're physical' instead. After all, running an ultramarathon requires an element of physicality (more on this in the next chapter). My man crush Chris Hemsworth is 'physical'. He's in great shape. Fit. Healthy. Ripped. Compliment.

So, my counter is that yes, and we could all do with being a bit more mental. Not in the sense of needing a lobotomy, or even the sense that everyone needs to go out and run an ultramarathon–for clarification, you don't have to run an ultramarathon; 'Phew,' I hear you say. But in the sense that we should all be able to tune into–and where necessary turn off–our mindset. We have somewhere in the region of 60,000 thoughts a day and these are predominantly negative because of the mind's survival instinct to protect us from anything that isn't homeostasis. No, don't do this, it'll be hard. No, don't do that, it'll be tiring.

'Take a couch to five km,' says Ollie. 'On the first day of your training programme you're lying on the sofa, dunking your biscuit in your tea, watching the TV, and you know you've got to get up and go for a training run. You've got to take action. But your mind wants to keep on doing the familiar because it knows that's safe. It'll say, "Just start tomorrow."' We've all had the thought and it's about as welcome as a fart in a spacesuit. It doesn't prompt action and doesn't help get the job done.

'The trouble is that people know how the operating system on their smartphone works, but they have no idea how their own operating system works and that tomorrow your mind will say the same, and the next day, and the next. You can't afford to keep on listening to that programme just because it is there to protect you. Instead, by contradicting what the mind is saying in that moment, we start rewriting our programme. And the more you do that, the more you build positive affirmations in your head, rather than the negative survival messages. Before you know it, you start to build a new habit and behaviour. It's the only way that you can really start to change, start to grow.'

Caroline and Ollie could not be from more different backgrounds. Their life experiences and knowledge are polar opposites. Yet the similarity in the conversations is uncanny. They have both talked in depth about how our brains are wired for survival and they've both mentioned operating systems completely independently of each other.

And while the notion of an 'operating system' conjures up scary thoughts of cyborgs stalking the earth, the analogy is important if we consider the body as the vehicle that is there to do the mind's bidding.

Another motivational Ollieism is: 'A goal isn't big enough if at some point you don't doubt your ability to achieve it.' In other words, anything that you want is likely to be hard. The bizarre irony is that it's the mind that dictates what we want but also the mind that tells us, 'Actually, fuck it, it's too difficult.' Or, 'I'll start tomorrow.' But by recognising the inclination to say no, we can discover the ability to contradict it.

In Chapter 12 we'll explore how, through building what I call mental fitness and making a conscious choice to overcome difficulties. It comes down to being more aware of our thoughts, our decisions and our weaknesses, in order to reflect better on the course of action that we wish to take.

Action. Remember that from Chapter 4? I won't repeat the Aristotle quote. What I'll do is give you two others:

- Benjamin Disraeli said, 'Action may not always bring happiness; but there's no happiness without action.'
- And George Bernard Shaw wrote, in the Epistle Dedicatory of his play *Man and Superman*, that 'the true joy in life' is 'being a force of fortune instead of a feverish, selfish little clod of ailments and grievances complaining that the world will not devote itself to making you happy.'

In short, if you want something, happiness or otherwise, you've got to stop dunking your biscuit in your tea and take action. You've got to climb the mountain and you can't take the path of least resistance to get to the top.

So, be more George Bernard Shaw. Be a force of fortune. Discover more, experience more, do great things. Move forward. Grow.

And be more George Mallory. Find reasons to. Not excuses not to. Take things on simply because you can. Contradict the no. Say yes to things. And when you've said yes, don't doubt yourself, even for a second, because then you'll give yourself the opportunity to talk yourself out of things. Don't put yourself down. Don't limit yourself. Push yourself out of your comfort zone.

'There's no comfort in the comfort zone,' quips Ollie.

Chapter 11:
Setting Up C.A.M.P.P.

Now bid me run, And I will strive with things impossible;
- *Julius Caesar*, **William Shakespeare**

If you're sat on your sofa reading this in your pants, whilst eating crisps–Nice 'n' Spicy NikNaks and Flamin' Hot Monster Munch were the go-to choices of my teenage years–you might not believe it but you, yes you, dear reader, are a finely tuned athletic machine.

'After six million years of separate evolution, we still share 95 percent of our DNA sequence with chimps,'[87] writes Christopher McDougal in the outstanding *Born To Run*, which explores the ability of Mexico's reclusive Tarahumara tribe to run seemingly endless distances barefoot or in flimsy sandals, and discredits the likes of Nike for ruining our gait with overly-cushioned running shoes. I'm not going to go into the science of barefoot running–I undertook all of my ultrarunning in a nice and comfy, padded pair of Asics–rather it's the evolutionary stuff that fascinates me.

Because it's the 5% that makes all the difference.

If you track down episode 10–'Food For Thought'–of the BBC's 2002 nature documentary series *The Life of Mammals*, you'll be entertained by the soothing tones of national treasure Sir David Attenborough as you're transported deep into south-west Africa's Kalahari Desert. Here, the camera crew follow the San People, 'the last tribe on earth to use what some believe is the most ancient hunting technique of all; the persistence hunt. They run down their prey … This is how men hunted before they had weapons, when a hunter had nothing more than his own physical endurance with which to gain his prize. Running on two feet is more efficient over long distances than running on four. A man sweats from glands all over his body and so cools himself … And a man has hands with which to carry water, so during the chase he can replenish the liquid he loses as sweat.'

In today's world of instant, well, everything, the concept of outrunning a wild animal for your dinner is one that's hard to get your head around. But, across the world, other ancient tribes are famous for the same method of catching their prey; the Aborigines in Australia, native American tribes like the Navajo, and the Tarahumara.

Drs Dennis Bramble, from the University of Utah, and Daniel Lieberman, of Harvard University, are two of the world's preeminent experts on how mankind has evolved as a species suited for stamina, outlining the subject in a number of their papers: 'Judged by several criteria, humans perform remarkably well at endurance running … humans are surprisingly comparable to specialized mammalian cursors such as dogs and horses' when maintaining relative speed over long distances and can 'adjust running speed continuously without change of gait or metabolic penalty over a wide range of speeds.'[88]

In short, we'd lose every time in a sprint against a tiger and then be mauled to death but, when it comes to endurance running (ER), we can outstrip any other species on the planet because 'human ER speeds, which typically exceed 4 m/s and can reach 6.5 m/s in elite athletes, exceed the trot-gallop transition speed of all other mammals, regardless of size.'

In the case of Attenborough's San People, a kudu collapses of exhaustion after an eight-hour hunt and the hunter's 'spear throw now is scarcely more than a symbolic gesture.'

This running prowess may come as a surprise to many but it's 'thanks to a diverse array of features, many of which leave traces in the skeleton. The fossil evidence of these features suggests that endurance running is a derived capability of the genus *Homo*, originating about 2 million years ago, and may have been instrumental in the evolution of the human body form.'[89]

This is where the 5% comes in.

Because, among these features are the Achilles tendon, which connects the calf muscle to the heel; the nuchal ligament, which runs up the back of your neck; and a whopping great gluteus maximus—your arse muscle—none of which our chimpanzee cousins have. As walking primates, they have no need for them because the 'nuchal ligament is useful only for stabilizing the head when an animal is moving fast; if you're a walker, you don't need one.' Aside from being admired by Sir Mix-a-Lot and fans of Kim Kardashian, whoever they are, 'Big butts are only necessary for running ... Likewise, the Achilles tendon serves no purpose in walking, which is why chimps don't have one.'[90]

So, if you think you're not cut out to be a runner, 2.5 million years of evolution says otherwise. I didn't think I was particularly cut out for it when I started out but I realised I didn't have an excuse. And neither do you, I'm afraid.

That said, I made the point in the previous chapter that you don't have to head out immediately and run an ultramarathon. In fact, if you'd prefer to stick needles in your eyes, I can appreciate your line of thinking. If, however, there is the tiniest chance you're considering a run longer than 26.2 miles, without the support of the crowds that you get when you take on an organised marathon, and suffering through the inevitable blisters, chafing and exhaustion–am I selling it?–here's my 'how to' of ultrarunning. I'm not an expert, by any means, but I've never had a 'Did Not Finish' (DNF) in an ultra, so maybe I'm doing something right. I've even coined a catchy acronym for your ease of memory: C.A.M.P.P. Though I won't go through them in that order. You'll see why.

C: Calories

Multiple ultrarunning world record holder, Ultrarunning Hall of Fame Inductee and arguably the greatest female ultrarunner of all time, Ann Trason, once said, 'Ultramarathons are just an eating and drinking competition with a little bit of running thrown in.'

A very approximate (since it varies according to all sorts of variables, such as altitude, elevation, pace, your size and women typically use less) gauge of the required calorie expenditure when running a marathon is 100 calories for every mile. So, the average runner will burn somewhere between 2,500 and 3,000 calories over the course of 26.2 miles. Of course, that doesn't include the rest of your day's movement, even if that movement extends only to easing yourself into and out of a hot bubble bath. After all, the figure of 2,000 (for women) or 2,500 (for men) calories burned every day is based on minimal exercise. Just thinking uses around 500 calories a day and you burn around 50 calories an hour while sleeping. A marathon *day*, then, is a 5,000-calorie day.

If you remember from Chapter 8 that a runner can typically store around 2,000 calories worth of glycogen, in the simplest of terms, you can't get through a running challenge which is more than 20-or-so miles (or around three hours of running at four-hour-marathon pace) without the necessary fuel. Your body then resorts to breaking down fat. 'The selection of fat for oxidation by the muscles is important since the stores of the most efficient fuel, the carbohydrates, are limited.'[91] But this is a far slower process and your energy levels aren't sustainable if you're relying on fat, and fat alone, for fuel. So, you need to be taking on calories in the run up to the event and during to replenish the ones you're burning through.

A note on carb-loading, incidentally. For a marathon, I'd say do it. Strategies vary but the principle is to maximise your glycogen stores before a long run, by first depleting them through a combination of exercise and reduced carb intake, and then building them back up again. What has worked well for me is cutting out carbs for two days, four and three days before a race, and doing a fairly quick paced five km to empty out the muscles. Then, for two days prior to the race, you rest and eat your body weight in pasta. However, once you get into longer distances, it's more your race-day intake that's important; it's continually fuelling the body that counts. The longest run I've done was a 145-mile ultra, more on which later, and I did so without carb-loading because I was on a short minimoon in the run-up and didn't fancy depriving myself of some decent grub.

When it comes to the day and the race itself, unfortunately there's no one-size-fits-all approach to an 'eating and drinking competition with a little bit of running thrown in.' Strategies, again, vary from runner to runner but, basically, you have to keep grazing. Sitting down for a three-course meal and a couple of yards of ale might get the calories on board but if you need a crane to winch you out of your seat afterwards, you're going to be hard pressed to run.

A lot of this is based on preference. I find dried snack bars (brands like Eat Natural and Nak'd) or a mix of dried fruit and nuts work well as a mix of sweet and savoury. You can't go far wrong with a bag of Haribo for a bit of a boost and I've also relied on Snickers bars, banana bread (homebaked, of course) and even squeezable pouches of baby food puree. Sounds bizarre but trust me. As an example, the 100g Ella's Kitchen Mango Baby Brekkie pouches each pack a decent punch of 112 calories, with a combo of natural sugars and brown rice. So, you're getting a double whammy of mushed up, slow release, carb-heavy goodness and tastiness, compared to energy gels that weigh 60g but only have 87 calories and can taste like a mix of cheap orange squash and Vaseline. (On which note, see the 'Admin' bit below.)

That said, energy gels have their place, but many people—myself included—feel sick after too many. It's also good to mix sweet with savoury. Why? Salt. Sodium and other electrolytes help with the control of how your muscles contract and a drop in levels can result in your muscles becoming over-stimulated by nerve signals freaking out and … hello agonising cramps.

Some people can't stand the idea of hot food halfway through an ultra but I always find a cup of tea or even soup picks me up from feeling like I've been run over by a rampaging crash–an excellent collective noun, in my humble opinion–of rhinos after pushing through three back-to-back marathons. You also have to be adaptable; as per my chat with Phil at the beginning of The Wall, there's always an element of 'seeing how you go'. In Chapter 14 I'll recount how I survived the second half of my first 100-mile ultra on nothing but Coca-Cola and slices of watermelon, since my stomach was in knots and refusing to accept any solid food.

'Food is mood' is a common saying across the ultrarunning community since your calories are crucial to your energy levels and how you feel. You have to eat the right food to keep you going but you should also enjoy it. If you're having to force it down, it'll add to your woes and you're unlikely to take on enough of what you need. Little and often is key.

Oh, and don't forget to drink enough too, obviously. You need to stay hydrated but you also can't eat if your mouth is too dry.

For this section, your task is to imagine a pie-chart broken into the five C.A.M.P.P. sections. In terms of importance, C: Calories takes up a wedge of about a quarter of the whole pie.

Score on James's imaginary ultrarunning pie-chart: 25%.

A: Admin

You've got to look after yourself and this means having the right kit. From a running backpack or vest to what you fill it with, including your calories, it should all serve a purpose in getting you over the finish line. It'll vary from race to race but I always have a first aid kit with me including anti-blister cream and a range of plasters for when the anti-blister cream doesn't cut the mustard. Spare socks. A lightweight, waterproof running jacket. A decent baselayer and a thermal blanket, just in case. More spare socks. A head torch, if you're running through the night. And ensuring that nothing rubs can be the difference between miles of comfortable cruising and miles of chafing—and chuffing—agony. Vaseline is your friend. Or coconut oil. Or Gurney Goo, an anti-chafe and anti-blister cream invented by some mad adventure racing Kiwis. Basically, anything that prevents chafing is good in my book.

It goes without saying that if you can get your admin right, you'll be in for more of an enjoyable time. Fewer snags, whether that's rough strands of clothing rubbing at your undercarriage or more general obstacles along the way, mean fewer stoppages but there's no such thing as a perfect race. If anything doesn't quite go to plan, it's not the be all and end all, provided you can manage eventualities as they come.

Score on James's imaginary ultrarunning pie-chart: 10%.

P: Pacing

As Leonard Hofstadter said in *The Big Bang Theory*, 'Who's ready for some science?'[92]

Energy in the body is derived from a variety of sources–mostly glycogen, which we explored earlier, and fats. Molecules of something called adenosine triphosphate (ATP) are synthesised from glycogen and are responsible for releasing the energy required to undertake exercise. Basically, ATP makes your muscles contract. But the body doesn't store much of the stuff and, when you exercise at maximum intensity, you rattle through your ATP in a matter of seconds. Meaning it has to be constantly replaced.

Oxygen is the key component in the production of ATP and at low levels of exercise intensity–during aerobic exercise–you're able to take on enough oxygen for the body to be a reasonably efficient ATP factory, churning the stuff out on a conveyor belt. But beyond a certain level of intensity–your aerobic threshold–the amount of oxygen needed by your muscles outstrips how much you can get to them. You're then exercising anaerobically and the energy release process isn't as efficient. Without oxygen, the ATP synthesis process is incomplete, less energy is produced, the heart rate spikes, and there are nasty chemical side products. It's a bit like the chlorine bleaching process used to make white paper, a by-product of which is dioxin, a highly toxic chemical and suspected human carcinogen that has to be heavily regulated.

In the case of our bodies, the dioxin is lactic acid, which produces the burning sensation you feel in your muscles when you've pushed too hard for too long.

Wow, that was boring. In short, 'During a long-distance race, almost all energy is derived from aerobic metabolism so the runner must maintain a speed that allows oxygen to be supplied to the muscles at the same rate as it is consumed.'[93] Or, slow the fuck down.

In simpler biological terms, you can't run two marathons at the same pace you can run one—or if you can, you didn't run the first one as quickly as you could. So, if you go out too fast, like I did in Paris, you're going to come a cropper later on.

If you can find the sweet spot at a level just below your aerobic threshold, in theory you can run all day. Well, in reality actually. It's not an exact science unfortunately, and again varies from runner to runner, but a golden rule is that if you can't maintain a conversation and speak in full sentences while running, you're probably pushing too hard. Recovering from overactivating your anaerobic system is possible, but it takes time and requires you to slow down.

Score on James's imaginary ultrarunning pie-chart: 15%.

P: Physical fitness

In the words of Olivia Newton-John, 'Let's get physical', because you need to be reasonably fit to complete a long run. No shit, Sherlock, right?

Right. To an extent.

As you put in your training miles, you'll improve your aerobic fitness and your body will become more efficient at breaking down fuel into energy. Physical conditioning helps get your muscles used to running long distances and you'll be less prone to injury the more miles you put in, since you'll improve your technique, perhaps even subconsciously. While out on your prep runs you'll also begin to learn what works for you and what doesn't in the other areas of calories, admin and pacing. You'll develop a preference for certain foods based on what your stomach can, well, stomach. You'll learn how much to drink and how often, and how many electrolyte tablets to add to your backpack bladder. You'll start recognising the signs that you're tiring and what to do about it.

It's also worth varying your exercise and not just because variety is the spice of life. Interestingly, studies have shown that training aerobically will only improve your aerobic fitness, but training anaerobically improves both aerobic and anaerobic fitness. Specifically, the finding of a study published in *Medicine & Science in Sports & Exercise* 'was that 6 [weeks] of aerobic training ... improved ... ˙VO2max ... but that the anaerobic capacity, as judged by the maximal accumulated oxygen deficit, did not change. The second finding is that 6 [weeks] of training using high-intensity intermittent exhaustive exercise improved ˙VO2max ... and the anaerobic capacity by 28%.'[94]

So, you might think that mile after mile of plodding 'up and down the same old strip'[95] will stand you in the best stead to be the running machine you aspire to be but a better bet is to mix it up. Head out for a run two or three times a week, for sure, but do some interval training too, some hill sprints, a HIIT class, or some leg weights in the gym. You'll challenge your muscles differently and gain more from their repair.

Score on James's imaginary ultrarunning pie-chart: 10%

But I said, 'to an extent'. Because I'm a firm believer that once you can run five miles, through a mix of all the above and the biggest piece of the pie, below, you can run any distance.

M: Mental fitness

Here it is, my dirty little secret. Drum roll please. You don't have to be that fit to run an ultramarathon.

Physically fit, that is.

Mentally, it's a whole different ball game. 'Of all the factors which make up a runner, mental strength is the most important. If you lose that, you might as well lose a leg. The body is there for the ride; it's the will that does the driving.'[96] This is the big piece of the pie. Served with a generous dollop of crème fraîche or a scoop of salted caramel–I told you they were two of my favourite words–ice cream, however you prefer.

There's no point sugar-coating it. Ultrarunning hurts. A lot. You have to be prepared to go to dark places mentally–and literally, if you're running through the night– and have the resilience to push on through. When your body is telling you that you can't take another step, it's your mind that wills you to carry on. It's the 40% rule of being able to call on the energy reserves that you might not have even realised you had. It's the difference between whether you end up crossing the finish line or not.

It's so important, not just to ultrarunning, but to life in general, that I'm going to devote an entire other chapter to it.

In the meantime, score on James's imaginary ultrarunning pie-chart: 40%

Let me just do a quick check of the maths there: 25 + 10 + 15 + 10 + 40 = 100. Phew.

Oh wait, you have to enjoy it too, that's pretty important. So, the acronym should be C.A.M.M.P.E. But now the figures don't work.

Balls (again).

Chapter 12:
Slipping Into Something More Uncomfortable

The illusion is that the finish line is the destination. But the act itself is the destination.
- **Phil Knight, Founder of Nike**

Even if you have no interest in basketball, *Air* is a compelling film about Nike's gamble to sign a young rookie in the 1984 NBA Draft. Under the vision of talent scout Sonny Vaccaro, Nike saw fit to plump their entire marketing budget on the North Carolina junior, who hadn't even stepped foot on an NBA court.

In case you don't know the rest of the story, the gamble paid off. Big time. The rookie's name was Michael Jordan. He was the NBA 1984 Rookie of the Year, a six-time NBA champion with the Chicago Bulls (and the Most Valuable Player in each of those Finals), a 14x NBA All-Star, a 10x NBA scoring champion, a twice Olympic gold medallist, and President Barack Obama awarded him the

Presidential Medal of Freedom in 2016. Hell, many people have called him the greatest athlete of all time and his accolades are far too numerous to list here.

And that's ignoring the financials. Nike was slightly off with its predicted $3 million in sales, through the Air Jordan brand, in the first four years of the deal with 'His Airness'; sales were $126 million in the first year alone, rising to just over $5 billion in a single year in 2022. A percentage of the sale of every shoe going into MJ's back pocket contributed to him becoming the first billionaire athlete and his current estimated net worth by Forbes of $3 billion[97].

Good for MJ.

But this isn't a marketing book, it's a part advicey, part ranty, part silly and part autobiographical brain dump that might even be called a self-help book, so the business case study isn't really the point. Rather, what struck me in the film was the portrayal (by Ben Affleck) of Nike Founder Phil Knight and his approach to going out on a limb to branch out from being a successful running brand and dip into basketball in the first place. Because signing MJ was a risk. A huge risk. And one hell of a tough decision for Knight, based only on a hunch that Vaccaro (played by Matt Damon) had on a 21-year-old, who was yet to play his first game for the Chicago Bulls.

While toying with the decision, Knight asks Vaccaro, 'Do you run?'

Damon's middle-aged, slightly pot-bellied Vaccaro rolls his eyes and replies, 'Is this going to lead to some Buddhist aphorism I don't want to hear?'

'Do you run?' Knight insists.

Vaccaro glances down at his paunch and concedes, 'No, Phil, I don't.'

Knight's next few lines are, in my mind, the most important in the film, not just for Nike's entry to the basketball market, but for the overarching theme of mental fitness that I'd like to cover off in this chapter:

'It's hard. It's suffering. It's difficult. The illusion is that the finish line is the destination. But the act itself is the destination.'*

---

*Side note:

The 'real' quote, from Knight's memoir, *Shoe Dog*, reads: 'It's hard. It's painful. It's risky. The rewards are few and far from guaranteed. When you run around an oval track, or down an empty road, you have no real destination. At least, none that can fully justify the effort. The act itself becomes the destination. It's not just that there's no finish line; it's that you define the finish line. Whatever pleasures or gains you derive from the act of running, you must find them within. It's all in how you frame it, how you sell it to yourself.'[98] In truth, the quote has absolutely nothing to do with Michael Jordan; the memoir covers the founding of the company and growth through the 1960s and 70s, before Jordan was signed. The film also makes out that Jordan was their first real basketball ambassador, when players like Spencer Haywood (then of the Seattle SuperSonics) and Paul Silas (Boston Celtics) were wearing Nikes more than a decade prior. Knight writes that, in 1977, 'Nike had a solid stable of NBA players, and sales of basketball shoes were rising briskly'.[99] But, this excerpt has so many parallels to life that I simply had to include it. Plus, as we said in Chapter 2, don't let the truth get in the way of a good story.

While Knight explains that running is physically demanding, it's his intimation that running is a metaphor for life that I love. Indeed, this is the premise on which my sobriety is based; that life is an endurance sport and we have to keep on putting one foot in front of the other.

***

'The times they are a-changin'', sang Bob Dylan, and it's true that our understanding of mental health is very different to what it was a few years ago, let alone half a century ago. 'We used to have a stiff upper lip as a society,' says Caroline Outterside. 'Back in the sixties, seventies, eighties, people didn't share emotional problems easily as it was seen as weak. Even women. There were scores of housewives on Valium in the seventies and eighties because it was prescribed quite liberally for anyone that wasn't feeling great. But they couldn't talk about it; they were just given these tablets. Now the pendulum seems to have swung right over, with everyone talking about it. And that is a good change but sometimes people have missed a key fact; that life is difficult. Talking and being open offers new perspectives but it doesn't change the fact that shit happens all through life and we do have to deal with it somehow.'

Or, as the @disappointingaffirmations Instagram account helpfully puts it: 'This too shall pass. And then some other bullshit will come and take its place. It never fucking ends.'

What Caroline can't–as a psychological therapist–say outright, but I can, is that there are a lot of people out there who are just having a good old whinge. There is no doubt that the supposed 'mental health crisis' is starker than ever before, with an almost 50% rise[100] in urgent referrals of young people to mental health crisis teams in the year to March 2023.

But–and it's a whopping great, massive but–there's a difference between a mental health disorder and just having a bad day.

As Caroline argues, 'We have to understand that every human suffers, it's in our nature and we have to learn how to deal with that. It's just about how we normalise it and bring it back into coping with life again.'

In my book–and this is my book, after all–in order to cope with life, we have to build what I call 'mental fitness'. You can call it mental health or wellbeing or wellness or whatever the hell you like really; there's a load of blurry lines between how you define the myriad terminology around the topic. But assuming they all refer to the idea of coping with life in some way shape or form, the point of using 'fitness' is that it implies that we can focus our attention on improving it, much like we do our physical fitness. We can exercise it, we can work on it, we can build it, all of which I'll also explain.

So, what is mental fitness?

For me, it's the ability to get through the challenges that we face on a daily basis. It's managing the difficult situations without our emotions getting the better of us, but it's also recognising the good situations and fully appreciating them. It's riding the ups and downs on the rollercoaster of life.

Because let's be honest, life can be tough. Exams, driving tests, deadlines. And, as Caroline pointed out earlier, life can be shit. Accidents, disease, family members fall ill–

and that's 'everyday' stuff, as opposed to the harrowing list of everything that's wrong with the world that I outlined in the Introduction. Plus, Caroline also points out that, 'The trouble is, the way we live now is very different to the way we lived a hundred years ago, let alone 30,000. So, even though our prefrontal cortex has developed to give us planning and logic, it can't work with so many new stimuli; everything's so fast, we're bombarded from all sides. We're using an outdated operating system which can't cope.'

We therefore need a mechanism so that we can, in fact, cope. But, as much as I'd like to be able to solve all of life's (and the world's) woes with a concrete definition of mental fitness and how we can build it, unfortunately it's not as easy as all that. It means something different to each of us. If that's about as useful as a chocolate teapot, let me give you a few more insights from some people who really know what they're talking about.

Ollie Ollerton's understanding of mental fitness goes far deeper than the resilience required to pass special forces selection. In fact, it was only after leaving the military, and subsequently fighting his toughest battle, that he began to address the demons that had been haunting him since his childhood. In particular, working abroad he found himself 'earning silly amounts of cash in a war zone, but haunted by the scars of a broken marriage and guilt-ridden about leaving my son behind. At best I was a functioning alcoholic.' In his autobiography, *BreakPoint*, he recalls: 'It seemed that suicide would make life simpler for me and everyone around me. Maybe I'd drink a bottle of whisky, take a load of pills and quietly pass away.'[101]

Ollie admits to me that he 'was in a very dark place; I hit rock bottom after trying to create a new life for myself away from warzones. But, without the stability of the military to keep me in line, I crashed and burned.'

His journey through recovery involved 'taking responsibility for the first time.' He therefore has a far deeper connection than most with what it takes to build mental fitness. For Ollie, 'It starts within.'

'The first thing anyone can do to build mental fitness is to become aware,' he explains. Caroline reinforces the need for people to 'raise their awareness and explore what they can do to balance themselves out in a way that is realistic and achievable.'

We touched briefly on tuning into our mindset in Chapter 10 and Caroline talks about a similar process of looking within: 'accepting life's ups and downs and tuning into the good when it's happening.'

Sciencey people who study sciencey things would call this metacognition. Caroline points me to a model designed by Dr Daniel Siegel, a Clinical Professor of Psychiatry at the UCLA School of Medicine, to explain this: the Wheel of Awareness. It's worth having a look at.

Imagine two concentric circles. Around the rim of the outer circle are sections that represent all of the things that we can focus our mind on, the most basic being our five senses, what we hear, smell, see, taste and touch. Every now and then we'll have a particularly sumptuous meal or we'll walk past a rubbish truck early in the morning on collection day and get a pungent whiff of rotting refuse. But mostly our senses operate in the background; we don't often focus on them. So too for our body's various internal functions—we know they're taking place but we don't pay any attention to them, unless, for example, our stomachs rumble—and our mental processes, many of which are so ingrained and programmed that it's as if we're on auto-pilot. Occasionally we focus on take-off and landing, but mostly the plane's flying itself while we're shooting the breeze with the co-pilot or joining the mile high club with an air hostess.

The inner circle—the hub—is your metacognition; your awareness. Caroline explains, 'You can choose to send spokes out from the hub to the different points on the rim and focus on them. For example, the joy of eating is taking time to appreciate what you're tasting. The same is true with thinking but most people simply operate on the rim without exploring the relationship between what's happening and how their mind is experiencing what's happening.' As Siegel himself says, 'Where attention goes, neural firing flows, and neural connection grows.'

In short, metacognition is thinking about thinking. It's reflecting on how you feel and why you feel. Like looking in a metaphorical mirror. By building a level of self-awareness, you start to develop a connection with yourself mentally and start to understand the emotions you feel as a result of different scenarios and experiences.

This is partly the premise of cognitive behavioural therapy (CBT), the clue being in the name; it explores cognition and the resulting behaviours, and how to move away from what could be perceived as bad emotions which can lead to the stigma associated with mental ill health. Instead, observing emotions for what they are, without judgement, gives you a far clearer picture of what you can do about them. It also helps develop your understanding of yourself, what picks you up and what brings you down.

Take exercise. Caroline explains that 'When

someone is mildly depressed, it's really helpful to look at their activities. More often than not they've become inactive in response to feeling low and lacking motivation. If you can turn that around, identify things they can do and get them to be slowly more active again, then that will start to help them feel better.'

I couldn't agree more. I never regret a workout. Exercise is my mindfulness. My discovery of running has allowed me to improve my ability to respond positively to situations that cause me stress–something psychologists refer to as 'healthy emotion regulation'. It has made me mentally fit and I have a mantra that if I can't solve a problem on a run, then it's not worth worrying about. I cast it aside. In *Air*, Phil Knight initially objects to Vaccaro's idea to sign a rookie and then does a u-turn, agreeing to risk his entire basketball budget on MJ. Vaccaro asks him what changed his mind.

'I went for a run,' Knight replies.

But your mindfulness could be anything; baking, knitting, building houses of cards, in fact, Caroline's keen to expand on the Stoic principle of living life according to your values with an 'effectively modified or extended version of CBT called Acceptance and Commitment Therapy, which is a terrible mouthful, but it has really taken off. ACT isn't based on just doing any behaviour that will make you feel good. Its focus is on tuning into activities that are meaningful to you and in line with your values, so it's different for each person. For example, if helping others isn't something that you have ever bought into, then there's no point suddenly becoming a volunteer. But if you find great value in having fun with other people and exercising, then joining a running club or similar is the best way to learn from the experiences that such an activity will entail and thus develop self-awareness.'

This should be music to everyone's ears. The beauty of building your mental fitness is that you can do it however you choose; however works for you. Personally, ultrarunning has taught me about myself. It has taken me on a wonderful journey of self-discovery and allowed me to push my limits further than I could have imagined. It has taught me metacognition, through experiencing the ups and downs of an ultramarathon and the associated emotions and thought processes.

But I've hopefully been clear on the fact that ultrarunning isn't for everyone, so I've asked the experts for some more general tips on how to build mental fitness without all the painful chafing.

Ollie says it starts from day one:

'We learn the most from the environment around us between the ages of zero and seven; that is when all your programming is done. For those first seven years, you have one brain functionality; you're like a tape player on record, just soaking in everything around you. It's only after seven that it starts to split, and you get the conscious mind and the subconscious mind.'

It's an age-old idea, even harking back to my venerable Greek friend who we met in Chapter 4: Aristotle. He supposedly said: 'Give me a boy until he's seven and I will show you the man.' (Although, depending on what you read, this quote is also attributed to St Ignatius of Loyola, the founder of the Jesuit movement. But Ignatius lived almost two millennia later, so I detect a hint of plagiarism. Naughty Ignatius.)

But don't worry if you're late to the table. It's fitness after all, so it's never too late to start. The trick is to recognise where you're starting from.

'It's like having a GPS system,' Ollie says. 'Even if you know your destination, if it doesn't know where you are right now, it's never going to get you there. So, you've got to be totally honest with yourself, sometimes for the first time. It's taking responsibility and starting to think of all the things that are holding you back. List down the things that are just not serving you any longer; the negative anchors in your life. Certainly for me, it was quite easy when I crashed and burned because it was the drink, the drugs; all that stuff had to disappear. At the time, I couldn't imagine a life without drink, even though I didn't want it in my life.'

Caroline suggests starting with your breathing: 'When you're mindful of your breath, you then start to notice other things too; you expand your awareness. You can become mindful of your body and the sensations within.' It doesn't have to be a strict mindfulness exercise, sitting in a cross-legged yoga position. Instead, spending just five minutes daily focusing on your breathing and drawing attention to certain parts of your body calms your nervous system, and importantly helps build what Caroline calls the 'noticing neuron'. When you notice a difficult emotion as it is happening and you can name it, such as frustration, then its impact upon you can be significantly reduced, or even disappear.

Ollie also advocates for starting 'with the small stuff. I'm a big believer in breathing, in cold dips, exercise. None of these require a pill. They're natural remedies to get your mind and body into a state of harmony. 90% plus of illnesses stem from stress, so we need to start listening to the thoughts that are going on in our heads and paying them the right attention.'

Ollie's simple argument is that the better we look after ourselves, the better we feel. 'It's three things; mind, body, nutrition. And if we haven't got a good grip on them, it's going to cause mental dis-ease within the mind and physical disease within the body.' By paying attention to 'the thoughts we have, the things we eat, the activities we do, the challenges we throw in front of ourselves,' we can 'build a basic structure of looking after ourselves.'

I run ultramarathons, Ollie climbs mountains—most recently Nepal's Ama Dablam, at 6,812 metres, and Mt Everest is in his sights—'but your mountain could be the fact that you want to spend more time focusing on healthy eating. So, forget climbing mountains if that's not your thing, we simply have a duty to look after ourselves.'

Aside from focusing on your breathing, there are plenty of ways to build mental fitness, according to what works for you. Again, everyone's different but here are some strategies that have served me well:

- Fitness is getting comfortable with being uncomfortable. Physically and mentally.

    So, do something that makes you uncomfortable every day. Physically or mentally. It doesn't matter what it is—exercise rigorously, take a cold shower, say hello to a stranger, dance down the cereal aisle in your local supermarket—the smallest things make a big difference because, by experiencing discomfort, you learn how you respond to it. You start recognising the emotions involved and by doing so, without judgement, you gain a clearer picture of what you can do about them. If you notice a difficult emotion, as Caroline suggested, you may even make it disappear.

- Don't be the guy in Chapter 10 who says, 'I could never do that.'

I understand that you might not *want* to run an ultramarathon or climb a 6,812-metre-high mountain, but don't limit yourself to being able to do so. Because if we tell ourselves we can't achieve one thing, we're subconsciously putting ourselves down in other areas. It makes us less inclined to meet that deadline, nail down that promotion, push ourselves out of our comfort zone, achieve happiness; *eudaimonia*, even. On the other hand, if you act like you can do something, the brain activates in the same way as if you were actually doing that thing. With that comes a confidence boost, increased self-esteem and improved self-belief. One study, by the School of Sport, Health and Exercise Sciences at Bangor University even showed that 'psychobiological interventions designed to specifically target favorable changes in the perception of effort are beneficial to endurance performance'[102]–half of a test group challenged to exercise until exhaustion recorded a 'placebo-driven 18% improvement,' when they were taught to use 'motivational self-talk,' compared to a control group who weren't. Why would you deny yourself the opportunity to feel better about yourself, simply by saying 'I can'?

So, the next time someone asks, 'Could you run an ultramarathon?' even if you have absolutely no intention of ever doing so, tell them, 'Sure thing.'

- Ask yourself 'How am I, *really*?'

    And don't just think 'I'm fine' and move on. Take time to *really* think about the answer. Time? What's that? Nope, the excuse that you don't have time isn't good enough. It takes five mins; three even. Do it while the kettle's boiling instead of scrolling through the Gram. Put your phone away and explore your mood. If it's good, why is it good? If it's crap, why is it crap? Are you just having a bad day or is there something niggling at you? If so, how can you resolve it? Would doing one of the things that Caroline or Ollie recommends help? Like focusing on your breathing or doing some exercise. You could even try writing down some of the situations that make you feel good or crap, and the emotions you experience as a result. An emotions journal isn't as hippy dippy as it might sound, especially if the outcome of it is to help you develop your understanding of yourself and build self-awareness.

Ollie bows out of our chat with an interesting conundrum: 'Your subconscious mind is a goal-striving machine which will stop at nothing until it gets what its dominant thoughts desire. Sounds great, right? Unfortunately, there's the major stumbling block that your conscious mind will flip out if it can't see the route to that goal. It will tell you it can't be done.'

But rather than this be a reason for us all to retreat into our sofa-sitting, biscuit-dunking shells, complain about life and everything that's wrong with it, and tell ourselves that we can't run an ultramarathon, climb a mountain or achieve any other goal in life because 'It's too hard,' let's flip things.

Let's be more aware. Let's spend time in our own thoughts; thinking about thinking. Let's understand how we react to certain situations and how these affect our mindset. Let's build our metacognition in order to reap the benefits of knowing when negative, survival-instinct thoughts are holding us back. Let's employ motivational self-talk to improve our performance—and not feel ashamed when we realise we're talking to ourselves out loud. Let's say, 'I can do this,' rather than 'I can't,' even if you've got zero inclination to actually do it. Let's all train ourselves in a basic level of mental fitness and confidence. Let's tackle setbacks, without being overwhelmed.

In doing so, let's be better human beings, capable of achieving more and getting more out of life.

Chapter 13:
I Love Your Socks

It's not what happens to you, but how you react to it that matters.
- **Epictetus**

Around the time Penny was sending me packing, some bright sparks in Los Angeles County were launching the latest app phenomenon that would sweep the world, and simultaneously be the best thing since sliced bread and a blight on society; Tinder. 'What, so you're saying all I have to do is flick my thumb and I have a chance of sleeping with that woman?' Swipey, swipey.

In theory, it was everything a newly single man could have wished for. In reality, though, swiping right left me flitting between meaningless flings and a series of relationships that ranged from vacuous to horrendous—which would also be an accurate description of some of the women—in a desperate attempt to overcome the woes of no longer having someone of significance in my life. There was the recovering alcoholic who initially told me she was doing

'Dry January' and only admitted to me several months later that she had an SFP. Which wouldn't have been so bad, given my own history of SFPs, had it not been that she was still in denial about having an SFP because her SFP was ongoing and involved her hitting the booze when I wasn't around. When I, not long sober, told her that I had to focus on myself and that I couldn't be sober for the both of us, she asked me why I was being such a selfish cunt. My response, which I thought was pretty reasonable, was that I had to focus on myself and that I couldn't be sober for the both of us. We might have gone round in circles a bit–her calling me names again, followed by an explanation that I had to focus on myself–but that was pretty much that.

There was an advertising director, a website designer, an accountant, a PT and a consultant in something to do with financial markets that I pretended to understand, none of whom lasted. And there was the charity worker and her two cats that I made the mistake of moving in with in her miniscule flat in a shabby corner of Harrow.

During the year that we were together–a year of my life that a small corner of my brain still niggles at me for not using more effectively, for example by spending the time repeatedly smashing my knuckles with a hammer–we jumped from argument to argument, often about the amount of exercise I was doing as I built up my tolerance to long-distance running and trained for *SAS: Who Dares Wins*. As I've outlined, though, the exercise was the root of my sobriety and, to put it frankly, more important than she was. The more she complained about it, the more I did; and the more I resented her for complaining about it.

This was the time when I was regularly running a half marathon before work and a part of this was simply a good excuse to get out of the flat before she woke up, so I wouldn't have to talk to her. I was then staying late in the office–often just watching Netflix for an hour–to avoid coming home and being subjected to the dross that is *Hollyoaks*, and minimise the time spent with her and the cats. But for some reason, our being poles apart in what we wanted wasn't enough to prompt me to do something about it.

That summer, I was honoured when Ollie–the friend I mentioned in Chapter 2, who would subsequently be my Best Man–asked me to be his Best Man. He and his beautiful bride Sarah got married at a gorgeous Northumberland farmhouse and it should have been a day filled with nothing but joy as my best mate tied the knot. But, if I'm very honest, it was a day of mixed emotions. On the one hand I was delighted for Ollie but, as I gave my Best Man speech and toasted the gorgeous couple–with a Biffy Clyro lyric, thanks to Ollie and I seeing the band together on multiple occasions–I selfishly felt an inkling of sadness and a smattering of jealousy at the thought of how unfathomably far I was from being in the same situation.

A couple of weeks later I did my usual early morning run into London, showered at the gym and stopped in at a coffee shop on the outskirts of Soho for a pick-me-up. As I sat in a corner with my cup of joe, an American drawl cut through my mindless scrolling of social media:

'Hey, I love your socks.' (They had avocados on them, in case you care.)

Slightly weary from my morning exertions, I wasn't sure who the comment was being directed at, but begrudgingly raised my eyes over the top of my phone to see a girl sitting across the coffee table from me. Who was spectacular. Slender physique, tanned skin, penetrating eyes. Shit almighty, I thought. She's talking to me.

'Thanks,' I sputtered. 'Life's too short for boring socks.'

She let out a giggle, ran her hand through her glossy brown hair and introduced herself. Her name was Leila and she was a singer-songwriter from California. Of course she was.

We chatted—she was in town doing singer-songwritery things—and the angel and devil on my shoulders battled over whether I should sack off work entirely, call in sick and spend the day acting tour guide. The angel won the first round on points and I excused myself but, as I did so, she asked if I wanted her number. The bell went and the angel and devil went at it again, only for the devil to come back from behind with a combination that finished with a powerful blow to the chin. The angel was out for the count.

'That would be lovely,' I replied.

I never saw Leila again but the realisation that I was at least willing to entertain her offer was the jolt I needed that I was in a dead-end relationship with someone that, in truth, I despised. She was controlling, abusive and borderline depressive, and was making me miserable too. And I couldn't stomach another fucking episode of *Hollyoaks*.

That weekend, I was in the crazy cat lady's Harrow flat watching a game of rugby on TV. Seven minutes before halftime, she asked me to help with the laundry.

'Sure,' I said. 'Can you give me seven minutes?'

'Why seven minutes, can't you just help now?'

'It's halftime in seven minutes, can you wait?' Which I thought was pretty reasonable.

'Oh, you sad twat.' Which I thought was pretty unreasonable.

It was the straw that broke the camel's back. I said that I didn't want to be in a relationship with someone who thought I was a sad twat and was willing to tell me quite so liberally. I vaguely recall her pathetically attempting to protest at me leaving but that was pretty much that.

I packed a couple of days' worth of clothes into a rucksack, checked into a hotel and spent the rest of the day assessing my next move, namely where to live. After all these dead ends and being called horrible names, I needed a fresh start; preferably somewhere a decent schlep away from Harrow.

On the recommendation of my friend Alex–the one of I-didn't-get-round-to-signing-up-for-The-Wall fame–who was living in Wimbledon Village at the time, I wound my way to south-west London. We coined 'Gilet Wednesdays'– which, in case it's not clear, involved wearing gilets on Wednesdays, because we were (and still are) pretentious idiots–and vowed to show the ladyfolk of Wimbledon a good time.

Full disclosure though, very few of the local ladies were shown a good time. Only one actually.

I was done with Tinder by this stage, it not having delivered on the true love it had promised*. But where Tinder had failed, Bumble came up trumps. Having shamelessly loaded my profile with various photos of my

SAS: WDW efforts, I was lying in bed one solitary evening, swiping through pictures of the opposite sex. A profile caught my eye. She was a lawyer, so obviously intelligent and motivated, strikingly attractive and her pictures were all outdoorsy, detailing a range of epic adventures from cycling trips to climbing Mount Kilimanjaro. No brainer. Swipe right.

> ***Side note:**
>
> Just to be certain of avoiding a call from Tinder's legal team, it probably didn't promise love at all.

A 'match' message flashed up immediately, meaning she had already liked my profile and, as women are empowered to make the first move on Bumble, I left the rest in the hands of the dating gods and turned out the light. The next morning there was a notification on my phone screen informing me of a message from Bumble: 'No way! Didn't think we'd match. But glad we did.' I asked why not and the response came in: 'You sound (and look!) incredible!' It's a message that I will mercilessly tease Krista about until we're old and haggard, even though I'd been thinking exactly the same thing, but it got us off to a hilarious start. Four years on, with a tiny human to raise, we're still laughing—and shitting ourselves at the prospect of keeping him alive.

Three days later I was scouring the Caffè Nero on Wimbledon Village High Street for an intelligent, motivated, strikingly attractive and outdoorsy brunette. After our coffees, we'd agreed to go for a walk on Wimbledon Common. Sat in a corner wearing hiking boots, she was effortlessly casual and comfortable enough to dress practically for an autumn stroll, rather than being glammed up to the nines. The attraction was immediate and mutual as proven half an hour later when Krista looped her arm through mine and pulled herself in close to me as we huddled under my umbrella in the November drizzle.

Not long afterwards, some dickhead in China was bitten by a radioactive spider, or had sex with a monkey, or was bitten by a bat, or ate a bat, or had sex with a bat, or did some other weird thing that they do with animals in the Far East. Whatever it was, unfortunately the outcome wasn't a crime-fighting, arachnid-human hybrid superhero, rather something called COVID-19. It was a nasty virus thing. You may have heard of it. It brought the world to its knees. We had to protect our health service instead of it protecting us. And clap our hands for the health service each Thursday evening despite not being able to get a doctor's appointment for six months because all the GPs clocked out and hit the golf course. Is this ringing any bells?

In the third week of March 2020, I was due to team up with some of my *SAS: WDW* buddies for a multi-day ultrarunning event through Sri Lanka's Udawalawe National Park. With the aim of raising money for the Mental Health Foundation, we were going to take on 250 km over five days.

I had an inkling of what this would feel like, having run a marathon around Phuket Island the previous autumn. After breaking up with the 'sad twat' ex, I treated myself to a week-long retreat on Thailand's biggest island. Although 'treated' is relative since I spent the week based at a Muay Thai boxing gym doing three or four workouts a day for five days, from kickboxing to CrossFit, in 30°C+ temperatures and 95-100% humidity. I then rounded off the week by running a marathon, including a pilgrimage up Nakkerd Hill–

and believe me, I was 'nakkerd' when I got to the top—to the Great Buddha statue. I have never sweated so much in my life. I filled up my two-litre bladder twice and also stopped into various little shops for sugary energy drinks for a total of about seven litres of fluids drunk in five hours.

For anyone training for a marathon, I wouldn't recommend upwards of 15 training sessions in the five days before the event, even if you're drinking gallons of coconut water and eating freshly-cooked Thai food. However, there's something satisfying about ringing out your t-shirt after a workout and the routine was exactly what I needed to clear my head, while the simplicity of my diet was like a detox, even if it was only from the 'sad twat'.

Six months later, I was liaising with fitness watch and sports clothing brands for support and, after an introduction through a mutual friend, corresponding with a former Permanent Representative of Sri Lanka to the United Nations for recommendations of sponsorship from local businesses. But, with flights grounded and borders closed due to the pandemic, the event was cancelled.

Rather than allow 1,000s of miles of training to go to waste, many of them in various layers to try and replicate the heat, I resolved to move the running from the Udawalawe National Park to the streets of London. I couldn't run 250 km across Sri Lanka but I was damn well going to run 250 km. I wanted to stay true to sponsors and generous supporters, even if there wouldn't be as many wild elephants snorting outside my tent at 2am.

Krista and I had a conversation about logistics and agreed a simple plan of me basing myself at her flat for the week. I'd head off running during the day and we'd share a big bowl of pasta each evening.

I set myself a few fun running challenges to entertain me over the course of five days and, on the Monday morning, started with some of the city's most iconic sporting venues. I headed down to Wimbledon's world-famous All England Lawn Tennis Club and from there ran via Twickenham, Wembley and The Emirates to the London Stadium (the former Olympic Stadium) in Stratford. Distance covered: 53 km.

That evening, Prime Minister Boris Johnson officially announced the UK's first lockdown, giving 'the British people a very simple instruction – you must stay at home.' Apart from 'very limited purposes' including 'one form of exercise a day'. What he didn't do was stipulate how long that exercise should last. So, ultramarathons were allowed. Technically.

Obviously there were those who protested; the naysayers, the keyboard warriors and the generally miserable fuckers who seem to have nothing better to do than try and spread their misery to everyone else. But I checked in with friends who are nurses and policemen and felt that raising money to support people with mental health issues was far more pertinent than not spreading a virus that I didn't have by not coming within two metres of other people. And, for the most part, the positivity was incredible. The solitude of running 250 km was going to be tough and this is one of the situations where social media can be a force for good. Messages of support poured in, validating my decision to continue the challenge.

That said, I didn't want to veer too far from home in the next couple of days, and though it best to avoid public transport, so I scrapped a plan to run the length of the Central line, the London Underground's longest line at 46 miles, and resorted to 1.25 km laps of the south-east corner of Wimbledon Common. Over the next couple of days, I covered 40 laps (50 km) clockwise and then a marathon anticlockwise. Total distance covered in three days: 145.2 km.

Fearing then for my sanity, I switched things up and opted to spread my geographical wings slightly for the final two days, running to Kingston and back along the River Thames (60 km) on the Thursday, and mapping out a giant 50 km Stegosaurus-shaped loop of Streatham, Dulwich and Crystal Palace on the Friday. 'Why a stegosaurus?' I hear you ask. To be honest, there was no particular reason for the route being in the shape of a dinosaur, other than it looking cool on my fitness tracker. Maybe I should have hired a fancy dress costume like the guy who I narrowly beat in the London Marathon and mapped out a T-Rex-shaped route instead.

On the Thursday afternoon I hit a snag as my right foot landed awkwardly on a tree root on the Thames Path. A shooting pain stopped me in my tracks and I panicked that I'd overdone it. I hobbled back to Krista's flat and spent the evening sitting with my foot propped up on her coffee table, hoping that the magic combination of an ice pack and generous lashings of ibuprofen gel would see me through my final 50 km.

The next day was agony. Eight hours of agony. My ankle had swollen up badly overnight and, even though I used what seemed like several miles of tape to strap it, I winced every time I planted my foot. On three separate occasions I stopped dead in the middle of the pavement and thought, 'I'm done. I can't go on.' But a little voice got me back up and running–well, walking–each time.

Hendri Coetzee was a South African adventurer who, in his autobiography, *Living The Best Day Ever*, wrote: 'I have learned that there is a place where the pain stops, where tiredness ceases, and where limits disappear. Unfortunately this place is guarded by plenty of pain, or at least what I used to think of as pain. The solace is in knowing that you can do just about anything, if you are willing to pay the price.'

I never found out the nature of the injury because chipping up to the local hospital would have been met with something along the lines of, 'We don't give a flying fuck that your foot hurts, we have more important things to be worrying about like a virus that's killing people', but it didn't really matter. Because a few weeks of limping around the flat recovering was barely even a price to pay. I raised a bunch of money for an important cause, so, in my opinion, the experience was worth every excruciating step.

Total distance covered in five days: 255 km. And girlfriends accidentally moved in with thanks to Boris' impromptu lockdown restrictions: One.

I wasn't allowed to leave Krista's flat to go home to my own flat. Maybe I could have swung it that walking home was 'exercise' but, in truth, I didn't want to. We hadn't thought through the prospect of us being locked down together but it seemed like such a natural transition that we simply rolled with it. Even though it was a small one-bedroom flat, we were perfectly comfortable together for the three ensuing months of confinement. More than just comfortable; blissfully happy, such that I asked Krista to marry me six months later.

So, in a way I have Boris Johnson to thank for my marriage. Which is a little weird. And for the same reason I also think COVID was brilliant. Can I say that?

Maybe, maybe not. The point is I'd sorted the missing piece of my life's puzzle that had eluded me for so long. And, it transpires, had eluded Krista.

Was it fate? Who knows, depends if you believe in it. Certainly the God of Bumble ordained it.

I've since read a definition of a soulmate as someone who allows you to experience a love so deep that you doubt you've ever truly loved anyone prior. When I was beginning to think that love was only true in fairy tales–thank you The Monkees–especially in the wake of the 'sad twat' ex, Krista has allowed me to understand what love really is. It's devotion, it's support, it's friendship, it's compassion. But it's also inspiration. I strive to be a better person because of her and for her–and for Freddie–although that's self-motivated because she would never push me to change. Love is based on being with someone for who they are, whilst bringing out the best in them and vice versa.

We laugh together daily. We have deep and meaningful conversations daily. She challenges my way of thinking. We also chat complete shit to each other daily. We shoot the breeze. We talk about everything, anything and nothing. We help sort through each other's problems, sometimes we even sort through other people's problems. We put the world to rights and we have righted each other's worlds.

In short, she is my fairy tale.

***

The Sri Lanka-cum-Wimbledon experience was, in the words of Green Day, 'another turning point, a fork stuck in the road'[103] towards learning more about myself. I have always added a charity element to my long runs but, from a selfish point of view, I'd achieved another milestone in my endurance journey. Where I could have easily packed it in only a few miles short of the finish line and justified my decision with the excuse of an injury, I'd battled through to the end. I'd furthered my ability to push through my limits, pushing through a pain barrier and completing 50 km on the final day whilst grimacing with every step.

I had also learned a valuable lesson in making the best of a bad situation, or what I call 'controlling the controllables'. My Stoic friends would have been proud of me, in particular Epictetus*, who I mentioned in passing in Chapter 2. He was one of the leading proponents of Stoicism while Marcus Aurelius was still in ancient Roman nappies. While he, like Socrates, never wrote anything himself, he's attributed with saying: 'It's not what happens to you, but how you react to it that matters.'

> ***Side note:**
>
> A note from Ben Harrison on Epictetus: 'He had been a slave and was lame, apparently caused by brutal treatment from his master, Epaphroditus, himself a slave. Freed by the emperor Domitian, you'd have thought Epaphroditus would have remembered what it was like to be treated badly–clearly it is the converts you have to watch out for! At least his leniency extended to Epictetus being allowed to attend philosophy lectures and, as a freedman, he became a philosophy teacher himself and attracted large audiences. Generally, poorer people,

> slaves and freedmen attended such events, as they were the ones that the current system wasn't working for–it was exactly the same rationale that made Christianity become increasingly popular among the lower classes during the latter part of the 1st century AD.'

While we're rattling through history and cultures, there was another famous playwright and poet who had a thing or two to say about the irrationality of letting a situation get the better of us. You might have heard of him. His name was William Shakespeare, whose arguably most famous character–perhaps second most famous after Romeo, or third most famous after MacBeth, or fourth after King Lear, or … stop it, he's definitely a top five Shakespearean character–was Hamlet. The Prince of Denmark knew that it's not what happens to us, rather how we interpret the events when he said, 'There is nothing either good or bad, but thinking makes it so.'[104]

A similar mantra is explored on the journey through sobriety by those in the AA programme. At the end of every meeting, attendees reel off a rendition of the Serenity Prayer:

> God, grant me the serenity to accept the things I cannot change, the courage to change the things I can, and the wisdom to know the difference.

Much like Step 3 of the programme, you can ignore the God bit if you like, or substitute it for a four-armed elephant, Yoda, a jar of Marmite or anything you pay homage to. What's important is the revelation that there's a difference between things we can control–or change–and things we can't. By accepting things beyond our control we can move past the point of them causing us stress and upset.

Like bank guy.

There's a number of variations on a story about a guy who's the victim of a freak accident. He's always an innocent bystander, whether in a bank heist, traffic collision or another crazy scenario; we'll go with the bank but don't worry too much about the specifics, it's the premise that matters.

A businessman jets off to The Big Apple on a work trip. Emerging from JFK arrivals, he tells the cabbie to take him straight to Katz's Deli for a mouth-watering, lip-smacking pastrami sandwich that would give Meg Ryan an orgasm. He checks into his hotel and gets some shut-eye before a big day of meetings. So far so good. The next day he's up bright and early, swinging into a Starbucks for a pumpkin-spiced latte before stopping into his company's New York office for a catch-up with the local team. Then it's a tour of prospective clients; he has a series of meetings all over town. The first couple go smoothly and he gets his prospects to sign on the dotted line. So far so good. The third will think about it. With an hour slot free in his diary to grab some lunch, he decides to pop into a local branch of his bank to pay in a cheque. Before you say anything, it's an old story; this was back in the day when people visited banks to pay in cheques. If you're a Gen Zer, Google what a cheque is. Anyway, while he's queuing in line to speak to the cashier–if you're a Gen Zer, Google what a cashier is because banking used to involve interaction, like with an actual, literal human–a trio of masked men run through the door brandishing handguns and fire a couple of warning shots into the ceiling to show they mean business. A cry of something along the lines of, 'Any of you fucking pricks move and I'll execute every motherfucking last one of you'[105], emanates from behind one of the masks. Over 200 banks in Manhattan and our poor protagonist has picked the one that is getting robbed. 'Never mind,' he thinks. 'Just keep quiet and it'll all be over soon.' He sinks to his knees, puts his hands behind his head and is minding his own business when another customer decides to play hero and go for one of the robbers' guns. The weapon goes off in the ensuing tussle and our man takes a slug to the chest.

He is rushed to hospital and, after extensive surgery to remove the bullet and repair internal damage, and a blood transfusion to replace the blood lost at the scene, he's hooked up to an antibiotic IV to ward off infection. A nurse comes to check on him.

'Jeez, Louise,' she exclaims. 'You are one unlucky son of a bitch.'

'Unlucky?' he replies. 'How so?'

'Well, of all the days to pay in a cheque, of all the hours in the day, of all the banks in Manhattan, you pick the one that's robbed. And of all the customers, you're the one that gets shot. What are the odds?'

'Slim,' he admits, 'but it was out of my control. And I'm lucky to be alive.'

I couldn't control breaking my neck in a freak rugby accident. But I could have not spent three years feeling sorry for myself about it. I couldn't control the fact that a freakish strain of mutated bat flu brought the world to a standstill, grounding international flights and cancelling my adventure to Sri Lanka. But I could still run. I couldn't control the government instating a 'moment of national emergency' and imposing restrictions on our freedom to 'protect our NHS'.

217

But I could still run close to home. I couldn't control the acute pain in my foot. But I could still hobble; I could control how I responded to each of those eventualities by adapting accordingly.

You guess that Epictetus wouldn't have run around complaining to all and sundry if he'd been shot in a bank–if guns had existed in ancient Rome. Unfortunately, rolling with the punches seems to be another skill that is fading from our life CVs. The term 'throw-away society'–coined to describe our changing behaviours and preference for disposable items as a result of consumerism–has extended from our day-to-day products to our hopes, dreams and relationships. Technology hasn't helped our inherent laziness–seriously, how can it be good for us as a species to be able to order a Big Mac meal by tapping our phone screen?–while dating apps have spawned 'a generation of sex-obsessed commitment-phobes … because of the hit-it-and-quit-it culture'.[106]

Shit happens; that's life, unfortunately. Whatever the scenario, be it during an ultramarathon or life, we're too quick to give up on everything, for all the reasons listed above. But as we outlined in the previous chapter, the more we challenge ourselves, the more we learn, the more we're able to adapt and make the most of a bad situation. There's always a positive side; you just have to be of the frame of mind to look for it.

Like bank guy.

That's not to say that you need to be completely devoid of feeling when it comes to receiving bad news, perpetually walking around with an inane smile on your face like a robotic imbecile. We'll explore difficult emotions further in Chapter 15 but, in short, expressing our feelings is a crucial part of metacognition and helps build mental fitness, as we discovered in the previous chapter. But the more we react negatively to bad situations, rather than reframing them to find the positives, like our bank heist victim, the more they weigh down on us and cause our mental health to suffer. If we continually think and act like the world is against us, it will seem more and more like it is.

If you struggle with the positives, gratitude is a habit that can be learned and practised. A daily gratitude journal–oh god, not another journal suggestion–works; another science lesson coming at ya.

Loads of studies have shown that when we actively focus on the things we are grateful for, the parasympathetic nervous system is activated. This is the 'rest and digest' system that is responsible for powering the state of homeostasis that our body loves so much. Yes, I know we discovered in Chapter 10 that it is essentially the root cause of our evolutionary laziness, but this is *active* laziness, and it's my book, so it's allowed. Our heart rate slows, our blood pressure drops and our digestion becomes more efficient, causing a state of relaxation. Gratitude lowers cortisol, the stress-inducing hormone, and boosts oxytocin, the love hormone.

It's proven then; just as 'motivational self-talk', i.e. telling yourself you're great, makes you feel, well, great, so does being thankful. So why wouldn't you do it? Writing things down is powerful but even if you're able to spend a few minutes each day reviewing what has gone well, you'll feel the mental and physical benefits. Daily is good, twice daily is better. Even in the darkest of times, it is possible to find something that is good in your life. Your health. Your partner. Your family. Your friends. Your dinner. Your goldfish. The key is a gratitude routine of some kind that helps you focus on silver linings.

I bet you bank guy had a gratitude journal that allowed him to see the positives. So, be more bank guy. Accept what you can't control without thinking that the world is against you. Adapt. Make the best of bad situations. Practise gratitude. Find the positives. Write them down if possible.

But try to avoid getting shot.

Chapter 14:
Finding The Funny

Cheerfulness in the face of adversity. Make humour the heart of morale.
- **Royal Marine 'Commando Spirit'**

All this brings me back to my own quest to achieve the 'impossible' and the lessons that *SAS: Who Dares Wins* had taught me:

1. Stress positions hurt more than a white-hot poker to, well, somewhere you don't want a white-hot poker.

2. When you think you've got no more to give, you've got plenty. Limits are in our minds.

The first of these wasn't of much practical use outside of a mock torture scenario but the second was the deciding factor in my quest to scratch the 100-mile itch. After all, I'd run 70. And pushed through 50 km with what could very well have been a hairline fracture. Surely I could manage the sacred three-figure distance ultramarathon? There was only one way to find out: sign up for one. So that's what I did.

***

Centurion Running's Thames Path 100 is pretty much what it says it is; a 100-mile race along the Thames Path. Starting in Richmond, London, and finishing in Oxford, the 2020 iteration was also affected by COVID, initially due to take place in May before the organisers were forced to postpone it. This was no bad thing personally, though. While 50 km on a swollen ankle might have been bearable, more than three times that distance would have been a different kettle of fish.

After hobbling around the flat for a few weeks, I was back at the training, gradually upping the mileage to upwards of 50 miles per week. Krista also convinced me to buy a road bike and I became an occasional lycra-clad wanker. With gyms still closed, pedalling through the Surrey hills became a welcome alternative to running around Wimbledon Common and Richmond Park, for the variation in exercise as much as for the change of scenery.

That summer, during a narrow window in which we were allowed to escape British shores, Krista and I made a dash for the south of France. We spent a week in a self-catered maisonette on a beautiful estate in the countryside outside the ancient walled city of Uzès. We lounged by the pool and read our books. We borrowed bicycles and ambled through gorgeous little village markets to buy fresh fish for dinner. We soaked up the history of the area and visited vineyards. Krista painted. And I ran.

A quick scope of the local geography revealed the relative proximity of the world-famous Pont du Gard. Spanning the River Gardon, which flows into the Rhône just south-west of Avignon, and standing almost 50 metres high, this is an unfathomable feat of engineering considering it was built in the first century AD. It forms part of a Roman aqueduct that carried water 30 miles from Fontaine d'Eure, near Uzès, to Nîmes and is the tallest of all Roman aqueduct bridges. It is impeccably well preserved, mesmerizingly impressive, and was designated a UNESCO World Heritage site in 1985. I *had* to run over it. So that's what I did.

As part of an attempt to tick off a 30-mile preparatory run, I mapped out a route through the fabulously named villages of Saint-Quentin-la-Poterie, Saint-Victor-des-Oules, Pouzilhac, Valliguières, Saint-Hilaire-d'Ozilhan and Castillon-du-Gard, over the Pont du Gard and back through Uzès to our little maisonette. It was, up to the marathon point, unquestionably the most stunning running route I have ever stretched my legs along and, after three months in lockdown, it was a privilege to be out plodding through the southern French countryside.

The 30 miles didn't quite materialise, however. It was a Sunday and, to add to that, the French basically do a grand total of sweet fuck all throughout the summer. So, there was barely a soul in sight, and my assumption that I'd be able to fill up my running bladder at a series of cute little boulangeries or cafés in the Gard department's unpronounceable villages left me waterless at the marathon mark, with little inclination to attempt the remaining 8 km in what turned out to be 35°C heat. Assumption is the mother of all fuck ups, isn't that what they say?

Fortunately, Krista hadn't yet partaken of her holiday afternoon glass of rosé and I was able to drop a WhatsApp pin and cower in the shade of a tree until she came in the car to rescue me. On arriving back at the maisonette, I fell straight in the pool, complete with all my clothes and running pack on, forgetting that my phone was in my pocket. It sprung back to life after a few minutes drying out in the sunshine.

So it was that, with a few extra training runs under my belt, including a double marathon three weeks prior, I got up early on the morning of 5th September 2020 to have a very large bowl of porridge loaded with bananas, most of a jar of peanut butter and lashings of maple syrup. I popped my mask on, boarded a bus in Wimbledon Village–the 493, if you must know–and trundled to Richmond.

As I've mentioned in previous chapters, part of the attraction of taking on a mass participation event–whether it's 50,000 running a marathon or even 500 running an ultra– is the 'mass' bit. As in the people. But COVID had put paid to all that, so the start of the Thames Path 100 was staggered. Although there's something to be said for this more relaxed approach of choosing when to start your own race, I'd enjoyed the reassuring chat with Phil at the beginning of The Wall. But no cigar this time around as there wasn't even the vaguest hint of pomp and circumstance to mark the start–no fanfare, no countdown, no fellow runners with whom I could exchange nervous banter, no nothing. I pitched up to the river, adjacent to Richmond Old Town Hall, visited a portaloo, and found one of the marshals. He shot me in the head with one of those thermometer gun things, confirmed that I probably didn't have COVID and told me I could start running. So that's what I did.

It was 8:12am. About six minutes later–remember what I said about pacing in Chapter 11?–my watch buzzed at me. I'd completed a kilometre. As we explored in the previous chapter, and in the section on reframing in Chapter

6, there could have been two sides to this situation:

The negative: 'Fucking hell, I've *only* done one km. The next 24 hours are going to be unbearable.'

The positive: 'Fucking right, I've *already* done one km. I get to do something I love for the next 24 hours.'

I opted for the positive and laughed to myself at the thought that it was 'just' 160 km to the finish line. It's a mindset that Henry Cookson would have been proud of.

***

It's not an exaggeration to say that Henry Cookson has rewritten the rule book on how to travel. As the founder of Cookson Adventures, a curator of some of the most incredible expeditions exclusively for the super-rich, he has developed a knack for scouting out the world's most remote locations. Think pioneering, world-first kind of stuff– superyachts in Svalbard, submersibles in the Southern Ocean and helicopters in the Galapagos Islands. Oh, and he was also part of the team that was the first to reach the Southern Pole of Inaccessibility using manpower alone, so he has taken, arguably more than any man on the planet, the road less travelled. Albeit everything, he admits, 'sort of happened by accident', and with a fascinating mental ill health subplot, as we'll discover.

Let's backtrack.

'From a young age,' Henry recalls, 'I didn't know what I wanted to do with my life. But I got a taste of adventure and the unknown when I went off to work as a horse riding safari guide in Kenya when I was 18. Even that I didn't have much of a clue about at the time; it was crossed wires because I thought I was signing up for a Land Rover safari. And then a message came through a couple months beforehand with an equipment list that included riding gear and I had to learn on Wimbledon common. So that experience sowed a seed, although I still didn't have a fucking clue what I wanted to do.'

He signed up for the military, expecting to do a short service commission, and got a bursary for university. He 'started to go down the expected path. I was fortunate to grow up in a relatively privileged background, which my parents worked exceptionally hard to make happen, and that meant that I thought the route to prosperity was in banking or lawyering. So, I realised, not to diminish the military, that I had to get a proper job and reluctantly got a job in the backdoor at Goldman Sachs.'

By this stage the idea of the wider world and all its opportunities hadn't really been on his radar and he admonishes himself slightly for not having a better handle on what his talents and strengths were. He sat in the Goldman Sachs interviews 'telling stories about being chased whilst on horseback by lions and around Kenyan campfires by horny single American tourists, and my heart sank because I knew I'd hate it and I was selling my soul.'

Nearly three years later, the call of the wild was too great to ignore. 'It was an itch that I couldn't get rid of,' Henry recalls. 'Finally, it grew to enough of a crescendo that I had to quit the job and follow my dream as a safari guide.'

As we've discovered, life can be cruel, and we'll come onto Henry's twist in the story in due course. For the time being, though, it was 'a whiskey-fuelled conversation' that proved the major crossroads for this soon-to-be-intrepid explorer and it was the Arctic, rather than Africa, that called.

'I was in Scotland with a friend called Rupert [Longsdon], salmon fishing, although there were no bloody salmon. And that's where he mentioned a ski race to the Magnetic North Pole because he'd also had a chance conversation with someone he used to pull pints with when he was making money in his school holidays, who was now the wife of the organiser. A bottle of Famous Grouse down, it seemed like a great idea,' he says with a wry smile. 'The fact that we didn't know how to put up a tent, we didn't know how to cross-country ski and we'd never been anywhere colder than a ski resort in the Alps didn't dawn on us. Despite sore heads in the morning, we couldn't really back down.'

Fast forward and some months later, as Team Hardware, Henry, Rupert and another recruited friend, Rory Sweet, found themselves in Resolute, Canada, as part of the 2005 Scott Dunn Polar Challenge. Faced with the prospect of crossing 350 nautical miles of Arctic tundra, 'we were just woefully ignorant and unprepared. And we were written off because we weren't taking it seriously. There was a TV crew to film it all and this was back in the days of normal tape, and they were told explicitly not to film us, because we were considered a joke and it would be a waste of footage.'

They had zero previous polar experience and were up against Arctic-trained Marines and professional long-distance athletes. 'There was a team called Commando Joe, who were active serving members of the Royal Marines; I think they were arctic warfare instructors or had done arctic warfare courses. And they were meant to win it. We were definitively the underdogs. Polar conditions aren't for idiots and fools, and, out of 17 teams, we were definitely the idiots and fools!'

But, speaking of the Marines, part of the Royal Marines' ethos is The Commando Spirit–Courage, Determination, Unselfishness and Cheerfulness, namely 'Cheerfulness in the face of adversity.' And Henry would argue there's something to be said for being the fools, or at least fooling around, in miserable circumstances; and Henry's experience, he is keen to emphasise, 'was miserable, really miserable.

'I mean there was this beauty and awe, but the average temperature was -30°C, which could feel like -60°C with the wind chill. Your skin would freeze almost instantly if exposed, I couldn't feel my hands, my balls and my inner legs were just chafed to bits and raw, our feet were just mush, blisters on blisters. There was sleep deprivation. The food we had was revolting because we were given all these ready meals and we just poured them all into one big sack to save time, so it was a mixture of like 10 different recipes. And there was a perversity to having paid an obscene amount of money—£16,000, which is a lot even these days but back then was a tonne—and my last bit of cash from Goldman Sachs, to put myself through abject misery.

'But you have to keep your sense of humour. It was so horrific that it was funny and the worse it got, the funnier it got. We had a giggle too; we found frozen polar bear shit and put it in Rory's sleeping bag, so it thawed through the night and he woke in this sticky mess because all they eat is seal blubber. We took a detour at one point because we saw a nice slope and we wanted to go tobogganing on our pulks. We played laxative roulette with our porridge and we'd wait and see who got hit because the mental boost for the other two far outweighed being doubled over behind an iceberg spraying shit everywhere. We wrote blog updates about being on holiday and expecting better facilities and where was the spa? It was sort of Monty Pythonesque.'

Long story short, they began as the underdogs but nine days, 11 hours and 55 minutes–with arbitrary 12-hour breaks at each of the two checkpoints for safety–they won the race, smashing the record by two days in a time that still stands. So, there's something to be said for a lighthearted approach to a serious endeavour.

'If you take these things too seriously, it slightly defeats the object. It's about having a bit of fun, not approaching everything militantly as some of the other teams were. The trouble is, of course, a really successful trip, when you get from A to B without incident, is quite boring and it makes for a really shitty story. And for adventurers, that doesn't get them column inches. Everyone wants to hear about your dick falling off or bears tearing you to shreds, or you fell down a crevasse, you know. It was Roald Amundsen that said, "Adventure is just bad planning." So, sorry, Sir Ranulph, but cutting off your own fingers in your garage because you lost them to frostbite possibly makes you shit at what you do!'

If you can have fun, without mishap, however, that's different. As Henry muses, 'Having those giggles kept the mental energy going, we got a good story out of it and we still have all our fingers.'

On the way back through Canada, the team had what Henry describes as 'an almighty session in a strip club in Ottawa, where we were the ones on the poles while the dancers watched us' and, despite the 'abject misery', they started looking at the expedition through rose-tinted glasses.

Henry admits that he 'certainly didn't grow up reading about [Robert Falcon] Scott and [Roald] Amundsen and [Fridtjof] Nansen and all the polar greats. I barely knew penguins were south and polar bears were north; it just wasn't on my radar. In fact, if I'd known how much suffering and hardship it would involve, I don't think I'd have done it. As for the race, we just wanted to finish it. That was our goal. We didn't have any aspirations to win it; just to get to the end. That would've been something to tell the grandchildren about. And it was going to be a one-off; an adventure and yet definitely never to be repeated.'

Remember Type II fun?

Well, within a week Henry and Co were already on the hunt for the next adventure and speaking about the Antarctic. But not just the run-of-the-mill South Pole; Amundsen, Scott, Shackleton, Byrd, Hillary, Fiennes, bloody hundreds have been to that wholly unremarkable point of the planet. 'Fuck that,' Henry exclaims, 'the South Pole's relatively boring, it has been done.'

Some research on Henry's part unearthed the Southern Pole of Inaccessibility, which sounds terrifying even without the -50°C temperatures and knowing it's at an altitude of 3,800 metres and thousands of miles from, well, anywhere. 'Defined as the exact centre of the Antarctic landmass,'[107] it's the most remote terrestrial point on the planet, 800 miles from the South Pole. You know, the average, everyday one where everyone and their uncle has been. Whereas practically no-one had been to the POI; in the late 1950s, the Third Soviet Antarctic Expedition had spent two years crossing the Eastern Antarctic in snow tanks and installed a research station at the POI, complete with a statue of Vladimir Lenin, pointing towards Moscow.

For Henry, being the first to get there without the aid of mechanical means 'wasn't actually about being the first, it was just something more interesting.'

The team brought in Paul Landry, a Canadian adventurer 'who actually knew something about polar exploration,' Henry jokes. Aside from being the official trainer on the Polar Challenge, Landry had 'led groups to the Geographic South Pole, across the Antarctic continent, guided four expeditions to the Geographic North Pole and one to the Magnetic North Pole and four times across the Greenland icecap.'[108] 'This is a guy,' Henry explains, 'who orchestrated and executed countless amazing trips, but he was rarely talked about when he'd be there patching up people's blisters, tucking them in and wiping away their tears. And he thought we were absolute buffoons on the Polar Challenge but we met up with him in Ottawa and said we'd like to consider something else. When we said we were going to the Pole of Inaccessibility, he just said, "No way. There's a good reason it's called the Pole of Inaccessibility." He was thinking about going into retirement because he'd been exposed to too many narcissistic, attention-grabbing personalities. But he liked the fact that we were doing it for the honesty of the trip and were doing it as a team, with us being very honest about his crucial role as a guide, a point sometimes 'forgotten' by others.'

The team rebranded as Team N2i, headed to the Novo (Novolazarevskaya) Antarctic research station, located on Queen Maud Land–around 2,500 miles from Puerto Williams, the world's southernmost town, in Chile's Antártica Chilena Province–and strapped on their skis.

53 days later, on 19th January 2007, Henry remembers 'A black dot on the horizon that got larger and larger and then we saw the silhouette of the statue sticking out of the ice. We were on the verge of collapse, but we just looked at each other and started laughing. It was surreal after travelling 1,750 km across the flat, white expanse of the Antarctic plateau.'

Whereas the Russkis had used vehicles, the efforts of Team N2i, as the first expedition to reach the spot without mechanised aid, using only a combination of skis and kites, will stand in the Guinness Book of Records in perpetuity.

What's the number one thing Henry credits for such an achievement?

'It was the mindset that got us there. The mind is much more powerful than the body and I'm a great believer that if your mind is in the right place, then anything is possible. With the ability to laugh at yourself, have fun and not take yourself too seriously, if something doesn't go according to plan, it's easier to accept it and deal with it. With that attitude, I've always found expeditions to be hugely enjoyable.'

Matt Fynn, who we'll meet properly in the next chapter, agrees. And he also knows a thing or two about gruelling endurance challenges, having been a running buddy of mine on the longest run I've ever done, more on which in Chapter 17. But that was a Sunday stroll in the park compared to the Wild Horse 200, which is, you guessed it, a 200-mile run–'across the trails and mountains of South Wales, along Offa's Dyke, traversing the Beacons Way before catching the Heart Of Wales Line on to the Wales Coast Path and finish line at Worm's Head,' on the Gower

Peninsula. So not for the faint-hearted then. Matt competed the 2023 race in 76 hours, coming fourth out of 50 crazy starters.

He recalls arriving at one of the aid stations and a volunteer asking him, 'Do you need anything?'

'I need this to end,' he joked. 'But she didn't get that I was joking, and responded bluntly that she meant food. So, I told her, "Oh, I'll just have some potatoes then!" I was about halfway through, still with about 100 miles to go and I couldn't help but laugh at how ridiculous the situation was. And that's the point; no matter how hard things are, you've just got to say, "This is ridiculous," and laugh.'

***

Henry Cookson has done more than most of us could dream of doing.

I mentioned superyachts, submersibles and helicopters earlier but that's just the tip of the proverbial iceberg—on another expedition he chartered a reinforced icebreaker yacht, so a client could see polar bears in their natural habitat. He has swum with whale sharks and orcas. He has spent three Christmases in Antarctica—wrong pole, Henry, but still fucking cool. He has stared into the depths of Erta Ale, a volcano in Ethiopia in the Danakil Depression—'It felt like I was looking into the soul of the earth.' He has witnessed a bear scooping salmon out of a river in British Colombia—'Surrounded by ancient, primary forest in the last refuge on the entire west coast of North America, that energy and that silence and that wisdom; to connect with nature like that is something else.' He has cycle-trekked through the remote province of Nagaland on the Indian-Bhutanese border, and attended a celebration hosted by a tribe who'd never encountered Westerners before–'The seniors came out and had tiger's teeth around their necks and we slaughtered a pig and they're banging drums. I remember sharing a beer with this old guy and the ring pull was completely bizarre to him.'

Yet, you wouldn't know it from meeting him; he is unassuming and wouldn't bring it up. He's not brash, he doesn't have a big ego. He's not the typical, chest-beating adventurer who's in it for the column inches. There is even a raw fragility to him that you wouldn't expect for a man with his list of accolades.

The truth is Henry has stumbled upon his fair share of crossroads and, while some have led to him being the guy that has crossed polar regions, rehomed giant tortoises in the Galapagos Islands, hosted a wellness retreat on a frozen lake in Iceland, and so much more, others have left him with deep-rooted demons that still haunt him today.

After handing in his notice at Goldman Sachs, Henry 'had Swahili lessons set up, was going to learn first aid, was going to go out to Kenya' and follow his dream. But the cruel twist of a fate I mentioned came in the shape of a car crash, which kept him in the UK. 'Then 9/11 happened,' Henry remembers, 'while I was serving my notice. I was in stock lending, so we were making a killing on shares going down in value and, even though I'd already made my decision to leave, watching this absolute feeding frenzy was the death blow to Henry Cookson in the corporate, cutthroat world.'

To cap it all off, his parents then told him they were getting divorced. 'They had a small travel company together and it became really toxic, with everyone dragged into it. And I don't know whether it was related to the car crash, or the family stuff, or a mix of things, but I started getting horrible depressions. Being a 20-something white male in London, privately educated, I felt a great deal of shame. I didn't share it with anyone, didn't tell a soul. I was just living with this horrible, really dark mindset.'

Henry tells me, 'Depression is something that still haunts me. It's not fully gone. I've done all the things I've achieved, I've grown a business, I've seen the world, but I've probably lost a quarter of the last few years unable to get out of bed. It's totally debilitating.'

Was the polar exploration and the setting up of a luxury travel business all an escape, then?

'I found it hard to connect with my emotions back then, even when I was doing the polar stuff,' he reflects. 'Some of it is a bit of a blur because I was in a very turbulent stage of my life. I'd pop out of my hole of depression to train and do these things and then sink back in again. But, yes, the North Pole was a massive escape and then suddenly it was all over and it was back to reality. Then came Antarctica, which consumed my life for two years. It gave me a focus and much needed distraction from the unhappiness and chaos around me. I did all the research, which is where the POI idea cropped up, worked with Paul and basically became the de facto assistant guide, did the concept development, sourced and designed kit modifications, doing everything under the guidance of the beyond impressive Paul, which was a privilege in its own right. So, it was an escape, to get away from the depression, get away from the family that was no longer the same unit that I knew growing up. But I had no vision for the future, nothing past the point of getting to Lenin. I was simply existing.

'The consensus was that Lenin wouldn't be there after almost 50 years of snow drifts, so when we discovered him, there was that moment of absolute elation, just pure joy, and such a sense of camaraderie that the four of us were jumping up and down, and hugging and screaming. And then, slowly there was a realisation of "Shit, what next?" My teammates were all going back to partners, wives and job security. I was going back to no money and the unknown. A void. And it was pretty quickly when I got back that I went back into my hole.'

With all that he has achieved, then, has come the full spectrum of emotions. And self-doubt may be the one that he's struggling with most recently. Despite Cookson Adventures 'nudging people towards conservation and giving back', resulting in the company being 'responsible for–that we can identify–about $14 million worth of donations to various worthy causes around the world', he wants to do 'something bigger and more meaningful. If a meteor comes out of the sky and lands on my head right now, and that's the end of Henry Cookson, I'd be accepting of that fate as I've been extremely fortunate in the rich life I've experienced. But, with seeing the world, I've also been unfortunate to see how humans behave and I've seen the catastrophe of our environment and the retreat of nature. And it's a fucking disaster.

'We are on a precipice and, unless we wake up and do something very, very quickly, we're all screwed. I've known for a long time that we're probably going to eventually destroy the place–and with it ourselves–but in the last couple of years I've come to the devastating conclusion just how imminent it is, and it's beyond upsetting. So, whatever grim future is incoming, I'm working out my next steps to see where, how and indeed if I can make a difference on the macro change level. Anything less in my view is futile.'

You feel this could be the basis of another book entirely, and if there's someone passionate and knowledgeable enough to write it, it's Henry Cookson. Perhaps that could be his next step. For the time being, though, we have a lot to take away from Henry's triumph and torture, which I'll summarise shortly.

***

My goal for the TP100 was to get over the finish line, but in the back of my head I thought I could run each marathon in the six hours necessary to complete the course in under 24 hours. And ever so slightly because the organisers issue two different medals (belt buckles actually). One says, '100 Miles Finisher'. The other says, '100 Miles in a Day'. To claim one of the latter I'd have to run an average pace of just under nine mins /km; 8:57 to be precise.

So, with one km down and the attitude that the remaining 160 would be a doddle, I settled into a gentle stride along the banks of the Thames. I find running next to water incredibly calming and the Thames has some beautiful stretches: Hampton Court Palace, built for Cardinal Thomas Wolsey, the chief minister of Henry VIII; Windsor Castle, weekend home of the late Queen Elizabeth II; Cliveden, a stunning National Trust property that was once the home of the Duke of Buckingham; Henley-on-Thames, home of the world's most famous rowing regatta; and more. It was perfect running conditions and the organisers reported not having a single drop out of the race until 8 hours and 30 minutes after the last runner had started, when many have usually quit in half that time.

Occasionally I'd overtake another participant walking, or vice versa, but for the most part I toddled along on my lonesome. Richmond to Kingston, Kingston to Hampton Court, quick stop at an aid station at the 10.5 mile marker, just before Walton-on-Thames. Walton to Chertsey, Chertsey to Staines, and before I knew it, I was arriving at the second station, at 22 miles. Having recce'd the first half of the course on my double marathon prep two and a half weeks prior, I knew it was a short hop to Runnymede, where King John sealed the Magna Carta on 15th June 1215. Which, incidentally, was an odd place to issue a royal charter, in a random field in Berkshire. But that's where he did so, thus establishing that the sovereign would no longer be above the law. Runnymede to Windsor, Windsor to Dorney, and I'd completed a pleasant, if uneventful, 50 km in just under six hours, at an average pace of 6:41 /km. Dorney to Maidenhead. Aid station in Cookham. Marlow. And on to Henley, just past halfway, still with a smile on my face, arriving shortly after 6pm. I'd covered the first half in less than ten hours. Could I do the same for the second half and even complete this thing in under 20 hours?

I had taken on what I thought was enough water, added in some salts, mixed sweet with savoury, and felt good. I sat down for the first time in over 50 miles, changed my socks, reapplied various creams and swung by the extensive spread of snacks available at the station. I popped a sausage roll in my mouth, chewed, chewed, chewed, and chewed some more, but couldn't bring myself to swallow. I resorted to swilling my mouth with a cup of energy drink and the resulting mulch of sugary, soggy sausage meat and pastry was only slightly easier to get down. In all of my previous races and training runs I'd never had a problem taking on calories before but now couldn't eat solid food, so I didn't entirely know what I was in for in terms of my energy levels.

As the day's light faded, I reached the 58 mile checkpoint at 8pm, just shy of the shithole that is Reading. I put away as much watermelon and Pepsi as I could without making myself sick, donned a baselayer and my head torch and kept on keeping on. From here on in, I was in uncharted territory. Nutritionally and geographically. Relatively speaking, of course, since following the UK's second longest river hardly needs high-tech GPS tracking equipment. But that didn't stop me making a wrong turn shortly after–a turn that I would correctly make ten months later, more on which in Chapter 17–fortunately realising my mistake after about 500 m. Of course, there could have been two sides to this:

The negative: 'Fucking hell, I've only gone and run an extra km.'

The positive: 'Thank fuck, I've only run an extra km.'

I summoned the latter thought, chuckled and made my way back to where I'd gone wrong. Reading to Pangbourne, where Krista was on hand to wish me well through the night and, from there, I'd love to give you a step by a step account of the next 30+ miles but 1) that would be incredibly tedious because there isn't really much to describe about running through the night and 2) it's all a bit of a blur. There were some checkpoints, there were some villages, there was a river tucked away behind a wall of darkness, and there were two floating lights. As I ran through seemingly endless fields just south of Oxford in the small hours of the morning, I rubbed my eyes and tried to discern whether or not I was hallucinating. When I was convinced I wasn't, I attempted to explain their presence, possibly as windows in a building off in the distance or maybe low level streetlights. Or, wait, is it...? Oh shit it is.

Smack. I ran into a cow, giving it and myself probably the fright of our lives. The dumb animal had obviously stood stock still on the footpath, mesmerised by my approaching head torch, the light reflecting off its eyes and rendering its half-tonne, black body invisible through the pitch black of the night. If there was a moment to laugh, after initially shitting myself, this was it.

There was also lots more watermelon and Pepsi, so much so that my teeth felt furry and were more than slightly sticking together by the time I ran into the outskirts of Oxford, crossed Donnington Bridge and ran under a giant inflatable 'Finish' sign.

It was 6am. The answer to the under 20 hours question was a no—my final time was 21:38:25—but this hadn't really been on my cards. I was well clear of my 24 hour goal, and finished in the top 50 of 230 starters, many of whom were exceptionally talented and experienced endurance athletes. Among them was Samantha Amend, an ultra distance legend, a GB ultrarunner, the 100 miles British record holder on a track, the England 100 km champion in 2018, the female TP100 course record holder and the race's female champion that year. She was the first woman to cross the line in 16:28:08 (28 minutes slower than her record from 2016) but the seventh overall, showing the quality of the pack.

I was ecstatic. Aching from head to toe. But ecstatic. On ultrarunning, comedian Michelle Wolf once said, 'You know, it does kind of make you feel like a badass.'

And I felt like a badass. I swooped up Krista, who was waiting for me at the finish line, into a great big sweaty hug, collected my race bag and treated myself to a steaming hot cup of tea and a bacon sandwich.

Had I really done it? Run the sacred distance of 100 miles in less than 24 hours? My '100 Miles in a Day' belt buckle seemed to suggest so. We joked that it was 'all in a day's work'. For another Disney quote, in the words of Maleficent, the Mistress of all Evil, it was, 'A most gratifying day.'

As the extent of my achievement began to sink in, I couldn't stop laughing. I realised I'd barely stopped laughing since 8:18am the previous morning when my watch announced one km completed. In a towering display of amateurism I'd made wrong turns, miscalculated my food and drink intake, taken several layers of enamel off my teeth and collided with a cow in a field. But it was this comedy of errors and the mindset of finding the positives that had kept me going.

Laughing doesn't make endurance events easy. Quite frankly, sometimes you feel as if you don't have the energy to even think about laughing. But it's in those moments that, if you can muster a smile at the very least, it does make them *easier*. No matter the situation, there are always two sides. At the finish line, they could have been:

The negative: 'Fucking hell, that was horrible.'

The positive: 'Fucking hell, that was incredible.'

The same goes for life. Laughter is the world's most natural painkiller, releasing endorphins, the pain- and stress-neutralising Alpha Team that we met in Chapter 7, and improving your mood. It relaxes you, helps you take on more oxygen, improves blood flow and studies suggest it could even improve your immune system over time.

So be more Henry Cookson.

Yes, Henry has his demons but he also believes that if your mind is in the right place, then anything is possible. He understands the power of cheerfulness in the face of adversity. So, find the funny in the misery, the hilarity in the horrific. Laugh at the ridiculous.

And hopefully I don't have to tell you this but, while you're at it, try and do your bit for the planet. Seriously, it's a fucking disaster.

Chapter 15:
Getting Busy Living

Starting your day with an early morning run is a great way to make sure your day can't get any fucking worse than it started.
- **Meme.**

Imagine you've made it through to the *Dragons' Den* and you've got the opportunity to pitch your business plan to Peter Jones and his merry band of billionaire stooges. You've crunched and double crunched the numbers, rehearsed your presentation so that it's as slick as an oil spill and your Windsor knot is immaculate in your silk, polka dot tie.

You open your mouth to address the panel and you're away:

'Thank you for giving me the opportunity to pitch to you today. With your investment, £100,000 in exchange for 33% of my business, I'm going to change the world.'

'That's a bold statement,' interrupts Jones. 'How are you going to achieve that?'

'First I'm going to start by making my bed,' you boldly reply.

At which point, Deborah Meaden gives you a quizzical look, rolls her eyes and exclaims, 'I'm out.'

But, when William H. McRaven, a four-star Admiral of the United States Navy and the ninth commander of the United States Special Operations Command (SOCOM), gave the 2014 Commencement Address at the University of Texas at Austin, that was exactly what he told the students:

'If you want to change the world, start off by making your bed.'

***

Matt Fynn, who I briefly introduced in the previous chapter, is a friend who I've met through my running endeavours. After connecting with each other on social media, we joined forces with my oppo from *SAS: Who Dares Wins*, Rick, for a 12-hour team endurance run during COVID-19, in which we collectively ran 300 km. And Matt and I have subsequently chewed the fat and chivvied each other through ultramarathons, with a friendly rivalry that has seen us challenge one another for podium finishes in some epic races.

One of the reasons I love ultrarunning is the people. No-one that runs ultramarathons is boring. That's just a fact. I'll admit I'm as guilty as anyone of droning on about my various pursuits over the years, including in this book, and *that* might be boring, but the fact you're taking part … not boring. Rather, the stories of why people are even on an ultramarathon starting line are nothing short of inspiring. Matt's no exception.

'I had a rough time at school,' Matt remembers. 'I'm dyslexic and I struggled. But I muddled through. Then there was a bullying incident. I was quite overweight, got picked on outside school and it came back into the school playground. After that, I was so stubborn about not going back to school that I was truant for the whole of Year 10.

'When you hear "truant for a whole year," you assume I was getting up to no good on street corners, smoking cigarettes or worse. But that wasn't me. I was at home, doing things around the house so my mum wouldn't be annoyed with me skipping school. Like DIY, anything that needed to be done at home. And I'd have dinner ready when she got home. So, I was learning life skills; probably more than I would've done at school.

'There wasn't much my mum could do about it; I'd leave the house at 6:00am to do a paper round and then I would just stay out until nine because I knew my mum would have to go to work and being out of the house would save an argument. But it got to the point—and this is where the system's broken—that my mum got a fine because I wasn't going to school, when it certainly wasn't for her lack of trying.'

This would dent most young lads' resolve. But not Matt's:

'When my mum was fined, I took my Xbox into town, exchanged it for cash and gave my mum the money. On reflection, I suppose I wasn't your average teenager. I always felt like I was a bit more mature than the other kids and that's probably partly the reason I didn't fit in all that well.'

Eventually the system did kick in and Matt received

therapy. He went through the CBT we've explored and learned how to deal with the feelings that he experienced at the thought of returning to school. The therapist, 'A young lady called Laura,' even worked Matt up to the point of sitting in a car outside the school gates, exploring his emotions.

It's not for me to denote what success looks like but, meeting Matt recently for a stroll in the Cotswolds, he's operations manager of an automotive company and drives a very shiny, smart white Tesla. If that's your thing. The point being that it was what Matt did next that defined him. He's not your typical 'drop-out', if I can say that, rather he's the boy who simply didn't go to school but has still managed to thrive. During work experience in a garage he 'was in [his] element.' An apprenticeship followed and from there he has excelled in a career that he loves. When he was more settled, such was his drive—if you'll excuse the automotive pun—that he went to night college to complete his GCSEs.

Unfortunately, though, the trauma didn't end there.

'In my mid-20s,' Matt continues, 'I was in a bad way. My mental health was in the gutter as a result of a bad relationship. It had been good for many years but she was going through mental health battles that caused her to self-harm very seriously. To the point that I'd be up in the middle of the night taking her to hospital and balancing that with getting back home at 3:00am and then going to work because we'd just committed to buying a house together and needed to pay the mortgage.

'I loved this person but couldn't understand how things had got to this point, and I simply couldn't cope with it. The only way I can describe it is that it felt like my head was going to explode. I kept saying to people, "The pressure in my head is just ridiculous." The difficulty of it all and ultimately a massive relationship breakdown led to me taking an overdose. I don't know what my full intentions were. I think I just wanted everything to stop for a minute, you know?'

For Matt, out of shape, having not taken care of himself through the relationship, physically and mentally, 'it was a wake-up call,' he proclaims. 'I wasn't living a healthy lifestyle. I was doing no exercise, so I'd put on a lot of weight and was very out of shape. I needed to do something and, while the end of the relationship was painful, it gave me a clean slate.'

He joined a local running club with the aim of completing a five km and found himself 'on a running path. I think the structure and the regular running were good and life started to get back on track. I did a half marathon, I did a marathon, then a quicker marathon.' You know, this is ringing some bells.

Nowadays Matt is the epitome of what Ollie Ollerton was referring to when he spoke about looking after mind, body and nutrition. He's regularly up at 4:00am on a long run into the hills around Abergavenny. 'I'm at my happiest when I'm training, which sounds insane when you're running 200 miles a month training and having to juggle everything else around that. But I'm a routine guy.'

He takes ice baths and makes time for mindfulness, reflecting over a coffee before heading to work. If that sounds extreme, that's the point:

'It's a bit of a cliché but, traumas aside, life is easy. The other day I needed a sewing kit. I ordered it at 7:00pm and it was delivered at 8:00am the next morning. My biggest gripe is that the nearest 24 hour gym is half an hour away. We've gotten soft and we're not challenging ourselves enough. So, when someone asks me how I can get up at 4:00am to go running, well, that's nothing compared to what I've had in the past. If I've had six hours' sleep, I'm golden. And when I rock up to the office at 8:00am and don't really feel like phoning that customer or dealing with that problem, I have this amazing feeling of knowing that I've already achieved something hard today. That something that I didn't want to do; I've already dealt with it.'

It'll come as no surprise that I'm a big fan of this outlook and the similarities to the section of Admiral McRaven's speech in which he told the students to 'start off by making your bed':

'If you make your bed every morning, you will have accomplished the first task of the day. It will give you a small sense of pride and it will encourage you to do another task and another and another. And by the end of the day, that one task completed will have turned into many tasks completed. Making your bed will also reinforce the fact that the little things in life matter.

'If you can't do the little things right, you'll never be able to do the big things right. And if by chance you have a miserable day, you will come home to a bed that is made, that you made. And a made bed gives you encouragement that tomorrow will be better. So, if you want to change the world, start off by making your bed.'

Matt's point is that we're no longer challenging ourselves to do difficult things willingly that make it easier to do difficult things unwillingly. And, as Admiral McRaven's speech highlighted, doing hard things or things that you don't necessarily want to do makes you feel good because of the sense of achievement.

It does beg the question, though—and this is something that Krista has put to me in the past—as to whether you have to have been through some kind of trauma to take on an extreme endurance challenge. I have. Matt has. The *SAS: Who Dares Wins* recruits all had a story to tell about why they were putting themselves through the 'toughest show on television'.

The truth is, I don't have the answer, nor can I be bothered to poll a bunch of ultrarunners to find out how many of them have experienced trauma. But haven't we all, to a certain extent, experienced trauma? And I'm not sorry to say that if you haven't, you will.

But we need to redefine the lines between difficult emotions, like trauma and grief, and the increasing trend of young people seeming to think it's fashionable to have a mental illness.

Sonja Jenkins is resolute on this point. A veteran family therapist and school counsellor, she spent 30 years helping adolescents and teenagers deal with complex emotional trauma, often rooted in their parents' relationship issues that have then had a domino effect on the children, causing crisis through the family. In that time, she has seen a paradigm shift in the relationships parents have with their children.

'Whereas parents are now very aware of positive affirmation,' Sonja explains, 'I grew up with criticism in my family. My father's generation went through World War II and all that went with that and troops coming out of the trenches never shared anything. They didn't have time for all of that. So, the next generation was never taught how to express themselves. It's fantastic now that it's become more of an accepted thing and people know how to express emotions but we've probably gone too far the other way. It needs to have boundaries.

'Self-gratification is also very prominent in the young because it's the way of the world now that parents are so busy, so stressed, that they don't want any conflict. It's easier to give in, it's easier to go along. Parents are too intent on being their children's friend, whereas there should be a hierarchy. Again, with boundaries. But boundaries come with conflict.'

The problem extends to schools, where 'Teachers didn't used to care if you didn't like them. That wasn't on their agenda. Teaching was on their agenda. It has now lost its way in the fact that children are ruling and we're indulging them, whether they're him, her, cats, dogs, or something else.' [I should add at this point that I've not broached the subject of children identifying as cats, as mentioned in the Introduction, with Sonja, so it's interesting she brought that up of her own accord—obviously, we're on a similar wavelength.]

We used to filter through this bullshit, quite frankly, and nip it in the bud. But, as Sonja continues, 'In today's world, liberal thinking has led us to have an imbalanced view of how to deal with certain behavioural traits and therefore we respond with a learned helplessness which in the long run has greater implications for young people. Parents struggle to put down boundaries and if teachers try, parents are very critical as a way of dealing with their guilt. We've changed how we deal with children because they no longer have the resilience or robustness to cope with being told off.'

The result is blurred lines between experiencing genuine mental ill health and simply having a bad day, as we touched on with Caroline in Chapter 12. Sonja believes that 'Often for adolescents it's about attention seeking. And social media doesn't help any of that either. Claiming you've got a mental health issue on social media is one way to get everybody jumping and hopping around.' On which note, The Daily Telegraph also reports that the 'Instagram generation are confusing normal stress and anxiety for mental health conditions because [of] increased awareness'[109], pointing out that feeling anxious is 'very different to a medically diagnosed mental health condition which can be horrific and debilitating.'

It's important to be able to recognise the symptoms of a serious issue in those closest to us, but also to be able to, well, filter through the bullshit. 'The person who is really mentally unwell,' Sonja continues, 'will show other symptoms. For example, they might not want to eat or drink or socialise. And people having a bad day might feel that way for a few hours, but not for a sustained period of time.'

For clarity, I'm not saying that we should be ignoring those who claim to be struggling, rather we should be paying more attention to emotions and learning to address them, but in a way that's healthy and productive for us and those around us. Sonja agrees that 'It is really good to be able to express our emotions but I would add as a caveat that we've also got to know where and with whom to share them. If we become the ever-open book, only talking about ourselves, we are never going to get those emotions acknowledged. And we are not listening. Sharing has to be a two-way street; it's not just about offloading.'

And what of the incidents where the trauma and grief

are genuine? Because, once again I'm not sorry to say it, life gives us terrible sadness. Grief is something we're all going to come up against at some point in our lives, if we haven't already, as a result of a multitude of scenarios. The passing of a loved one is the obvious example but it could equally be a relationship failing, the loss of a job or learning of a terminal diagnosis. Sonja is herself no stranger to grief, following her husband's diagnosis of Parkinson's disease and subsequent decline.

He's tragically 'not the person I married,' she says, 'and Parkinson's is bloody awful. I hadn't realised how awful. I've therefore gone through a grieving process because I know that the time will come but, when it does, my grief will be very different to how it might have been had it happened suddenly.'

The grieving process is commonly broken down into five stages, as pioneered by Swiss-American psychiatrist Elisabeth Kübler-Ross in the 1960s. The Kübler-Ross model, which has also been applied to generic change–which we'll cover in Chapter 20–sees victims of grief go through denial, anger, bargaining, depression and acceptance.

As Sonja explains, 'First of all, it's, "Oh my God, I can't believe this is happening."' Individuals question whether there's been a mistake, perhaps with the diagnosis.

'Then anger. We blame God or whoever.' Maybe medical staff for not doing enough. We might lash out at others.

'Thirdly, we bargain: "What if I'd done this or done that. How could my life be different? What if I give up smoking or alcohol, for example." The sadness follows.

'Then we come into acceptance because at some point we've got to see the hope again, even if it's a small appreciation for things, like a nice day.'

And how long might that take?

'There isn't a time limit to any of that, but you definitely need time to process it and to go through all of those stages in order to accept the grief. Everybody experiences grief at a different pace but it may even come to the point where it's dragging on. If it goes on too long, it becomes self-indulgent. Then you have to ask what the purpose of this grief is? Is it to get attention? Do you want somebody to rescue you? Well, there comes a point when you've got to start thinking of rescuing yourself. Maybe you'll tell yourself that you need to pull yourself together and move on.'

Easier said than done, of course, but 'It comes down to looking after ourselves and support,' Sonja continues. 'Human beings are quite tribal. Once upon a time, the whole family would live on one street, so that support network was readily available next door. Now we've moved far away from families and we're dotted all over. The family of the church and religion also played a huge part. And with the family of the church came hope, even if it was just hope that you were going to go to heaven. Nowadays, we don't have that.'

Surround yourself with people you love and trust, then. Look after yourself. And don't be afraid of grief; you're allowed to experience it. In fact, doing so can be healthy. Nor should you be ashamed of it. As Pip says as he heads off to London to claim his inherited fortune and learn how to be a gentleman, 'Heaven knows we need never be ashamed of our tears, for they are rain upon the blinding dust of earth, overlaying our hard hearts.'[110]

Sonja concludes, 'We have to create our own hope, our own positiveness, and we have lost the wherewithal to do that. Focus on things like good exercise, good nutrition, maybe meditation or breathing properly; all the things that are going to help your wellbeing' can all help with the process of grieving healthily.

***

If you've never run an ultramarathon, the chances are very slim that, having read the previous 60,000-or-so words, you're now desperate to do so. In fact, the likelihood is you'd rather be strapped to a chair and forced to listen to Nickelback's entire discography. And that's fine.

To be clear, while I firmly believe everyone *could* run an ultramarathon, I'm not insisting that everyone *should*. Rather, ultrarunning is my metaphor for life. You experience some cataclysmically dismal lows during an ultramarathon and your mind will tell you, over and over again, to give up. Call it a day. Go back to your sofa-sitting and your biscuit-dunking.

But, as Phil Knight writes, 'You must forget your limits. You must forget your doubts, your pain, your past. You must forget that internal voice screaming, begging, "Not one more step!" And when it's not possible to forget it, you must negotiate with it.'[111]

When you find yourself suffering, knowing how to deal with the pain requires self-awareness and an understanding of what your body is going through. Have you not eaten enough, are you low on salts, are you sufficiently hydrated, do you have a blister? There will be a reason you're feeling that way and, by discovering the source of your pain, you can learn to push through.

Translate that into an emotional awareness and there you have it, ladies and gents; mental fitness. When you've been through tough stuff, it puts things in perspective. It empowers you. It allows you to banish those negative, limiting thoughts so that, ultimately, you can cross the finish line. As a result, the highs are all the more precious and special. The satisfaction at having achieved something–even making your bed–is greater.

As Andy Dufresne says to his fellow inmate and best friend, Red, in (my favourite film of all time) *The Shawshank Redemption*, 'It comes down to a simple choice; get busy living or get busy dying.'

The difference between the two is the willingness to push ourselves and experience a little bit of short term pain for long term gain. Making your bed might seem like a right royal pain in the arse, and heading out for a run might hurt, but that's the point; as the hero Wesley says in *The Princess Bride* (possibly my second favourite film), 'Life is pain, highness. Anyone who tells you differently is selling something.'

But the rewards more than justify the means. You'll feel better for it and, if you don't, at least 'your day can't get any fucking worse'.

So, be more Andy Dufresne. Get busy living.

Chapter 16:
King Of The Cotswolds

It does not matter how slowly you go, so long as you do not stop.
- **Confucius**

In the months leading up to the pandemic I'd extricated myself from PR agency life–and subsequently had an argument with my shyster of a former employer who had fabricated a clause in my contract in order to threaten me with legal action–and put my entrepreneur's hat on. I'd had an exciting idea to start a travel company offering restorative retreats to those experiencing burnout and the woes of business life, calling on my network of inspirational people in the physical and mental health spheres. But the restrictions of the pandemic thoroughly squashed that dream.

The torrid world of freelance PR consultancy therefore beckoned, and Krista and I spent the COVID first lockdown cooped up in her one bedroom flat in Wimbledon Village, albeit perfectly content in each other's company.

As we huddled around her kitchen table each day for three months, whilst attempting to avoid diary clashes that involved us shouting over each other on video calls, the realisation that there was more to life than the hustle and bustle of the Big Smoke hit home. When the lockdowns lifted, even after only six months together, it was therefore clear the direction we were heading, namely doing grown up stuff together, like moving to the country. We'd even had the serious chats, the ones which couples shirk for fear of sounding too commitmenty. Like, 'Do you want kids?' You know, adult shit.

So, when an opportunity to join an independent law firm based in Bath presented itself to Krista, she stuck in an application for the role. And Krista, being Krista, bagged the job after one interview. Having never stepped foot in Bath before in my life, an upheaval across the country didn't immediately strike me as an option, especially as the role could have been fully remote, but we opted to spend a weekend in Bath, 'Just out of interest.' And Krista, being Krista, arranged a couple of flat viewings while we were there, 'Just out of interest.' When we liked one, we put in a cheeky offer below the asking price, 'Just out of interest.' Long story short, the offer was accepted and we were moving to Bath.

But not once did we question or doubt our movements. We barely discussed it; it just happened and we were happy to go along for the ride.

Meanwhile, unbeknownst to Krista I was planning out how to ask Krista to marry me and did so two weeks before we were due to move, cunningly (I like to think) combining a beautiful setting with Krista's no.1 love (after me, of course); cycling. I spent an evening catching up with friends from my old rugby club in Kent, while she was at home in Wimbledon, and we agreed to meet at Hever Castle the next day for a cycle around the local country roads. The childhood home of Anne Boleyn, the ill-fated second wife of Henry VIII, the 750-year old castle boasts stunning grounds which were to be the setting of the tryst I had planned. Krista, however, was determined to take the guided tour of the castle, the final room of which houses a grisly display of medieval weapons and torture contraptions, including implements that were used to slice off women's breasts for adultery. Which somewhat put a dampener on the romantic mood that I'd had in mind.

Adding to the distractions was the annual Hever Triathlon, taking part around the aforementioned grounds, and it took some effort to prise Krista away from more cycling exploits and wanting to cheer on the competitors. Finally able to find a quiet corner overlooking the castle, I got down on one knee and asked her to make me the happiest man in the world. Despite the torture instruments and the beheaded former owner, she said yes.

Two weeks later, we were on the way to Bath. Which wasn't the worst thing. To borrow from my friend Bill Bryson, if you have never been to Bath, go at once. Take my car. It's wonderful. Finally free of COVID restrictions, we were a stone's throw from the World Heritage Site that is the historic city centre. Out of our front window, our flat overlooked the Grade I listed Royal Crescent, one of the finest examples of Georgian architecture in the country. Out of the back? The Cotswold Way.

***

A designated National Trail that spans six counties, the

Cotswold Way runs from the market town of Chipping Campden, in the north of the Cotswolds, to Bath. Stretching 102 miles as it weaves between the two, it follows the Cotswold Edge escarpment, a geological phenomenon also known as a hilly ridge. Very hilly. A total elevation of half the height of Mount Everest, to be exact. But also stunning. Very stunning, with views out over the Severn Estuary, the Forest of Dean, and as far as the Black Mountains and Brecon Beacons in Wales. When you're not traipsing up a hill on the route, you're meandering through one of the most beautifully quaint villages in the world and passing places of interest, such as Sudeley Castle (home of Catherine Parr, the lucky, surviving wife of Henry VIII); Cleeve Hill (the highest point of both the Cotswolds and of Gloucestershire—did I mention the route is hilly?); and the site of the Battle of Lansdowne (fought during the First English Civil War, to prevent the Royalists from advancing out of south-west England). Not forgetting the Royal Crescent and Bath Abbey.

Having just spent 20-or-so hours running along a flat river, the idea of challenging myself to a few inclines seemed like an obvious next notch on my ultramarathon belt. And, after a little pottering around on t'interweb, I learned that no-one had completed the route unsupported, only as part of an organised race. A Fastest Known Time (FKT) is a speed record for a given route and particularly popular on longer trails. On fastestknowntime.com, the record for conquering the Cotswold Way supported was a smidge under 17 and a half hours, but the unsupported record was up for grabs. An image of a lovestruck Wayne Campbell sprung to mind and I thought to myself, 'She will be mine. Oh yes, she will be mine.'[112]

Early one morning the following spring, Krista drove me to Chipping Campden and my mission was simple; run home. Well, not quite that simple, since I'd resolved to do so whilst carrying all my own calories and plodding the length of the Cotswold Way on my lonesome. And the sub-mission of completing the task in less than 24 hours was again loitering in the back of my mind. At 7:00am, I started the day standing on the disc of limestone that marks the start of the route–with a similar marker at the other end in front of Bath Abbey–with a brass acorn at its centre (the National Trail symbol) and a T.S. Eliot quote engraved around its circumference, from the second poem of his Four Quartets: 'Now the light falls across the open field, leaving the deep lane shuttered with branches, dark in the afternoon.'

The overly pretentious National Trail website states that, 'For those about to embark the words will hold the promise of the adventure to come, and to those arriving they will be a reflective focus for the journey they have made. The flow and human liveliness of well-designed hand carved lettering along with the visual impact of a contrasting circle within the paving make a striking and visually enticing focal point in front of the Market Hall.' Flow and human liveliness? Of a stone engraving? Fuck my life, really?

The website goes on to explain that 'T.S. Eliot visited in Campden several times in the 1930s and was inspired to write the first poem Burnt Norton, through his walking experience here.' Though they could have just said he visited and avoided the Georgian-style olde English.

Not that I was too worried about this over-pompous verbosity–maybe the promise of adventure bit–as I tentatively took my first steps along Chipping Campden High St. The route's first climb, out of the town, rewarded me with incredible views over a hazy mist engulfing Worcester and Warwickshire.

The early start gave me a sense of having the English countryside all to myself, as I enjoyed the bliss of not seeing another living soul for the best part of an hour. It was only after climbing to Broadway Tower, at the second-highest point of the Cotswolds, and descending into the village of Broadway that I saw the first sign of life of the day, another runner plodding in the opposite direction. We gave each other a knowing nod of approval and it crossed my mind that he might be about to pip me to the post of the unsupported Cotswold Way record. But, I assured myself, the chances were slim that he'd started his run in Bath the previous day.

I made good progress through the quintessential English villages of Stanton and Stanway, with narrow streets lined with thatched cottages, and hit half marathon distance without incident. Winchcombe (at 20 miles) was the first opportunity to stock up on liquids and a climb out of the town then turned into rolling fields. The scenery was a smorgasbord of stereotypical Englishness, changing in the blink of an eye from hills to woodland carpeted in bluebells, to tracks lined with thistles, to farmland, with sheep and cows watching me inquisitively as I ambled past.

As the hills became increasingly brutal, the reward was beautiful views out over Cheltenham and beyond. The Cleeve Hill summit and marathon distance came and went without too much drama.

After a hill up to Lineover Wood, I enjoyed a gentle stretch of wooded flat running and made it to my next drinks stop at the Crickley Hill Visitor Centre (around 37 miles), where I proceeded to buy the shop out of all of their bottled water and treated myself to a can of Coke. It was here that I also treated the first hint of a blister on my left heel but, with the power of Compeed, it proved to be only a mild irritant and nothing to slow progress too dramatically.

As the tiredness (and laziness) set in and I ran through woodland with a view over Gloucester (at around 45 miles), I made the mistake of tempting fate by thinking to myself, 'I'm really enjoying this,' only to badly stub my toe on a tree root … twice … the second time so badly that I genuinely thought I'd broken it. I hobbled on, smirking to myself as I recalled an article I'd once read on the Runner's World website, titled: 'Do Runners Even Need Toenails, Anyway?' As John Krebsbach, a podiatrist, said in the piece, 'We can live without them.' Onwards then, James. What are you moaning about?

The going got really tough through Edge Common and up to Haresfield Beacon, at the halfway mark, though more spectacular views (this time over the Severn Estuary) were the prize. The Co-op in Kings Stanley served as my next stop for liquids and an hour later, with the light fading, the head torch went on.

If the hills had been bad up to this stage, they became hellish just north of Dursley, where there's a point on the Way with a gradient of 35%. For context, according to Rouleur, a leading cycling magazine, one of the hardest stages on the 2023 Tour de France peaked at 'a maximum gradient of 24%.' Riders needed 'strong mountain legs [to] slog it out on the climb.'[113] As darkness fell, and with still around 40 miles to go, the 'slog' up to Cam Long Down was an enormous drain on my resolve and fatigue–and my increasingly weary non-mountain legs–especially as going down the other side wasn't any easier. This was followed by a succession of huge climbs and brutally steep descents in and out of North Nibley and Wotton-under-Edge. It was slow going in the dark, with the uphills taking their toll on the legs and lungs and having to take the downhills carefully to avoid turning an ankle on rocky ground. Remember what we learned in Chapter 8 about eccentric exercise?

At 75 miles, a mini natural waterfall in Splatt's Wood and some water purification tablets gave me the liquids that would see me through to the end. Through the night I had waves of good and bad moments, in particular enjoying a decent second (or more like fourteenth by that stage) wind with about a marathon to go. I stuck to a pretty solid pace for a couple of hours but deteriorated quickly just after I made it south of the M4, at around 4:30am. Not even the hint of the sun emerging in the east could stop a hideous wave of nausea and feeling like I was going to pass out. I sat on a bench outside the Dyrham Park estate, fighting the urge to have a nap.

After 20 minutes, I fought another urge to give up entirely and willed myself on. The next few miles were hell, but I got a boost of adrenaline at completing a big climb up to Lansdown and reaching familiar training run territory around Bath Racecourse and Kelston Roundhill, for which I held the Strava 'Local Legend'. I knew the views over Bristol and the Severn Estuary wouldn't disappoint and a low morning mist made the local and far off hill tops look like islands floating in a choppy sea. I had a final surge of energy as I descended into Bath, passing the Royal Crescent, running into town and, at 8:15am, curled up in a ball on the second of the limestone circles in front of Bath Abbey, delirious with fatigue but ecstatic at getting the job done.

I hadn't completed the Cotswold Way in the 24 hours I'd have liked. But I was the first recorded person to do it solo and unsupported. Unfortunately, despite no-one having run the route in that fashion previously in the 14 years since it was inaugurated as a National Trail on 24th May 2007, someone clinched the unsupported FKT some five months later, two hours faster than my time. When I saw this on fastestknowntime.com and joked with Matt Fynn that, 'Some fucker has bagged my Cotswold Way FKT,' he responded, 'Are you going to moan about it, or get back out there??'

I'm going to moan about it, Matt, but I like your attitude.

Chapter 17:
To Quit, Or Not To Quit

You cannot fail unless you quit.
- **Abraham Lincoln**

Full disclosure, though; the Cotswold Way was technically just a training run.

After the exploits of the Thames Path 100, I'd immediately lined up my next 'official' race, somehow convincing myself that even a 100-mile run wasn't enough. And, on deciding that we'd be moving to Bath, something that involved running through a vague geographical proximity to the city seemed appealing.

Short of the 'silly' races–like Matt Fynn's Wild Horse and the Spine Race, held over almost 270 miles of the Pennine Way–the ultras organised by Canal Race C.I.C. are among some of the UK's most iconic. The company stages three races each year, along the canal towpaths between Leeds and Liverpool (the Leeds & Liverpool Canal Race), London and Birmingham (the Grand Union Canal Race), and London and Bristol (the Kennet & Avon Canal Race). And, while Tennessee has its Lazarus Lake, the eccentric inventor of the Barkley Marathons, pegged as one of the toughest foot races on the planet such that only 20 people have completed the race since 1989*–the Canal Races have their Dick Kearns. The Gandalf of ultrarunning, Dick and his flowing white beard have been ever present as part of the organising committee since he was on the start line of the first Grand Union Canal Race in 1993.

> ***Side note:**
>
> The figure of 20 people completing the Barkley Marathons is following the 2024 edition, which saw five runners finish the event, two of whom, John Kelly and Jared Campbell, did so for their third and fourth time respectively. In an astonishingly heroic performance, British runner Jasmin Paris also became the first woman to successfully finish, doing so in 59:58:21, just 99 seconds inside the 60-hour cut-off time. The videos that did the rounds online of her collapsing over the iconic yellow gate that marks the finish line are nothing short of inspirational.

The Kennet & Avon ticked all the right boxes; 145 miles from Little Venice, London, along the Grand Union Canal to Slough, the Jubilee River and Thames Paths to Reading, the Kennet & Avon Canal to Bath, and finally the River Avon Path to the centre of Bristol.

Before taking on that most epic of adventures, though, I had something more important to do; get married.

***

Krista and I tied the knot in a beautiful ceremony, in a beautiful church, in a beautiful village, in the beautiful Cotswolds. Having spent much of the ten months since our engagement still flitting through some form of lockdown, it had become a pleasant distraction from COVID to systematically mine our way through the myriad logistics involved with saying 'I do', from organising a florist (Krista's job), to liaising with the band (my job).

The process wasn't without its challenges, though, mainly on account of the bizarre system of rules imposed by the government, which made about as much sense as hole punching a condom. For example, all the guests had to wear masks in the church, except the bride and groom who were seemingly immune from COVID for the day, and singing hymns wasn't allowed. But speaking tunefully was. Needless to say, when the organ piped out the first few bars of Jerusalem and one of Krista's bridesmaids, a former professional opera singer, belted out a mesmerising rendition of 'And did those feet …' absolutely no-one cared that it wasn't allowed. As the congregation joined her in the second verse—'Bring me my bow …'—I had tears streaming down my face for the second time in an hour. The first, I'm not ashamed to admit, was on seeing the vision that I was about to call my wife walking down the aisle towards me.

We also had to navigate the issue that standing up and mingling wasn't allowed at gatherings. Guests had to be seated and the venue operate a table service system for drinks, since apparently you couldn't catch COVID whilst sitting down. Games, on the other hand, were allowed, but for some reason the venue didn't appreciate my suggestion that we invent a game called 'Stand Up Drinking', the rules of which were simple; all participants would have to be standing up, and drinking. As it was, after the champagne, a French rosé and a locally-sourced cider and ale had been flowing for about four and a half minutes at the drinks reception, our guests were playing Stand Up Drinking whether the venue liked it or not.

Moronic rules aside, it was a perfect day. A group of people, gathered in the same room for the first time in over a year, and all those we care for most in the world, no less, was more than we could have hoped for amid the uncertainty of global events. The fact that Krista and I got to celebrate our love, and make vows to each other, and have all these wonderful people promise to 'support and uphold our marriage' was the icing on the wedding cake that consisted of four stacked wheels of cheese.

The day was also symbolic, marking the end of lockdown. With everyone desperate to escape their COVID cocoons and craving a good old fashioned throw down, the evening's entertainment made for an incredible party. The rule that you couldn't order drinks from the bar quickly went out the window as several guests demanded that the bar staff furnish them with trays of Jägerbombs, which were promptly brought onto the dancefloor. Oh, and dancing was also 'frowned upon' but that didn't stop everyone getting incredibly sweaty, hugging each other and jumping up and down like idiots to Bryan Adams' *Summer Of '69* and all the other cheesy wedding classics. For the first time in a long time, no-one gave a monkeys about COVID.

Krista and I then spent a blissfully relaxing few days on a minimoon in Cornwall, in a quaint little National Trust cottage overlooking the English Channel. We loaded the cottage's fridge with the leftover cider and ale, and I performed my husbandly duties of keeping Krista's glass suitably topped up. We newlywedded our little hearts out; got up to watch the sun rise, took little jaunts to local beaches, and did other things which are absolutely none of your business. We also ate. A lot. All the Cornish staples; from fine dining to fish and chips at Lizard Point, the most southerly point of the UK, with daily pasties and scones with jam and clotted cream in between, taking care to adhere to the Cornish way of spreading the jam on first. Not that it makes a blind bit of difference to the taste, but don't tell any Cornish people I said that. And did I care that I was supposed to be carb-loading for the biggest endurance challenge of my life? Not one single bit.

***

We got married on Saturday 17th July, two days before the official end of COVID restrictions. From Monday to Thursday morning we were in Cornwall, then, on the Thursday afternoon we missioned it into London. My task again: run home (and a bit more).

On the Friday morning, at 6:00am, Matt Fynn and I were two of the 75 mad individuals that congregated on the canal towpath in Little Venice to take on the KACR. If anyone remembers the summer of 2021, there was a mad heatwave in mid-July, when the temperatures topped 30°C for a week. This was awesome for our wedding; Krista, being half-French, had maxed out on the homage to Provence, with the expensive rosé, boundless amounts of brie, as much lavender as any person could cope with, and our wedding car was a Citroën 2CV called Fifi. And being on the beach on Cornwall in that heat was like being on the French Riviera.

But if running 100 miles is tough, running 145 in 30°C heat is brutal. It slightly kiboshed my C.A.M.P.P. equation, given how essential it was to keep cool and take on enough fluids and salts. While I'd opted to rely on the route's aid stations for all my supplies, Matt had asked a friend to crew for him. Rich kindly carting a cool box across the breadth of the country proved our lifeline as each time we met him, we removed our running caps, filled them with a handful of ice, popped them back on our heads and enjoyed a slow, cool dripping down our face and the backs of our necks as we went on our merry way.

6:00am, then, six days after getting married, thanks to my extremely accommodating wife, and I was away, heading west out of Paddington, along the Grand Union Canal. I would find out later that amongst the pack was the legendary ultra distance runner and walker, Sandra Brown, who holds the world record for the highest number (more than 200) of 100-mile ultras completed, as well as the official World Walking Records for the 100 km, 100 miles, 12 hours and 24 hours track events. She was also the Land's End to John o' Groats (LEJOG), a distance of 830 miles, record holder for nine years, with a time of 13 days 10 hours. Some pedigree then.

I usually find running alongside water to be very calming and having done much of my training along the 10-mile stretch of the canal between Bath and Bradford-on-Avon, for example, I knew I was in for a treat in the later stages of the race. I could look forward to old fashioned locks, tree-lined stretches of the canal and the rolling countryside of Wiltshire and Somerset. Before then I had to make do with half submerged shopping trolleys, barbed wire-lined security fences and the urban sprawl of Kensal Green. It was the reason Krista and I had left London in the first place, quite frankly, and not much changed until after Slough, when we joined the Jubilee River at around mile 22. Matt and I chatted about everything and nothing, enjoying the company of some of the other runners and occasionally leaving the other to walk for a short stretch. We were very middle of the pack and happy to be so, with no intentions to break into anything other than a gentle, steady pace.

It was a sign of what was to come that the heat was already pretty excruciating when we reached the second checkpoint, at mile 27, at 10:15am–it would stay floating in the high 20s °C and nudging above the 30°C mark until 7 o'clock in the evening.

But we kept in good spirits. Val Kilmer may have played Iceman but we had our very own in Rich as we systematically took chunks out of the route by dousing ourselves in freezing cold water and running off with our ice-filled caps on our heads.

From miles 28 to 52, we followed the same route as the Thames Path 100 (from Maidenhead to Reading, through the likes of Cookham, Marlow and Henley) and then, in Reading, the wrong turn I'd made ten months prior was now the right one. Krista being there to meet me with an ice lolly meant that the second time of running through the shithole that is the UK's largest town-that-isn't-a-city wasn't quite as bad.

It goes without saying that following a canal doesn't take complex map reading or acutely honed navigational skills. Every now and then you have to cross a bridge and run along the other side, which is nice if only to add a bit of variety as to which side the water is on. That said, I felt the next major milestone for me was Newbury, at 72 miles. As part of my prep I'd done a recce from Newbury back to Bath, a run of about 55 miles, some three weeks prior. When I arrived in the town at 7:45pm, it was some consolation that, despite being only halfway through the race, I at least knew the rest of the route. A small consolation, but I was willing to take whatever I could get at this point.

At some point, Matt and I parted ways. I suspected he was ahead of me but wasn't sure. Night fell and I was grateful for the temperature dropping even by a couple of degrees, though I was still sweating buckets as the humidity had been slowly rising throughout the day.

I took my longest break of the day at checkpoint seven, just shy of 100 miles. I hadn't anticipated sitting down but one of the crew offered me a bowl of rice pudding and this sounded like the best and most heavenly idea in the history of ideas. I sat there, probably bumbling absolute shit to the poor guy, for ten minutes, before peeling myself out of the chair and making tracks. Having not paid the blindest bit of attention to how many people I'd passed—or been passed by—along the way, I was staggered when I asked how many runners had been through before me. 'You're the fifth,' he replied. WTF? I was fifth?

From there, with the energy of the rice pudding surging through my veins, I kept up a decent pace—decent for someone who had already run 100 miles—into Devizes as the weather finally broke. I felt like I had front row seats to the grandest and most brilliant light show in the world as shards of lightning streaked across the sky in the distance, filling the sky with a vibrant red hue. Alone with my thoughts and the magnificence of nature, it's moments like this that make these things worthwhile.

As the rain inevitably came, I didn't mind getting absolutely drenched. It provided a change from the brutal heat of the previous day and I covered off 17.5 miles to the next checkpoint at a reasonable lick. It was the early hours of the morning by this stage and I passed some other joggers, who I assumed were just out enjoying their Saturday morning, taking on their own section of the canal between Devizes and Bradford-on-Avon. Arriving at the pen-penultimate checkpoint, at 116 miles, then, I was even more taken aback when I asked the same question: 'How many runners have been through already?' The reply: 'Just one.' What. The. Actual. Fuck? I was second? Stop it.

The final marathon is a bit of a blur. In hindsight, I'd probably taken the previous section too quickly and it took Krista meeting me near our flat in Bath to push me over the finish line. If there was any doubt as to why I'd married her–there wasn't–her joining me with 20 miles left to go, having driven to the finish line and cycled 15 miles back to Bath to meet me, was proof that she was the other pea in my slightly crazy pod. She encouraged me, propped me up when I felt nauseous, and didn't once complain at the staggering distance she had to cover, for someone who hadn't been training for an endurance event. Not to mention putting up with me doing something so insane six days after marrying me, travelling into London with me to reassure me at the start line and systematically feeding me ice lollies along the way.

Having slowly chipped away at the distance and most of the leaders–in a rice pudding-powered push–I crossed the finish line, hand-in-hand with Krista, just after one o'clock on the Saturday afternoon, in a time of 31 hours, 9 minutes. The leader had beaten me by almost five hours but I couldn't have cared less. Second. Given my only aim was to complete the race before the 45 hour cut-off, I couldn't believe it.

The Saturday coincided with the first British and Irish Lions test match in South Africa, so the rugby fan in me had wanted me to get back to the flat in Bath in time for kick off at 5:00pm. After a cup of tea (the best I've ever had), Krista drove us home and I took a shower (the best I've ever had) and sat in my dressing gown with a non-alcoholic beer (the best I've ever had) in front of the game. I couldn't tell you a single thing about it; the next day I even had to look up who won (the Lions). All I can remember is taking myself off to bed as soon as the final whistle was blown and sleeping for 15 hours straight.

Incidentally, Matt wasn't one of the runners I passed in the small hours of the morning, but he did his own job of ticking up the leaderboard, crossing the line in third place, just under an hour after me. We'd had an awesome run together and it was a remarkable achievement for his first ever 100-mile (and a bit more) ultra, and a delight to share the (non-existent) podium with him. Afterwards, he wrote the following on Instagram:

'I thought about [the bullying he experienced at school] a lot in the night section of this run. To continue that run in that moment felt impossible. However, I refused to quit. I even remember saying to myself out loud, "Being bullied was easier than this shit." That was a dark moment. I'm not sure if that statement is true or not, but it's how I felt at 3:30am plodding along the wet canal.

'I feel with this run I've gained some inner satisfaction I was looking for. I now know that when things get tough, I'll no longer quit.

'I guess my point of sharing this little story was, if you're not happy with where you are now, be kind to yourself. It will be okay, do the best you can do in that situation, your time will come!

'Don't be frustrated with who you are now or the situation you currently find yourself in. Be excited for who you can be in the future or where your current situation may lead you.'

Which is just lovely. Matt Fynn: from the kid that quit to the guy that didn't.

So, be more Matt Fynn. When things get tough, do the best you can do in that situation. Your time will come. Most of all, don't quit.

Chapter 18:
One Steppe At A Time

I'm not crazy; I'm just colourful.
- **Butch Cassidy**

I asked Krista to marry me during the afternoon of Sunday 27th September 2020. So, maybe it was fate that I received a promotional email from an adventure company that very same evening.

The email subject was: '2022 Patagonia: Glacier to Glacier – Entries Now Open' and the adventure promised, 'a huge canvas on which we have painted an extraordinary adventure,' amid 'Towering mountains … huge glaciers carving off into stunning lakes, interspersed with forest, alpine meadows, steppe and other uniquely Patagonian flora and fauna.' But this wouldn't be taking in these incredible sites the way that most normal people take them in, no siree; it would involve 'serene biking', running along 'exciting trails' and 'scenic kayaking', covering almost 250 miles through 'this wild and alluring place' in 'six glorious days'. This would be a little different to running 145 monotonous miles along drab canals.

Krista and I had talked about a few destinations that were on our bucket list–Patagonia among them–and, with this concept seeming far from a typical honeymoon, I semi-jokingly forwarded it to Krista, saying, 'For our honeymoon, darling?!'

Krista's response: 'WOW. Yes please.'

This was one of the many reasons I'd asked her to marry me. She'd taken on her fair share of epic endurance events–namely covering hundreds of miles across Europe in various multi-day cycling challenges–and her sense of adventure more than matched my own.

The email was promoting the 2022 Glacier to Glacier but spaces were still available for the December 2021 iteration. We knew that sitting on a beach–as serene as the Maldives or Mauritius might be for some–wouldn't cut it for us; beaches all look the same. And this had to be the trip of a lifetime. So, whether it was fate or not, after some to-and-froing with the organisers because of the ongoing international travel restrictions, we signed up and built our honeymoon around this most incredible of adventures.

***

Five months later Krista was drinking free champagne in the business class lounge at Heathrow Terminal 5, and I was living it large with a plate of as many assorted pastries as I thought I could manage. We had respectively agreed to drink and eat our way through Argentina's finest and I had some stomach-stretching to do to accommodate the amount of steak that I was planning to consume in the following three weeks. Even getting that far seemed like we'd beaten the system, since the weeks preceding our travel had involved jumping through so many hoops and navigating so much red tape that we were no longer sure if we could be bothered to make the trip. Before leaving we'd had to get NHS COVID Passes, send saliva samples off for testing to secure a Certificate of Coronavirus rtPCR Testing, completed a Ministry of Health, Welfare and Sport health declaration for travellers and applied for something called an EC Certificate. Even though a sealed tin can, 35,000ft above the planet, on which everyone had gone through the same level of testing to ensure they were free of the virus, was the safest place imaginable on or above the earth, we had to be tested on arrival in Buenos Aires to pass through immigration, and do the equivalent paperwork–including the Detección de Coronavirus COVID-19 (SARS-CoV-2) RT - PCR–and Passenger Locator Forms on the way back.

In short, we fucking deserved this trip.

After a quick stopover in Paris–more champagne and even better pastries–we were on an overnight flight to Buenos Aires. We did a bit of exploring of the city, but mostly we were excited to visit a restaurant on the recommendation of a friend of Krista's; Don Julio. The steak eater's mecca, the place is notorious for serving slab-sized cuts of 21 day-matured Aberdeen Angus steak that barely need to see a grill. We only found out afterwards that the restaurant was ranked highly on the list of the World's 50 Best Restaurants. A T-bone the size of my head later, and I was off to a good start in my mission to eat Argentina out of cow.

From the capital we flew south to El Calafate, the southern city from which you access the Southern Patagonian Ice Field, the second largest extrapolar icefield in the world (the largest is in Canada). In the Argentine province of Santa Cruz, El Calafate is named for a little bush that's common in the area, with yellow flowers that produces a dark blue berry; the calafate. The city arose in the early twentieth century, originally as a sheltering place for wool traders making their way to the coast. We treated ourselves to a night at the nicest hotel in town and hit the spa, in preparation for a week of camping and hostelling. The next morning, we returned to the local airport to meet the rest of our contingent and boarded a minibus bound for the start of our challenge–135 miles away across the Patagonian Steppe–knowing we'd be doing the journey in reverse (and some more) under our own steam over the course of the next week.

It's unsurprising that visitors to El Chaltén, a small village to the north-west of El Calafate, are greeted by a sign that proudly welcomes them to the 'Capital Nacional del Trekking'; Argentina's trekking capital. Sitting at the edge of the Southern Patagonia Ice Field, the village is a gateway to the Parque Nacional Los Glaciares. El Chaltén therefore boasts incredible access to some of the world's most epic hiking and climbing. But glaciers aren't the region's only attraction; rugged granite peaks soaring above 3,000m dominate the skyline.

The most imposing of these is the spire of Mt Fitz Roy (3,405m), to which the town owes its name. *Chaltén* is a Tehuelche word (a local language that went out of use when its last speaker passed away in 2019) meaning 'smoking mountain'–it is more often than not shrouded by clouds and high winds mean these are constantly swirling around its peak. These winds, and Fitz Roy's sheer faces, make the mountain very technically hard to climb and only a scattering of people have achieved the feat–far fewer than have summited Everest. This would be the backdrop of the start of our Patagonian adventure.

DAY 0: Admin day and warm-up hike – distance covered: 13 miles

With a day to ourselves before Glacier to Glacier officially began, we sought advice from the locals on the best hikes to help us stretch our legs after several days of travelling. We opted to head out of the town to the south and make for a point that would give us spectacular views of Laguna Torre and Laguna Capri, two lakes to which we'd be hiking over the next couple of days.

We gathered under the 'trekking capital' sign with four of our fellow adventurers and set out for the hills. Accompanying us were Anna, a lawyer from Florida in her late 50s, and three lads from Sheffield; Ben, Andy and Kristian, of similar age to me and Krista. Anna was an absolute hero, while the guys were hilarious, knocking back bottle after bottle of Malbec each night and constantly taking the mickey out of each other.

As we climbed, we enjoyed views back over the town and up the valley behind it. Running alongside the Rio de Las Vueltas, which meandered through the valley, would form part of our first foot stage the following day.

A beautifully clear day, we were lucky to be able to see the peak of Mt Fitz Roy throughout the climb. The vegetation at lower altitudes slowly turned to a rocky, lunar landscape higher up as we approached the Loma del Pliegue Tumbado viewpoint. From here, even before we'd started the expedition, the views were unlike anything we'd ever seen before (and they were only going to get better). Laguna Capri was a beautiful deep blue away to our north, while Laguna Torre, with Fitz Roy behind it, appeared murkier to our north-east. Spinning round 180°, the vast expanse of Lago Viedma, which we'd be cycling round on Day 3, stretched out to the south-east.

In hindsight, we could have taken it a little easier on our rest day–the 'warm-up' turned into a half-marathon hike, with almost 1,200m of elevation, involving over four and half hours of moving time–but it was worth it to take in the magnificence of the area and get a taste of what was to come.

DAY 1: Foot Stage 1 – distance covered: 22 miles for Krista; 26.2 miles for me

Briefings done, day bags packed, GPS trackers stashed alongside the calories we'd need for a day of running and trekking, we gathered by the El Chaltén sign again.

12 of us in total, which we felt was a perfectly-sized group, the remaining six consisted of a foursome from the Caribbean island Turks and Caicos, and another couple, James and Jennifer, who were also on their honeymoon. We couldn't believe there was another couple as mad as us and they were great company.

Leaving El Chaltén to the north this time, the town's Avenida San Martin became Ruta Provincial 23, which winds its way up into the Andes. Less a road and more a gravel track as soon as you leave the town, it was hard going on the legs, but the course alongside the Rio de Las Vueltas provided a beautiful backdrop, with rainbows shining over distant glaciers. Belonging to the Santa Cruz River basin, the river's source and mouth are two of the region's biggest lakes; it begins as drainage from Lago del Desierto (Desert Lake) and flows into Lago Viedma como 15 miles downstream.

After 10 miles, we reached our first checkpoint, where we fuelled up with the first of many empanadas and biscuits dipped in dulce de leche. We turned off the road, following trails that led us into the Parque Nacional Los Glaciares, and were increasingly taken aback by views that just got better and better.

With the Piedras Blancas Glacier to our right and its ice cascading into the Laguna Piedras Blancas below it, we covered a few miles through the woods, before taking a right turn onto the beautiful Sendero al Fitz Roy. This is an iconic trail that leads from El Chaltén to the base of Mt Fitz Roy and Laguna de Los Tres. 'Lake of the Three' in English, the number represents the three peaks towering above the lake–Fitz Roy, Cerro Torre, and Mt Poincenot–and seeing these mountains loom over the turquoise-coloured lake was a stunning reward for the 500m ascent to the viewing point.

Dragging ourselves away from the most magnificent view we had ever seen took some doing and, with Fitz Roy now behind us, we followed the Sendero al Fitz Roy back down to El Chaltén. On the way we stopped by the side of Laguna Capri, to take in another breathtaking view of Fitz Roy, and at the Mirador Rio de las Vueltas, a viewpoint overlooking the valley we had run up earlier in the day.

At 22 miles for the day, Krista was done, but I'd set my sights on running a marathon whilst in South America– the fourth continent on which I'd done so. Much to the bemusement of the rest of the group as they tucked into their first bottles of malbec of the evening, I therefore ran a few out-and-backs from the centre of the town, to add the all-important four miles to the total distance. Someday I'll get around to Africa, Australia, and maybe Antarctica.

DAY 2: Foot Stage 2 – distance covered: 20 miles

Stepping out of the back door of the Hosteria Alma de Patagonia, our lodgings for the duration of our stay in El Chaltén, the Senda a Laguna Torre took us out of the town to the west. While we'd enjoyed two days of clear skies and sunshine, there was lower hanging cloud in the air this morning and a hint of drizzle. But this lifted our spirits, rather than dampened them, as it meant a rainbow arched its way across the sky in front of us for most of the morning.

Snaking alongside the Rio Fitz Roy towards Cerro Solo (2,121m), we followed the trail along the valley floor for six miles and reached the lake's frontal moraine, before dropping down to the water's edge. Icebergs drifting across the lake would have formed over 10,000 years ago and slowly 'flowed' down the mountain as part of the glacier, before breaking off into chunks and floating away. Brilliant blue tips showed above the water line, while fragments lay on the shore, making for some amazing photos.

From here, we continued along the lake's northern ridge for another mile and soaked up the glorious views of the glacier from the Maestri viewpoint.

Leaving the glacier, we struck back along the trail to its junction with the Sendero Madre e Hila and turned off to the north. At first obscured by the lower peak of Loma de las

Pizarras (1,691m), Fitz Roy eventually hoved into view. The weather was on our side again as the sun burned off the clouds, meaning we had an idyllic couple of hours of hiking past two lakes, Laguna Hija and Laguna Madro, and a beautiful descent back into town.

Amongst the crew, resident chef Sebastian was local to El Calafate. That evening, he fired up the BBQ and we feasted on a selection of locally sourced meats and sausages.

DAY 3: Bike Stage 1 – distance covered: 68 miles

After calling El Chaltén home for four nights, the time had come to start making our way back towards El Calafate. Rickety mountain bikes at the ready, we prepared to cross a section of the Patagonian Steppe.

The eighth largest desert in the world, the steppe covers an area almost three times the size of the UK. Although the sparse shrubs and plants mean that animals require vast areas in which to graze, cattle, sheep and horse husbandry are the primary land uses, and Argentina is the fifth largest producer of wool in the world.

The 135 miles back to El Calafate (with some meandering kayaking also to come) seemed plenty daunting enough at this stage, but we were thankful we didn't have to cross the whole desert and set off in good spirits. With Fitz Roy now behind us, we climbed briefly out of town on RP23 and cycled along the north shore of Lago Viedma, on the straightest road we have ever seen. For miles and miles the road stretched out in front of us, more often than not simply disappearing into a mirage in the far distance, and we wondered if we might cycle off the edge of the world.

Despite the barren surroundings, there was wildlife in abundance; we spotted condors, foxes, and guanacos (closely related to the llama), although the occasional skull or carcass could also be seen amongst the shrubs or stuck in the barbed wire fences that lined the road.

After 55 miles we came to the intersection of RP23 and Ruta Nacional 40. This iconic road is one of the longest in the world, stretching more than 3,000 miles from Punta Loyola near Rio Gallegos in the south to La Quiaca on the Bolivian border in the north. It crosses 11 of the country's provinces, 20 national parks and 18 major rivers, and its highest point is at an altitude of 5,000m.

Turning right onto RN40, we now found ourselves cycling into a 50mph headwind and were relieved we only had just over ten miles to go. After a brief stop on the bank of Lago Viedma, with Fitz Roy now a distant speck on the horizon, we finished the day's ride, arriving at the Hotel La Leona.

Sitting on the banks of the Rio La Leona, this guesthouse is steeped in history. It was originally built as an estancia by a family of Danish immigrants but has more recently served as a base for Andean climbing expeditions, including the first summit of Fitz Roy in 1952, and has welcomed many other famous guests over the years.

None quite as famous–or infamous–however, as Robert Leroy Parker and Harry Alonzo Longabaugh.

Better known as Butch Cassidy and the Sundance Kid, the outlaws had settled in South America after a spate of train and bank robberies in the US in the late 1800s. Despite the intention of becoming respectable ranchers, it wasn't long before they were tempted back into crime. In February 1905 the pair held up the Bank of London and Tarapacá in Rio Gallagos and fled north, along with Sundance's girlfriend, Etta Place. They wound up at La Leona, where, under false names, they were treated as distinguished guests for an entire month.

Our stay wasn't quite as distinguished, camping in the field at the rear of the hotel, but drinks and stories around the campfire brought the day to a close perfectly.

DAY 4: Kayak Stage – distance covered: 24 miles (+ 17 miles by bike)

Kitting up on the banks of the Rio La Leona, we climbed into tandem seakayaks for the next leg of the journey. Another river whose source and mouth are lakes, the river meanders 30 miles from its origin in the south-east corner of Lago Viedma down to Lago Argentino.

This was a serene morning, spent enjoying the gently flowing current, while gazing in awe at millions of years of geological history represented in the layers of rock in the surrounding hills. The area is among the greatest paleontological centres in the world, with vast numbers of fossils found from the Cretaceous period (about 145 million to 66 million years ago).

Along the way, we pulled up on shore to explore an abandoned estancia, complete with derelict Cadillac and more guanaco skeletons.

After several hours of being crammed into a plastic

tube and the ensuing cramp in my legs, I was glad when the wind picked up–and the current too–and we were told we had to disembark the kayaks. A short blast on the bikes got the blood flowing again. Our second night camping, we again stayed by the side of the Rio La Leona, this time on a cattle ranch, next to a pen of very noisy cows. But, after the day's exertions, and with a belly full of Seb's homemade stew cooked over an open fire, the mooing didn't keep us awake too long.

DAY 5: Bike Stage 2 – distance covered: 56 miles

Getting back onto the bikes–to the dismay of some with sore backsides–we covered around 12 more miles of RN40 before cutting right onto Ruta Provincial 11. Now making for El Calafate, we wound along the south shore of Lago Argentino, the biggest freshwater lake in Argentina. Striking turquoise, yet cloudy, the colour of the water is due to a very fine sediment produced by glacial abrasion, also known as glacial flour.

20 miles later we were back in El Calafate. The town was originally founded in 1927, but it was another decade before the Parque Nacional Perito Moreno was created, sparking growth and the building of better roads. They weren't something that we were able to enjoy, however, as we wound our way into the hills above the town. Another 20 miles of gravelly track awaited us, wreaking havoc with our bums and backs.

Along the way we passed the *Monumento a los Caídos de las Huelgas Rurales* (the *Monument to the Fallen of the Rural Strikes*), erected in honour of labourers who were shot during the Patagonia Rebelde. This was the name given to the violent suppression of a rural workers' strike, held in 1920 and 1921, that demanded an increase in wages and better living conditions. Many surrendered but were still executed by Argentine Army firing squads. The monument's plaque reads, 'In memory of the 1,500 rural labourers shot in defence of dignity and freedom.'

A few short (but still painful) miles later, we arrived at the remote Estancia Rio Mitre, where we were surrounded by inquisitive goats and a tame baby guanaco. Our hosts cooked a whole lamb on an open fire and, with remarkable views over to the Península de Magallanes, which juts out into Lago Argentino, we were left feeling insignificant thanks to the staggering vastness of the landscape before us. As the sun set, the crew lit a campfire and we watched the colours changing over the mountains in the horizon.

DAY 6: Bike Stage 3 – distance covered: 24 miles

On the final day of the expedition, we rose early to get back on the bikes. Six km of bumpy gravel was quickly forgotten when we joined the tarmac road that would take us to our finish line. The reason for the early start? To arrive at the Parque Nacional Los Glaciares boundary by 7am, an hour before the park officially opened to the public, thanks to the crew bribing the park rangers with new gun holsters. In doing so, we had a road that was worthy of a *Top Gear* segment completely to ourselves.

Skirting around the southern edge of the Península de Magallanes, the gently undulating and winding road slowly teased us with glimpses of the Perito Moreno Glacier, named after Francisco Pascasio Moreno. A *perito* (meaning 'expert'), Moreno was a prominent Argentine explorer and academic, who studied the region in the 19th century and played a major role in defending the territory of Argentina in the conflict surrounding the international border dispute with Chile.

Around 20 miles further on from the park entrance, we hit a steep incline and climbed the final stretch to the finish line.

Walking down the boardwalks that accommodate the large crowds during the day, but doing so alone, without the masses, we admired the magnificence of the glacier from the viewing platforms. It is unquestionably the most immense and spectacular thing I've ever seen; three miles wide, 20 miles in length and covering 100 miles^2, it towers 70m on average above the surface of Lago Argentino and extends 170m below the surface.

And, while global warming is causing many of the innumerable glaciers worldwide to retreat, Perito Moreno is one of the few that maintains a state of equilibrium, thanks to the mass of snow and ice that accumulates at its higher altitudes. In winter, the glacier even advances (at speeds of up to two metres per day), reaching the coast of Península de Magallanes and cutting off the southern arm of the lake called the Brazo Rico (Rico Arm). With no outlet, the water in the Brazo Rico can rise by as much as 30m above the level of Lago Argentino, causing immense pressure on the ice barrier. When the ice ruptures, it does so in cataclysmic fashion, sending a massive outpouring of water into the main body of the lake and the Santa Cruz River.

As we were soaking up the sight, nature gave us a demonstration of its awesome power; a deafening crack was followed by a chunk of ice the size of a house carving off the front of the glacier and crashing into the water below.

To cap off an incredible morning (and week), we boarded a boat and drifted closer to the glacier–outside of the 300m exclusion zone from the ice. While celebrating our achievement with a glass (well, plastic cup to be accurate) of fizz, we were awarded our medals by race director, Rob. But this wasn't about the validation of getting a medal on completing the challenge, it was a journey of discovery for us both, as individuals and as a couple, and we will cherish it forever. The experience is something we'll remember and draw on for the rest of our lives.

As for the rest of the honeymoon, well, after the exertions of the week, we'd arranged to tag an element of relaxation onto the end. A hop, skip and a jump–and two more flights–later, and we were in a villa on a vineyard in the Malbec region for more wine (for Krista) and more steak (for me).

Chapter 19:
The Eternal Student

Perfection is not attainable but, if we chase perfection, we can catch excellence.
- **Vince Lombardi**

Remember Socrates? The wisest of them all? The guy who was, in fact, so wise that he 'was conscious that [he] knew nothing at all'[114]?

Socrates was the eternal student. And I don't mean one of those bums that floats from degree to degree, eking as much as they can out of the taxpayer as possible while pretending they're some real life incarnation of Peter Pan and refusing to grow up. Take Luciano Baietti, a 75-year old Italian who has 15 degrees. He was recognised in the Guinness Book of Records in 2002 for clocking up his eighth degree, in motor skills–having previously graduated from Rome's prestigious La Sapienza University with degrees in sociology, literature, law, political science and philosophy–and has since added seven more to the list; including in criminology, military strategies and tourism.

Jeez Louise, man, live a little. Put the book down and

take your long-suffering wife—30 years his younger—out for pizza occasionally. And don't tell me that studying motor skills is living.

No, I mean Socrates was the eternal student in terms of his continual willingness to learn and we should all be taking a leaf out of his orchard. The trouble is that that's easier said than done, if something called the Dunning-Kruger effect is anything to go by. In 1999, David Dunning and Justin Kruger, social psychologists and professors at the University of Michigan and at New York University Stern School of Business respectively, demonstrated, in the Journal of Personality and Social Psychology, that 'people tend to hold overly favorable views of their abilities in many social and intellectual domains.'[115]

So, where Socrates knew that he knew nothing at all, the rest of us are ignorant of our ignorance. We overestimate our capabilities. Dunning states that 'the scope of people's ignorance is often invisible to them.'[116] In particular, 'poor performers in many social and intellectual domains seem largely unaware of just how deficient their expertise is. Their deficits leave them with a double burden—not only does their incomplete and misguided knowledge lead them to make mistakes but those exact same deficits also prevent them from recognizing when they are making mistakes'.

***

After the honeymoon, life sort of got in the way of any attempts to sign up for another crazy challenge. In a good way.

Two days before we headed out for Patagonia, Krista and I visited a Grade II listed cottage in the Wiltshire countryside, about half an hour outside of Bath. As much as we'd loved renting in the centre of Bath, the downside to trying to buy a property in the middle of a World Heritage City is that if you want anything larger than a shoebox, you have to have a seven-figure budget–and then double it. So, we'd cast a fairly wide net outside of the city and Krista had spent six months going down the Rightmove rabbit hole. As we aimed to lay roots, we visited umpteen listings before landing on the one we knew we wanted.

So, amid the free champagne and pastries at Heathrow, we were frantically refreshing our inboxes in anticipation of the email that would mean we could truly enjoy the next three weeks. Just before boarding, it came through: 'The property will now show as Sold Subject To Contract … No more viewings will be undertaken and any potential buyers will be advised a sale has been agreed.'

And relax.

Or at least as much as you can relax when you're buying a house. Which isn't very much, since it's one of the most stressful of life's experiences, especially when the sellers constantly move the goalposts, threaten to put the house back on the market if you don't buy their cooker on top of the asking price, insist that they redo the kitchen before you move in without you having any say in the design, therefore pushing back the completion date, and stand resolute that you go along with things if you really want the house. Sorry, had to get that out of my system.

Stress or no stress–but mostly stress–four months after coming back from our trip of a lifetime, we were moving to the country and focusing much of our attention on our dream home. So much so that I wouldn't take on my next challenge for another nine months; that next challenge coming after seeing news of the actor Tom Hardy turning up unannounced to compete in a Brazilian jiu jitsu competition.

According to psychology's four stages of competence, when learning a new skill we begin in a state of 'unconscious incompetence'. We don't know how to do the skill and probably aren't even aware that it needs doing. We go about our day like the story of the two young fish who are asked by an older fish, 'How's the water?' One turns to the other and says, 'What's water?' From there we move into 'conscious incompetence', where we become aware of the skill, but haven't yet learned how to do it. We decide we're going to take a crack at learning it and enter stage three: 'conscious competence', where we have learned the skill but are yet to master it, having to concentrate hard to do it. When we practise some more, and then some more, and then a little bit more, we learn the skill and it becomes second nature. We achieve 'unconscious competence'. We no longer have to think about the skill in order to do it. Driving's the obvious example. You shit yourself the moment you're first behind the wheel of a car but it's not long after you've passed your test that you're brushing your teeth with one hand, flicking through DAB radio stations with the other and somehow looking at your phone at the same time. Basically, doing everything but actually driving the car.

Apart from, my mum reminds me, a couple of taster classes as a youngster, I have never studied a martial art or combat sport. I don't regret for a second the amount of time I spent playing rugby as a kid, but you can't help imagining other routes that might have been taken. Who knows, maybe I'd have been fencing world champion if I'd opted to pursue that, but we make our choices—or at least we should–based on the things that ignite our passions and bring us joy.

Brazilian jiu jitsu, then, was very much an unconscious incompetence. But seeing Hardy, competing under his real name Edward, show up to the 2022 BJJ Open Championship in Milton Keynes and dominate the blue belt division in the medium heavyweight class got me thinking about the poor fucker who, at the beginning of a match looks up and realises he's about to fight Bane. I mean, if the guy can snap Batman in half, sales manager Andy doesn't stand much of a chance, does he?

Afterwards, Hardy posted a photo of himself on Instagram, wearing a gi, head bent in contemplation, alongside the following caption:

'Addiction is difficult and complex stuff to navigate; as is mental health. Subjects which are both deeply personal for me and extremely close to my heart.

'Simple training, for me (as a hobby and a private love) has been fundamentally key to further develop a deeper sense of inner resilience, calm and well being. I can't stress the importance it has had and the impact on my life.'

I had read about Hardy's history of alcohol and drug addiction and hugely respected him for the openness with which he had shared his experiences, including waking from crack cocaine binges and visiting rehab in 2003. Anyone in the public eye who is willing to be open like that gets my vote. So, the impact of this regime for him was interesting. And it also got me thinking about my next challenge.

I had by no means 'completed' running–nor achieved unconscious competence–but coming second in a nigh-on 150 mile race hadn't been too bad a high to go out on before a hiatus from such gruelling challenges. I didn't have anything further to prove to myself and no longer felt compelled to find the next level of my limits. Ultrarunning had served its purpose as my short-term sobriety mechanism and a means of channelling my emotions into something positive. Plus, not having to stick to an arduous training programme had meant more time available to focus on the important things in life: Krista, the house, and a new job secured a month before we moved. Another thing that's supposedly no good for the stress levels. Hey ho.

A little more digging and BJJ seemed to be the growing trend amongst a wide crop of pretty prominent names; Keanu Reeves, Guy Ritchie, Ashton Kutcher, Dave Bautista, Jason Momoa, even Barack Obama. To be honest, you had me at Tom Hardy.

Pioneered by the Brazilian Gracie brothers in the 1920s as a hybrid of Japanese jiu jitsu and judo, the sport rose to prominence in the 70s when Carlos Gracie moved to the US to coach it. Although derived from the Japanese words ju (柔) meaning 'gentle' and jutsu (術) meaning 'art', you could argue that the aim of trying to cut off the blood supply to your opponent's brain or trap one of his limbs in a position that causes him to fear that it's about to be snapped off is far from gentle or artistic. A meme describes BJJ as 'the gentle art of folding clothes while your opponent is in them' or 'involuntary yoga'.

And, with positions like the 'mount' and the 'rear naked choke', it also sounds like the Gracie brothers were leafing through the Kama Sutra while pioneering the sport. But watching the experts go at it, you wonder if they might have made it as ballerinas, such is the grace and fluidity of their movements.

Most importantly, it is a sport centred around learning. It encourages you to embrace the fact that you know nothing at all. Whether you have previously been a champion weightlifter, a gold medal-winning Olympian or once upon a time played semi-professional rugby and more recently came second in a 145-mile ultramarathon, none of that matters. BJJ is the ultimate leveller; everyone starts from the beginning.

As Chris Baugh, a performance coach with 30 years of combined experience in boxing and martial arts, says, 'The number one reason that I would advocate [for someone] to take up combat sports is not to lose weight or protect himself, it's for the simple fact that it will teach you to be an eternal student. What I mean by that is if you start Brazilian jiu jitsu as a grown adult, you will be crap for quite a long time. I'm not saying that to put people off, I'm saying it because, once you realise that, you have a really clear choice to make and that choice can tell you a lot about yourself; am I prepared to keep showing up, week in week out, being the crappiest person here and humble myself in the pursuit of progress? And if people can say yes to that, there's nothing more rewarding than watching your really crap self become slightly less crap every week. And God knows, maybe one day you'll be good.

'But what I don't like to see is coaches taking people on and telling them, after a short time, "Oh yeah, you're really good now." You shouldn't need to hear you're good to stay in the game. If you do, you're dealing with the wrong currency. You should be able to hear you're not very good, you're *still* not very good, but you're better than you were last week. That should be enough to keep you in the game.

If it's not, it tells you that you're desperate for ego stimulation all the time. That if you're not being patted on the back every step of the way, you're going to give up.'

Or as another meme puts it: 'What are your jiu jitsu goals? Suck less at jiu jitsu.'

Chris attended an elite public school and a top London university, and is now a performance coach to the city's high flying professionals, having had an unbeaten professional boxing career. Since retiring from professional boxing in 2016, Chris has also taken up Brazilian jiu jitsu.

But things could have gone very differently for him. When he was just four years old he came within a hair's breadth of being sent to a Primary Pupil Referral Unit, an institution that's one step shy of a juvenile detention centre, that takes in the kids that schools don't want; among them the neurodiverse and the ones with serious behavioural issues. Chris was one of the latter.

Seemingly triggered by his parent's divorce and the tumult in the wake of his father's departure from the family home, Chris displayed increasingly challenging behaviour in school. Top of the list was extreme violence, wreaking havoc to the extent that he was excluded from school aged just four, following various assessments by educational psychologists. Fortunately, after several months of juggling full time work and childminders, his mother found a private school that was willing to take him, and from there he achieved a scholarship to an elite private secondary school.

This environment was at odds with the South London neighbourhood from where he made the 75 minute bus and train journey each morning. So, 'all the time I was at public school,' he recounts, 'I was not making many friends, I'll be honest with you, and not feeling like I fitted in with the jock crowd. Instead, from 15, I was in a boxing gym.'

As mobile phones became a thing around the time he was entering his teens, 'suddenly everybody had something on them that was worth nicking, and I was wearing a uniform with a big pound sign on my chest, because everybody knew the school and assumed I was minted, so I was getting jumped all the time. I got to a point where being an average size, bespeckled private school boy wasn't cutting it. So, I thought "I'm going to learn the nastiest thing I can think of"; I'd watched *Kickboxer* and wanted to do what Van Damme was doing.

'At 19, I converted from kickboxing to boxing and was sparring a lot harder. I started getting hit in the head and I realised how scary that was.'

Training in kickboxing and boxing gyms 'with big West Indian men', as opposed to his white, middle class classmates, he 'got a different perspective of what masculinity looked like and started to develop a mindset that was commensurate with that environment—an environment where you shut your mouth because you are not the toughest guy in there. And if you talk or act like you are, you will get battered. You have to learn how to portray yourself. But there's also no hiding. You have to learn when it's your time to step up and when it's your time to shut up.'

This was a world away from being surrounded by white middle class boys in a privileged school setting, giving Chris 'an outsider's view looking in on lots of people who fancy themselves as being just generally good at life. They're decent looking and make decent money. They're confident. They can sit in a room full of other white men like them and sound like they've got half a clue about most things they open their mouth about. There's a certain sense of entitlement, they can open their mouth and wax lyrical with very little knowledge about politics, football, almost anything.' At which point I explain the Dunning Kruger effect to Chris and he responds, 'That makes perfect sense. I think too many people talk too much with too few consequences; none of these guys have ever been put to the test. No-one has ever called them out on their bullshit.'

I'm as guilty as anyone of having been the public school boy bullshitter stereotype that Chris has described, and it's undoubtedly the fact that I thought I could breeze through life without any setbacks that was ultimately my downfall.

But the beauty of sucking at something, especially a combative sport, is that you will have setbacks every time you step into the ring or onto the mat. Setbacks that will invariably leave you either battered or fearing for your consciousness, competent or otherwise.

Rich Sheppard is the coach who has had the unenviable task of trying to make me suck less, ever since I took on my first taster session. By coincidence, he also started boxing at a young age: 'I boxed all of my childhood and had a really good boxing coach called Tony Stannard, who received an MBE for services to boxing and was like a second father to me. He was very strict but compassionate as well, so he was really good for me because I didn't have a lot of good structure in my life in my childhood and I was a weird kid in a lot of ways. I was quite anxious but also very hyperactive and wanted to do a bit of everything. One good thing about boxing was that it gave me control. People wouldn't start fights with you because you boxed and I enjoyed the training.

'I had my first bout as young as possible, which was 11 years old at the time. Years later, when I was invited to train with some MMA guys, I didn't know anything about it. I thought I'd done well at sparring and it would be kind of the same thing. But I got picked up, dropped on my head, arm-barred, strangled; my boxing didn't help me at all. When I got out of that session, it just sort of took me. I thought, "O my God, this is amazing, man, I've got to learn this." And it's been a force for good in my life. I'm not naturally very focused. I'm not naturally very good to myself a lot of the time. But jiu jitsu seems to sort that out. I find it really easy to stay focused on jiu jitsu.'

Having achieved his black belt after 14 years of studying BJJ, Rich somehow moves differently to us average joes; it's as if he flows. Watching him roll is like witnessing Robert Patrick's shape-shifting, liquid metal T-1000 in *Terminator 2: Judgement Day* glide through a door made of metal bars. Except Rich's opponent is the metal bars. One minute you'll be lying on top of him, in what you think is a fairly advantageous position, the next, without you knowing how he has done it, he'll have his arms locked around your neck as he unleashes a deadly anaconda choke and you try in vain to avoid passing out. But he's also the most gentle and unassuming individual you will ever meet. If the special forces were on a hunt for the epitome of the Grey Man, Rich would be it, and he'd come complete with a potent array of deadly choke holds for close combat situations. I genuinely think we should give him a balaclava and send him into the Kremlin to sort out a certain Mr Putin, although Rich is so lovely the pair would probably end up shooting the breeze. Vladimir might not be even the slightest bit interested in guitars and motorbikes but after a few minutes with Rich, he wouldn't have a choice but to be. (Although, ironically, Putin is a black belt in judo–you can even pick up a copy of *Judo mit Wladimir Putin* from t'interweb–so martial arts would be common ground.)

In that first session, to say I was nervous was an understatement. I don't like sucking at anything–big surprise, I know–and, despite ten years of supposedly learning that I don't have to be the big, strong, macho, fit guy I described to you in Chapter 4, I felt I had something to prove. Rich says I was 'a monstrous rugby idiot'. Which is astonishingly accurate. At one point, an opponent had his legs around me in what's called the Guard position, and I thought it would be appropriate to pick him up and slam him into the ground.

Unfortunately, it's not WWE. I'm not The Rock. Body slams are not allowed and no-one can or wants to smell what I'm cooking.

Amusingly, though, Chris recounted an identical story about his first ever BJJ session. Let's back up a bit though.

From boxing as a hobby, then at university, followed by unlicensed fights, collar fights, and amateur fights, Chris bumped into a boxing promoter who remembered him from a previous fight and suggested he chat with a pro coach. Suddenly, 'it was like a dream I'd never allowed myself to have because I never thought I was good enough.'

Chris turned pro, giving up his career and flat, and moving into his mum's spare room to do so. Unfortunately, after a series of complications, including medical issues that delayed his pro licence and injuries, he was forced to quit after two years, albeit undefeated in four fights as a pro.

'Eventually, after retiring,' he says, 'I was training pads with a friend who did MMA and he suggested I give jiu jitsu a go.' This was at the gym where he trained and worked as a boxing coach, where MMA classes were also available. 'After two years of smashing people in the face every week and being smashed in the face,' he admits to 'looking down on the jiu jitsu players and basically being a prick because they had a different profile to the boxers. They were normally very cerebral, educated people and *not* in the business of getting smashed in the face every week. We'd say, "Look at you guys, rolling around in your pyjamas, hugging each other."'

Note Chris' use of the word 'player'. Someone who practises jiu jitsu is known as a player, practitioner, athlete, student, competitor; but never a fighter.

With the rage that he was carrying from his childhood, kickboxing and boxing were what he calls an 'investigation into [his] dark side,' as he expressed and examined his violent tendencies in doing maximal damage to the opponent *fighter* across the ring. But BJJ was Chris' second steep learning curve; this time transitioning to a sport in which you place your trust in your fellow players and work with them to improve your technique. 'In boxing, if I tell you how to improve something that you are doing and you then do it more and build confidence next week, that results directly in more blows to my head, more pain to me. There's an inverse relationship between encouraging your teammates to improve and the impact on your own health. So of course you're not going to help each other. You become very insular; it's not supportive, it's not team-like and it's always a competition. Everyone's holding their cards as close to their chest as they can.'

BJJ is different, with a culture based around trust and helping others. There's no choice in the matter; when you roll with someone, you place your life in their hands. Quite literally. The sport is based around various choke holds that restrict the flow of blood to the brain through pressure on the carotid arteries in either side of the neck. Fail to tap–on your opponent's shoulder, the mat, or shouting 'tap'–in the event of such a 'submission' and you're unconscious in a matter of seconds; possibly dead in minutes. There is a beautiful vulnerability to the sport that forces even the most testosterone-fuelled of men to put complete trust in each other.

'That is what is at the heart of jiu jitsu culture,' Chris continues. 'When you tap, they have to stop doing the thing which could shortly kill you and they do so every time. That is miraculous, really. Not only have you been released from near death, I might then put my arm around your shoulder and say, "Look man, maybe do this differently." So, not only am I not killing you in an act of combat, not only am I giving you the opportunities to ask me to stop and you see that request is listened to, but then I help you. In doing so, I might not be able to make you tap like that again, but that gives me something new to think about and work on.'

And there's always something to work on.

Rich says, 'You never complete jiu jitsu. When you learn to be ok with that, it's liberating.' Or, as the modern day Socrates, except not really, Damien Rice, sang, 'It's not hard to grow, when you know that you just don't know.'[117]

Think about it though; we never truly complete anything. Completion implies perfection. No-one in the world is a complete master of a sport, or a field of knowledge, or a musical instrument, or of any skill such that there is no room for them to improve. Vince Lombardi, the celebrated NFL coach who led the Green Bay Packers to multiple NFL Championships and the first two Super Bowl titles, famously said, 'Perfection is not attainable but, if we chase perfection, we can catch excellence.'

It's the opposite of the Dunning-Kruger effect; the more we study something, the more our ignorance becomes visible. The more we realise how much there is still to learn. The more expertise becomes nuanced. The easier it is to identify where to improve. For example, at the moment, Rich is 'really into the inverted north south [which, I'll admit, sounds like another sex position]. I'm trying to branch out from a front headlock, arm in arm out choke sequence that I go through. What I'm trying to do is expand that.' If you don't have a clue what he's talking about, don't worry, that's the point. His knowledge is so in depth that he talks in levels beyond most people's comprehension. Whereas I just want to suck less.

My liberating moment*, a couple of weeks later, came when a guy 20 kg lighter than me and 10 years older than me bent me half and choked me so hard that I lost my voice. Which, obviously, I thought was awesome.

> *Side note:
>
> My witty 70-year-old neighbour had also brought me down a peg or two by quipping, when I mentioned that I'd taken up Brazilian jiu jitsu, 'What does that involve? Getting a wax beforehand?'

It made me realise that it was ok to suck. In fact, it wasn't just ok, it was great, because in accepting that you suck–that you know nothing at all–you become willing to learn. You open your mind to the possibility of improving and sucking ever so slightly less than you did the previous time you practised, studied or trained. You become an eternal student.

Since then, I've made it my mission to become less of a monstrous rugby idiot. At the time of writing I have notched up four stripes on my white belt, meaning I'm one step shy of earning my blue belt. When will I get it? I don't know and I'm fine with that. That's the whole point. My only aim is to suck less to the extent that Rich thinks I deserve it. He tells me that the difference between having four stripes on a belt and the next colour belt is 'about refining everything you're already doing. You don't need to do anything necessarily differently, just more accurately. Think of it like driving a car. When you start out, you go to change gear and have to think about it. And you might occasionally miss and the gearbox makes a clunking sound. But after a while, it's smoother and you don't have to think about it.'

Sounds like he's talking about being more unconsciously competent to me. Or at least being less 'clunky'. In other words, sucking less.

It's a very different perspective to the one I used to have when I was clocking up hundreds of miles of running each month. Ultramarathons are finite. They take place on set days, over set distances and with set cut off times. You either complete them, or you get a DNF–Did Not Finish–next to your name.

But there's no line in the sand with BJJ and the sport itself only has limited rules that are in place to prevent serious injury. According to Rich, 'Unlike sports like judo and wrestling, which are very specific in terms of moves—all the judo throws are listed, for example—jiu jitsu is completely free form. So much so that when you start, it almost seems too much to have to learn everything. And when you're 10 years in, you start thinking, "This is great, but I've still got so much to learn."'

This extends to the level of self-awareness that comes with studying the sport, in that the more you learn, the more you realise you still have to learn. Sounds like the opposite of Dunning-Kruger again.

From there comes the pursuit of more and more precise movements, so that you give your opponent less and less of an opportunity to counter what it is you're trying to achieve.

As John Danaher, one of the world's most renowned BJJ instructors, wrote on social media: 'The more precise you are with your mechanics the more effective your moves will be when applied with whatever strength you have. However, we have to be realistic. The more stress and chaos we are subject to in sparring and competition the harder it will be to maintain the ideal of perfect mechanics. Don't despair. You don't have to be perfect in application - just good enough to get the job done. Your goal in drilling is to get as close to perfection as you can. Your goal in sparring is to be good enough to get the result you seek. The more precise you are in drilling, the more there will be a carryover effect into your sparring that increases your precision; but be realistic, it'll never be perfect.'

'It'll never be perfect'; to paraphrase Vince Lombardi.

Rich gives the example of the guillotine choke, which

is a notoriously brutal submission if done correctly. But 'Sometimes you'll see someone do everything right apart from one thing and that's the thing that causes the entire move to go wrong, or not complete the submission, or allows their opponent to escape. The guillotine choke is very interesting because the first instinct when you've caught your opponent's neck is to pull your hands up your chest towards your head and basically elongate the neck. But my elbows should really come down when I'm doing a guillotine, not up. And there's a specific motion of the wrist like checking my watch that will help nail the submission.'

And what of mental fitness, since it's something I've brought up with each of my interviewees?

'I think any difficult endeavour helps you,' Rich says, 'And jiu jitsu is difficult. There are days when you lose, when you think, "That was hard." I've never wanted to give up jiu jitsu, but I've left some training sessions thinking, "God, that was tough." I've seen fully grown men crying. It just happens. But life happens too, doesn't it? You've got to go through the motions with jiu jitsu, as with other things.' Even a match or roll is itself a succession of tiny improvements, as Rich adds: 'Jiu jitsu is getting from one position into a slightly better position, and then a slightly better position, and so on until you're in a good position.

'You have to just carry on doing jiu jitsu and that's the same as life. Just do the steps, even when it's getting hard.'

For Chris, mental fitness 'is about self-awareness.' Ah, there it is again. 'It comes down to you knowing about yourself, what matters and what doesn't matter. If you're finding yourself in situations where something really matters to you, but you can't muster up the courage to take a setback and keep coming back to get it done, then we should have a conversation about your mental fitness.

'When I work with people, many of them ultra-high-performing guys, I want them to have clarity. I want them to understand what they really want, what they really need, and what really matters to them and what doesn't. And that is obviously an exercise in self-awareness; to scparate the often very neglected little voice in your head that is telling you what you are and what you want, from the voice that is shouting what you *should* want and *should* be and *should* have. Because too many people are hanging their hat on certain labels, goals, outcomes; and that's their whole sense of self. So, you put yourself under pressure to get results and if you don't achieve them, it seems like life or death. In contrast, BJJ teaches you to look in the mirror and be OK with yourself.'

It's a far cry from the high performing guy Chris mentions, who is set on the next aspirational goal because of the expectations of society's consumerism and materialism, as discussed when Tyler Durden was the focus of our attention all the way back in Chapter 1. If that's your sole purpose in life, Chris says, 'It's a slippery slope.'

Talking to Chris reminds me of my own inability to recognise my desperate need for purpose and quick fixes when I was struggling in the wake of my rugby injury; my inability to be a human being, rather than a human doing; and my inability to be present in the moment. Society had me under its sordid little spell and I felt I had to toe the line with those around me. I was desperate to fit in, while being unaware of the discontent this was causing me.

If Aasmah Mir's column–also mentioned back in Chapter 1–is anything to go by, a worrying number of people are in a similar situation. They're seeking the success that society says they should be seeking, rather than being who they truly want to be. They don't have a level of self-awareness that gives them clarity. Or humility, for that matter.

As Chris continues, 'There's a massive contrast between the values learned in high performing environments and in combative sports, both on a philosophical level and in the practical application of those values; between what being braggadocious gets you and what humility gets you.'

Learning the humility of the eternal student mindset has been liberating. I don't have an 'overly favorable view' of my ability in jiu jitsu because the scope of my ignorance is most certainly visible; BJJ puts me to the test every time I show up to roll and I've only just begun to scratch the surface of what the sport entails. But sucking less is enough of a goal for the foreseeable future. As I progress, I'll endeavour to be more precise, like John Danaher, with the goal of being good enough to get the result I seek; less clunky, like Rich Sheppard, such that I'm constantly aiming to refine everything I'm doing; and more like Vince Lombardi, to the extent that I'll get as close to perfection as I can, whilst being happy in the knowledge that I'll never achieve it.

I'll settle for excellence. Even if it's a long way off.

Chapter 20:
Performing At Your Peak

Set your sights upon the heights; don't be a mediocrity.

- **Merlin**

On 7th February 2009, the England rugby sevens team reached the final of the New Zealand leg of the World Series. And not the 'World Series' where only American baseball teams are able to compete.

Playing in the cauldron of the Westpac Stadium (now Sky Stadium) in Wellington, in front of a vociferous 50,000-strong crowd of fancy dress-clad, beer-soaked Kiwis, the side then faced the prospect of going 17-0 (three tries) down to the hosts, who just so happened to be the best team in the world, by half-time.

The captain that day, Ollie Phillips, remembers, 'We were staring down the barrel of a gun, thinking this was only going to go one way and we were going to get stuffed.'

No-one would have blamed them if, as Englishmen, they'd have chosen to stick the kettle on and sack off the second half. But that's not what goes through the head of the world's elite. So, what does?

'Probably "Oh shit," if we're being totally honest and transparent,' Ollie quips. 'But I don't think we were thinking about anything else other than us as a group. We knew that we were in a hostile environment, we knew that it was going to be challenging, but we also knew that we had the talent and capability, we trusted in each other and believed in the process. There was a belief that if we worked together as a collective unit, we would overcome this. I don't think we ever felt like we were out of touch.'

Rugby sevens is fundamentally the same in terms of the rules and regulations of the 15-a-side version of the game, but with the obvious difference of there only being seven players on each side. But still on a standard-size pitch, meaning there's a lot more space and a LOT more running. Non-stop running, in fact, for two seven-minute halves.

'There is a mental application that you need to have throughout the course of the game to get you over the line,' Ollie explains. 'You're there for a short time but oh my god it's going to be intense. You blow a gasket for as long as you're on the pitch and it never gets any easier but there's also the realisation that this is short lived. Short term pain for long term gain. Let's work our socks off and take it to the wire.'

England blew a gasket and took that game in Wellington to the wire, winning 17-19 at the final buzzer to record their first win against New Zealand on New Zealand soil, with the tournament title being the icing on the cake.

'Yes, we had a mountain to climb,' Ollie admits, 'but if you look at the mountain as a whole, if you stand at the bottom and think, "How am I ever going to get to the top of that?" it can become overwhelming and insurmountable psychologically. You start to panic. Whereas, if you approach it by just looking at what's in front of you, you can break it down into more achievable targets as you progress towards the summit. We never focused on the end goal. It was more a case of thinking how we get one foot back in the game over the next seven minutes, score a try, 17-5, then another which was converted, 17-12, then a third and Ben Gollings converted that one too. Bang. 17-19. It's special; even when I think about it now, it excites me.'

Ollie is one of those annoying people that accomplished more before the age of 40 than most people do in several lifetimes. We played rugby together at Durham University, where, while I was arguably focused on laying the foundations for my future drinking problems, he was destined for greater things. To be honest, between nights out in Klute–an urban myth tells of this minute sweatbox that calls itself a nightclub being awarded the dubious 'second worst nightclub in Europe' accolade by FHM magazine before the worst one, in Belgrade, burned down–the prospect of playing professional rugby didn't even cross my mind, whereas a contract with the Newcastle Falcons saw Ollie playing alongside some of the game's greats, like Jonny Wilkinson and Carl Hayman. But it was in a ten-year golden era of sevens for England, when the side was ranked no.1 in the world and regularly winning tournaments, that Ollie really made his mark. He captained the side for much of this time and was voted the IRB (International Rugby

Board, now World Rugby) Sevens Player of the Year in 2009. 'It was a phenomenal time to be involved in England rugby sevens,' he reminisces.

That famous victory in Wellington was followed by a lucrative contract with Paris' Stade Francais, where he was named Best Overseas Player in Europe in 2011. The successes continued and an Olympic Games beckoned. (Rugby sevens was announced, in 2009, as an additional sport at the 2016 Games in Rio.)

'You have plans, aspirations, hopes and dreams,' Ollie muses, 'of things you'd like to achieve, whether they be big or small. I certainly had bits left in the game that I really wanted to do, one of which was an Olympic Games. I was excited, and maybe a bit ambitious and hopeful, that I could make it to Rio. I would have been 32, but it was a target that I felt I could achieve.'

It wasn't to be. In a training camp ahead of the 2013 Sevens World Cup, he dropped to the floor with a pain in his lower leg. He'd severed a nerve in his calf, with no real diagnosis as to why or way of treating it. 'Within three hours of that happening, all of the plans, aspirations, hopes and dreams vanished. And it was difficult to accept. I told myself all I needed was some time; an interlude so I could rejuvenate and recover, defy the odds and medics, and wouldn't it be an amazing story to come back from the jaws of injury and defeat to play in an Olympic Games?'

It was the denial we talked about in Chapter 15 with Sonja Jenkins; the first stage of **the Kübler-Ross model because**, 'When you believe in something so vehemently and it means so much to you, and someone else tells you it can't happen but can't really tell you why, you look at other avenues and ways of proving them wrong. You never want to let go of a dream.'

Not one to sit around twiddling his thumbs, the 'other avenues' that Ollie looked at during his 'interlude' included what he describes as a series of 'distractions'. Most people's distractions involve taking up, depending on your level of athleticism, cross stitch or CrossFit, bingeing Grey's Anatomy or playing Angry Birds. But not Ollie. The first was taking part in the Clipper Round The World Race, spending 11 months at sea and sailing, well, around the world. 46,000 miles, to be precise.

'The narrative,' he explains, 'was to take the time off, sail around the world, come back in a blaze of glory, prove myself fit, get into the GB squad and play at the Olympics, whilst having had an amazing life experience. And I continued to believe it. I came home and trained like an absolute dog for six months, went to play in a tournament in Dubai with an invitational squad and my calf wasn't right. In order for people to believe in me and take a risk on me for the GB squad, I needed to pull through in that moment, and I didn't.

'But I still had too many distractions in my life which kept me from accepting it. For example, because people had seen me being a bit of a lunatic on the Clipper Race, I'd been approached to go to the North Pole.'

In 2015, the Arctic Rugby Challenge saw Ollie as the captain of one of two teams that trekked 100 km from northern Canada, 'surviving harrowing winds, avoiding polar bears and facing temperatures of -30 degrees'[118], built a pitch and set a Guinness World Record for playing the most northerly rugby match in history, at the certified magnetic

North Pole*.

> ***Side note:***
>
> So, Ollie is my second world record-setting polar explorer interviewee. Not that I'm bragging. Much.

'Maybe it was a mistake to juggle all these things and think my rugby might happen again, I'll never know. Perhaps I could have focused all my energy on one thing, rather than trying to spin a few plates at the same time. But I felt I gave it my best shot.'

We're ten years on from the end of his rugby career and it has taken much of that decade, some deep soul searching, and some 'slow and painful and confusing' therapy for Ollie to arrive at that sentiment. You see similar stories of sport's superstars questioning their raison d'être throughout the elite world.

Sir Bradley Wiggins, Britain's most decorated Olympian and the first British cyclist to win the Tour de France, retired in 2016 because he 'had stopped enjoying [cycling].' He told Men's Health, the four years after winning Olympic gold in 2012 were 'probably the unhappiest period of my life. Everything I did was about winning for other people'.

Adam Peaty, the 100 metres breaststroke world record holder, not just for the single fastest time, but the 20 fastest times in history over the distance, and triple Olympic Champion, pulled out of the 2023 British Swimming Championships citing mental health issues. In an interview with The Times, he revealed, 'The devil on my shoulder [says] "you're missing out on life, you're not good enough, you need a drink, you can't have what you want, you can't be happy" ... I got to a point in my career where I didn't feel like myself – I didn't feel happy swimming, I didn't feel happy racing, my biggest love in the sport ... The dedication and sacrifice – weekends and all your time are spent chasing that goal for this one opportunity of Olympic glory. I don't know why I'm still doing it, to be honest. I don't know why I'm still fighting.'[119]

Meanwhile, Krista's most recent issue of Women's Health comes through the door and Mary Earps, goalkeeper extraordinaire, winner of the UEFA Women's Championship and World Cup runner-up with England, and BBC Sports Personality of the Year 2023, is interviewed about burnout. She talks about her obsession with success as 'a gift and a curse ... When you can't stop thinking about something'. Her days off are 'not days off any more' and she suspects 'she's sleepwalking towards burnout', trying to 'base [her] life around gratitude because [she feels] like that is the most powerful way to stay motivated; stay happy.'

Ollie, too, thought that the constant pursuit of success and the resulting adulation was making him happy but, on reflection, it wasn't *him* that it was for.

'I had a great childhood until I was ten,' he recalls, 'and then in my teens it was very disrupted and confusing. My parents went through an ugly divorce and I didn't really see my dad for two or three years. I was old enough to know what was going on, but not old enough to really understand why. He couldn't really tell me why either because he's quite a disconnected individual.

'The fallout from that as a kid was wondering if it was something I'd done and wanting recognition or praise when he was just incapable of giving it. He may have been super proud, but he could never say it. I remember getting picked for England and his response was, "When are you going to get a proper job?" For him that was rational. But that wasn't what I wanted or needed to hear.

'I thought when I was made captain of England and then voted the best player in the world, surely he would say, "That's amazing," but he never did.

'I wasn't aware that my drivers throughout my professional rugby career were centred around insecurities stemming from my dad and craving his validation. A lot of my decisions in life, probably until my early thirties, were driven by that, and sport was an environment where I was accepted and people valued me. Maybe not my dad, but 80,000 people at Twickenham, the media, the IRB voting me as the best player in the world; all huge privileges but ultimately feeding an unhealthy insecurity.'

The tragedy is that all sports careers are finite and Ollie's not ending on his own terms made the pill all the harder to swallow. 'To be honest, you refuse to swallow it.'

Intriguingly, though, while the possibility of the Olympic comeback remained at the forefront of Ollie's mind, 'and then everything else would have got dropped', emerging at the back was the acceptance that it wouldn't. The result was a contingency plan–a job at PwC–even if he still didn't fully believe he'd need to activate it. Only on returning from the North Pole, donning a suit and tie, and sitting down at a desk in the PwC offices, did it dawn on him that 'this was never happening again. Ollie Phillips the rugby player was no more.

'And whilst it was an incredible career and I loved it, it all started falling apart when I stopped because the thing that gave me this sense of meaning, sense of purpose and sense of self-worth had gone. So, holy fuck, who's going to tell me that I'm great now, who's going to praise me?'

Ollie has never touched drugs and barely drinks, so, where many get their instant gratification from these quick fixes, he admits that he sought his in the fairer sex. When the Twickenham crowds were no longer screaming their appreciation of his talents, he had a series of women in his early thirties, well, screaming their appreciation of his talents. If you get my meaning.

'I had a vision of how I wanted my life to be,' he reflects. 'An incredible family, something that I didn't have as a kid because it was disjointed, a really strong, solid relationship with my wife, where she is my best friend, and beautiful kids that are loved unconditionally. But my behaviour was totally contradicting that, jeopardising that vision at every opportunity because my drivers were based on needing people to love me. I got my gratification from women and relationships, and multiple girlfriends simultaneously. And I'd convince myself that because I would never necessarily tell them that it was exclusive, I was absolving myself of any responsibility. I made some really bad decisions.'

This all came to a head just prior to leaving for the North Pole, when a girl he was seeing fell pregnant. They found out they had lost the baby at the 12 week scan but, rather than this being a tragedy for Ollie, he found himself feeling relieved. 'Even though we were quite rocky at the time, that [feeling of relief] sat badly with me because of the vision of what I wanted. But, because of my narcissistic ego, my reaction to her being in mourning, being distraught and understandably so because she didn't think she could have children, was that she was being miserable.'

The need for gratification took over.

'I start chatting to an ex-girlfriend, telling her she looks amazing and I'd love to see her, basically being a horrible human being. Then the current girlfriend finds this ream of messages and rightly tells me to leave. So, I move out, and am in a different flat two days before I leave for the Arctic. I come back and am full of my own ego because I'm all over the news for setting a world record at the North Pole. I go out, get with a girl and she comes back to my house and at one o'clock in the morning, the girlfriend who had been pregnant turns up on my doorstep, hysterical, uncontrollably bawling her eyes out, and begging to see me. So, I have my ex outside screaming, and she eventually falls asleep outside my front door. The other girl is in the bedroom doorframe wondering what the hell is going on and I'm pretending that the girl outside is just a nutty ex-girlfriend, even though I was going to have a kid with her and betrayed her, and she's now so emotionally distraught that she's a broken woman.

'And I just remember thinking, "Ollie, you've no-one to blame but yourself for this situation. You've created it. Neither of these people have done anything wrong, they've been nothing but genuine to you. And the truth is this is a repeat pattern. You've jeopardised or sabotaged situations that had all the ingredients to be exactly what you wanted and ruined them. Then you've been ignorant enough and arrogant enough to blame everybody else." So, that was the moment when I knew I needed to go and see somebody.'

Cue the therapy we mentioned, luckily available to Ollie through the support of the Rugby Players Association, 'the representative body and collective voice of professional rugby players', founded by former England international Damian Hopley. What followed was 'a shit load of hard work' to get to the crux of the deep-rooted problem that was driving his 'narcissistic and egotistical ego.'

He continues, 'We need to explore our mental health, because too often we can get caught up in the moment, and you don't realise that you're neglecting other parts of your life. You're busting a gut, pedal to the metal, and before you know it the whole world crumbles around you, and you suddenly realise it's too late.'

Even our conversation seems cathartic for Ollie and I'm honoured that he's willing to share. Now that the ego is in check, there is a vulnerability to him that is remarkable when you consider his CV. It really has been an astonishing couple of decades for him; on top of his playing highlights, he has also completed an MBA, worked as a TV commentator and pundit for Eurosport and Sky Sports, written a rugby column for London's business newspaper, City AM, coached the Wales women's sevens team, acted as Head of Olympic Performance for Rugby China, and set three more world records, one of which was for the highest game in history, played on a plateau 6,331 metres up Mount Everest. He now runs a thriving behavioural change platform, Optimist Performance. Anyone in their right mind would also call his post-rugby career a resounding success and I sense Ollie has finally come to the same conclusion.

But he has done so for him, not for anyone else. This, he explains, should be at the heart of elite performance: 'The first element of high performance is being aware of your drivers; why you are making decisions. That requires developing a willingness and an openness to be vulnerable, and it takes bravery and courage to admit that some drivers are going to be unhealthy in the long run. For example, insecurities that can be deep rooted in our childhoods, whether it's a difficult relationship with a parent or an event that's the trigger, can give rise to a determination to either prove people wrong or to feel liberated, strong, valued, important, successful. And then when you experience those feelings, in contrast to how you felt before amid the insecurities, it almost becomes addictive. You've suddenly found something you're really bloody good at and everyone's praising you. You want more, and more, and more. If your drivers, like mine were, are based on needing a reaction from someone else, then that's not healthy. Because you've got no control over the outcome, or how others will react. All you can do is hope. And that's a mug's game. Equally, if things are going well, you won't want things to change because of the perception that it's all bringing you success. And normally people only have these epiphany moments when it all starts to go wrong.'

Ollie is, it would seem, another of my interviewees who advocates for building self-awareness and this is also the key to sustained levels of high performance: 'Doing something for you, for the right reasons rather than for the gratification of someone else, is also how you get longevity. So, if you're turning up in the pissing rain in the middle of winter for a training session, great, but if you're only doing so because you need people to think you're incredible, it'll be short-lived. Whereas if you are fully in control of what you want, what you need as an individual and why you are doing this, then your energy is infinite. Because it won't change. You know that it's built on super solid foundations and there's a reason behind it all.'

Imagine a graph charting your performance levels over time. The line rises as you continue to excel but, if you're unclear as to what's underpinning it all, the energy will eventually peter out. The graph will ultimately peak and drop off again in the shape of a bell curve. Like Sir Bradley Wiggins, Adam Peaty and Mary Earps, the result will be burnout as you are left questioning your 'why'. Ollie agrees that 'there's different stages of high performance and how well you transition through those phases is critical. As you move through that performance curve, you need a really great level of self-awareness as to what's driving you. If you're unclear as to why you're putting in the graft, you'll struggle to produce consistent levels of performance. Eventually you crash down the other side.'

Of course, even if Ollie was disappointed not to live out his Olympic dream, his professional rugby playing, globe circumnavigating, world record breaking, successful businessing CV still puts most people's to shame.

***

In *The Sword in the Stone*—because you know by now I love a Disney quote—Merlin sings, 'Set your sights, upon the heights. Don't be a mediocrity.' Of course, Wart goes on to become King Arthur, which is just about as high as sights can be set. And as much as we'd love for Freddie to achieve greatness, we're not expecting him to overthrow the monarchy. I joke that we'd love him to play rugby for England but only the top percentile hit the lofty heights of performance that someone like Ollie can claim. So, what if you don't? What solace can us mere mortals take from not being in the top fraction of a fraction of elite performers on the planet? Is it fine being 'a mediocrity', or at least being average? And should we have contingencies, as Ollie did, or, if we're setting our sights on the heights, should we just go full whack at them with the risk that we might not hit them?

Ollie says, 'That depends on how willing and capable you are to accept and deal with the ramifications and fall out of disappointment. And, how thick-skinned and bloody-minded you are to keep going. That's a really dangerous line to walk but if you can genuinely give everything in the hope of achieving your dream and be content with having done so, you should be congratulating yourself. But that takes strength of character and there are not many people that will do that when they're so emotionally invested.

'It comes back around to building the self-awareness to know that you have done everything that you possibly could, but also being acutely aware as to why that thing is so important for you.

'You might not be a professional rugby player, but if you have that same level of dedication and application and your drivers are the right things, it'll manifest elsewhere. It's adapting the concept for different environments and how you excel in other areas of life. For example, if you really want to experience being part of an incredible team, build an environment of excellence and strive to be competitive, to challenge for honours, to be recognised for your behaviours and output as the best in your sector or industry, that is a strong set of values. It doesn't matter the arena that you're in. Similarly, having an incredibly healthy, vibrant relationship with your wife and your kids and your family; that's high performance too, just as much as winning a gold medal.'

Remember, in Chapter 4, how Michael Maisey said,

'That's the gold in life'? Ollie's is a similarly beautiful sentiment, coming from someone who, like Sir Bradley Wiggins, Adam Peaty and Mary Earps, has won his fair share of gold medals, even if they don't feature the Olympic rings.

The Olympic founder, Pierre de Coubertin, is credited with saying, 'Winning medals wasn't the point of the Olympics. It's the participating that counts.' Some might say that's a cop out mantra–second place is first loser, and all that–for all the athletes who *don't* win, many of whom dedicate their whole lives to the pursuit of their sport's most coveted prize. But, where today's society equates high performance to these perceived achievements, the sentiment here is that high performance shouldn't be driven by the outcome. People might not remember the athlete that comes second but if being remembered is your sole motivator, you're in it for the wrong reasons. More applicable is the *pursuit* of excellence–which we explored in the previous chapter–a consistent application of understanding the self, and being in total control of your emotions and what drives them.

Ollie concludes by saying, 'The rollercoaster ride that we're all on is driven by how we feel. How you feel ultimately determines the level of success that you believe you've achieved or not achieved. How we feel determines our emotions, our emotions fundamentally drive and shape our behaviours, and how we behave dictates our decision making. Depending on the situation, if you feel confident, encouraged, enthusiastic, fulfilled, you're more likely to reflect on your capability and experience as a positive one, and feel valued, irrespective of whether you've done a brilliant job.'

So, be more Merlin. Set your sights upon the heights and go at them with everything you've got. Give it your best shot. But be self-aware enough for that to be sufficient and take pride in the satisfaction of a job well done; or at least a job done as well as can be. While you're at it, be more Ollie Phillips, but in his self-aware, late 30s, rather than his adulation-seeking 20s. Work hard on understanding yourself, on **developing a level of cognisance and self-awareness,** and make sure your actions, your behaviours and your decisions are driven from a place of security and good health.

Chapter 21:
Finding Your Iceberg

I'm here to tell you, you're perfect just the way you are.
- Peter La Fleur

There you have it. Some advice, some rants and–for me–a cathartic penning of the ups and downs of my life. Hopefully you've taken as much from reading it as I have from having the various fascinating conversations and writing it.

If not, well you've got this far so it can't have been all bad. And claiming the experience was a waste of your time and money now would be the equivalent of sending an empty plate back to the chef, having mopped up the sauce with your last piece of bread, French-style, with a complaint that your steak wasn't cooked to your liking. So, no refunds, sorry.

As per the famous Dodgeball quote–no, not the 'If you can dodge a wrench, you can dodge a ball' one–you might be entirely confident you're 'perfect just the way you are.' If so, that's amazing. Crack on. Go back to your smug life, Smuggy Smuggerton McSmugface.

But, no offence, that's unlikely. Worryingly few people are who they truly want to be. They're seeking the success that society says they should be looking, rather than being content with their lot in life in the moment.

So, if my ramblings have had you thinking about how you could be more Maximus Decimus Meridius, Franz Stampfl, Henry Cookson or Andy Dufresne, or how you could take a leaf out of the books of any of my fascinating interviewees that have formed the basis of the preceding 20 chapters; if you've had an epiphany and been inspired to get more out of life; if reading this has sparked a desire to change just the tiniest part of your existence for the better, well, then you've got some work to do.

Because no-one likes change. Not even penguins.

Our Iceberg Is Melting, written by Dr John Kotter, the Konosuke Matsushita Professor of Leadership, Emeritus, at the Harvard Business School–so he probably knows his shit–tells the fable of a penguin colony in Antarctica. One of these waddling chaps, the hero of our tale, is an 'unusually curious and observant' little fellow, ironically called Fred.

Fred starts to notice that something is wrong. The structural integrity of the iceberg is in jeopardy because of the changing weather conditions. Melting ice is causing fissures and underground caves in the ice and there is a risk of water penetrating these, freezing, expanding and cracking the iceberg apart. So, some potentially pretty catastrophic consequences for our penguin folk.

Fred takes the issue to the senior penguin Leadership Council and expresses his concern. But 'As far back as any of the penguins could remember, they had always lived on that iceberg. "This is our home," they would tell you if you could ever find their world of ice and snow.'[120] So, any alternative would cause a great deal of panic and be a major upheaval. And Fred's no meteorologist, which is a stupid word, because it should really be someone who studies meteors. But that's a meteoriticist. The Latin for weather is *tempestas* so tempestologist would make much more sense and just sounds cooler. But Fred's not a meteorologist—or a tempestologist—and 'had no track record as a credible iceberg forecaster.'[121] He's just a curious and observant, mid-level penguin with a theory that he can't prove, and the penguin who *is* the resident meteorologist shouts him down, accusing Fred of 'wild speculation' and 'fear mongering'.

Fortunately, Fred has Alice on his side. Alice, Alice, who the fuck is Alice? Alice is the hard-ass penguin known for getting shit done, and she convinces the Leadership Council to host a general assembly to create a sense of urgency amongst the colony and get the ball rolling with their next course of action.

Melting strategy sessions, SWOT analyses, a bunch of confused penguins, an experiment with a glass bottle filled with water that freezes, expands and cracks the bottle, a seagull, and Dr John Kotter's eight step process of successful change later, and, well, spoiler alert coming up ... the colony ends up with a better outcome than its original situation. The penguins move to a 'better iceberg, larger and with richer fishing grounds.'[122]

Curious penguins aside, the fable's overarching message is that the world is changing and we must change with it. Dr Kotter says: 'I'm convinced that more and more and more people have to understand how the world is changing, the need for change, how change works when it works well, or [we're] going to have a heck of a time adapting to an increasingly turbulent environment that we find out there. And the rate of change is not going to slow down. The evidence is overwhelming about that.'

So, the question is, what is *your* iceberg? Your rock bottom, your lowest point, your 'extreme moment', as Ollie Phillips called it.

***

I said you've got work to do. That's because there are no two ways about it. There's no point sugar-coating it, dipping it in treacle and sprinkling it with Hundreds and Thousands; change is fucking hard. In Chapter 15 we talked about difficult emotions, such as grief, and the five stages of the Kübler-Ross Model. Intriguingly, this same model is more widely called the 'Change Curve', since we experience the same emotions when we go through change. We don't like change; we actively resent it because it goes against our basic instincts. In fact, we fear it because it is contrary to what we know is safe. It represents uncertainty and could impact our survival, so is a source of great anxiety.

Jim Hughes overcame that uncertainty when he made the enormous change of giving up a well-paid job running an engineering business in Australia, opting to start his own business whilst living as a digital nomad.

'I had no qualifications as an engineer,' he recalls, 'no experience, no knowledge of the industry and no contacts. As somebody who thrives in chaos, who loves it when the chips are down, the job was great for a while. It was exciting, it was a growth opportunity, I was learning loads. But, when the owner of the company slowly backed out of the door, amid the worst mining recession in Australia's history, leaving me with a corner office and no clue what I was doing, gradually the cracks started to appear. The enjoyment started to fade and the stress started to increase. Or maybe the stress had always been there, but I could suddenly see it. It was no longer being overshadowed by the positives. I was getting angrier. I was drinking more, but aggressive drinking, not fun drinking. I wasn't sleeping well. And I started to forget who I was. I started to lose that spark essentially. It's incredible the shit we do that doesn't serve us in the name of sticking to an identity that we have created for ourselves.'

A rock bottom doesn't have to involve drink–as it did for me–or drugs.

Referring again to Aasmah Mir's column, she went on to write, 'But I think success is actually finding the lowest point in your life – a horrible childhood, a job that you hated so much it made you ill, the most punishing relationship – and measuring how far you've come.' Which is lovely. For Jim, his iceberg of 'a job he hated so much' sparked a period of soul searching which unearthed the realisation that he had effectively been living a lie; that there had been a gap between the life that he was inspired to live and the reality of living it.

'I had made big life decisions before then,' he says, 'like moving to Canada, but they were all instinctive and fairly low risk. They came very easily. Whereas in Australia, I had to start quantifying how much that job was costing me, in terms of my health and my relationship.'

It led to Jim travelling the world as a digital nomad,

learning from different people and cultures. On his first day of nomadic living, he launched Untamed, his coaching business, which is centred around connection. Often, as Jim did, his clients have lost that connection with who they truly are and it takes a period of conscious reflection to rediscover that; to reconnect.

He reflects, 'I'd never had to consciously think about who I am, what I'm good at, what I like to do, what lifestyle I want to lead.'

Have you?

Dr Kotter's eight-step process is largely geared towards organisational change, exploring how to guide a team through the process, and considering the impact on a large number of individuals across different backgrounds, skill sets, and possibly even geographies. Components such as the vision and strategy, communications required to deliver them, and the need to engage colleagues in the process are overly complicated for our requirements, so Jim has simplified it to three steps. The Push, the Pull, and the Resistance. You need all three to make a change successfully.

As a precursor, part of Jim's focus is based around digitally detoxing and silencing the daily distractions that have given rise to a variety of unhealthy, modern habits.

Take the fairly new concept of 'phubbing'. Think about the last time you were having a conversation with someone and you subconsciously reached into your pocket to check your phone for notifications. You're guilty of phubbing; phone snubbing. A recent paper published in the Journal of Applied Social Psychology 'revealed that increased phubbing significantly and negatively affected perceived communication quality and relationship satisfaction.'[123] So our digital actions are causing us to have lower quality interactions. The irony being that a brief flick through a social media feed should, in theory, make us feel *more* connected but it is, in fact, causing all of our relationships to deteriorate.

For Jim, this connection is with each other but, more importantly, with ourselves. 'Everyone's different,' he says, 'but the only way we can connect is to silence that stuff at least temporarily and ask how do I feel in this moment? We need to distance ourselves from these daily distractions because we're adding layers that are stopping us connecting with who we really are. And the only way to really check in on what inspires us, on what we're driven by, on whether we're living authentically, is to make time and silence all that.'

We've explored comfort zones and wanting to just do the same old shit because we know that it's safe. We've gone through the reluctance to want to challenge ourselves even if we know it's going to do us good in the long run. On top of that, we even challenge our ability to make change by undermining its importance.

Change, then, takes conscious effort. It's about moving past these debilitating mindsets, even to the level of tweaking the language we use. Jim explains, 'Our subconscious can reinforce a narrative that isn't serving us. For example, we frequently say "find the time" to do something, when it's not like looking for your keys. The time is there to do the stuff; it's about *making* the time. When you say, "find the time," you are telling yourself that your most valuable time is better spent elsewhere. It promotes the mindset that your goal is one step further away; that much harder to reach.'

We're chatting on a stroll down a country lane in Wiltshire, and Freddie is strapped to my chest in a (very manly) sling. Jim points out, 'In contrast, you don't *find* the time to feed Freddie. No, it's absolutely sacrosanct. Everything else fits around it. The point is we *make* time for things that we value.'

Remember how we reframed language in Chapter 14? I'm certainly one for the power of the smallest things to change our outlook on how achievable something is and, if something as simple as our use of language can spark our greatest successes, I'm all for it. Crucially, though, if you can't make the time for something, there's no point making excuses or judging yourself. Rather, that should serve as the realisation that you're prioritising other things and now you have the awareness to do something about it.

So, how much do you value a connection with yourself? The answer should be 'a lot' and making yourself the priority can be the difference between *wanting* to change and actually doing so. In finding your iceberg.

Because it's only in identifying it that we can then seek to change it. Sounds blindingly obvious, doesn't it? But we're terrible at spotting there's even a need for change, let alone doing something about it.

Jim says, 'For us to seek change, we have to have a Push; a motivation to move away from the situation we are currently in. Until you realise that situation—the job, relationship or habit—is undesirable or painful, you are unlikely to change. Equally, if we have no alternative—the Pull—we're unlikely to make any change. And the third element is resistance. You've got the Push, you've got the

Pull, but these have to be great enough to overcome the million resistances you'll face that will get in your way and stop you making the change. There's always resistance.'

Let's walk through each of them and by the end of the chapter, you'll be 'itching like a man on a fuzzy tree'–a lyric from Elvis Presley's *I'm All Shook Up* and, no, I don't understand it either–to get out into the big, bad world and pursue your dreams.

There'll be nothing stopping you.

The Push

The basis of change is knowing where you are and where you want to get to. That can require being daring enough to take the leap into the unknown.

However, 'Doing daring things,' explains Jim, 'goes against our basic hardwiring of eating, reproducing and continuing to propagate the species. Change isn't in our makeup, so we've got to quantify how bad or painful our situation is. If we don't realise what the job, or the relationship, or the poor physical health, or bad habit is costing us emotionally, physically, financially, we're not going to make the change.

Let's, as Ollie Ollerton did, take the couch to five km analogy as an example.

'So, you're overweight. So what? The Push needs to be the motivation as a result of that. Maybe you're tired of getting out of breath walking up the stairs, maybe you feel insecure, or maybe you feel undesirable to other people, so you are unlikely to meet the woman or the man of your dreams. You have to ask what your situation is costing you and that takes honesty, that takes humility, and that takes courage.'

The Pull

'Motivation is a word that's overused, though, and isn't enough on its own. It only goes so far. We also need inspiration; the Pull. The trouble is motivation requires energy. If you rely purely on motivation to get you fit, you'll put your trainers on for the first few days but it's unsustainable. After a while, there's a net loss in energy, the willpower wears off and you stop or default to old habits.

'That's why you need to clarify what the alternative could be, visualise it, surround ourselves with people who already do it or share that vision, and then get to a point where it's a must-have, rather than a want. When you fall in love with the alternative, which is success, performance, presence, fulfilment, happiness, all of those other good things, then the change can start to become a reality.

'For example, I'll imagine doing this five km and how good I'm going to feel about myself, how I'm going to fit in my clothes, sleep better. Maybe I'll speak to other people who are really fit, get their opinion on it. Maybe I've tried it a little bit; I've run one km and that felt good. I got sweaty and felt the endorphins. I can see how running five km is going to be good for me physically and mentally, and encourage me to improve other areas of my life.

'So, you have to have a reason to move away from one thing and a reason to move towards another. Step one is motivation. Step two is inspiration. But a lot of people don't do step two. They know that they're not having a great time and want to change. And they're motivated, but motivation is not enough in isolation.'

The Resistance

No, not Muse's fifth studio album. The barriers. The hurdles. The things that are going to hold you back from making the change. Jim continues, 'You think, "I'd love to run a five km. But my job is getting in the way, I think it'll be painful, I'm feeling tired, lazy, I don't like the sensation of being out of breath, the weather's shit, I don't own a pair of trainers."

'The key thing is to understand the difference between a genuine resistance and the story we tell ourselves or other people. I believe most resistances come from fear, and we make them up ourselves.

'It could be a fear of failure. What if I can't finish the five km? What if I do it and I hurt myself?

'It could be a fear of judgement. Running a five km should be achievement enough, but what if I get a really bad time and I get judged and laughed at?

'It could be a fear of rejection. What if I get judged by others who don't want me to change? Perhaps they resent me for wanting to make improvements in my life. Maybe they want me to stay overweight so that they can feel ok about themselves. Your environment and people you spend time with are key in your ability or willingness to change because they can be a major resistance. You need to ensure your friends are able to support you in your change and encourage you to do the five km, rather than saying, "Mate, don't bother, let's go for burgers." Rejection can also take the form of being told no, with a job application or asking someone out on a date, for example.

'It could even be a fear of success. One of our biggest needs is certainty and the way we meet that need is through our stories. We create stories of who we are and what we're capable of. Over time these develop and become ironclad. We rely on them in order to know who we are and where we fit. If our story is that we're not athletic, or we don't deserve a better job, or we're stupid, that has enormous power. The prospect of succeeding in something which goes against the story can provide an unbelievably powerful resistance to making the change.

'Those resistances can stop or at least massively slow down any change and the scarier the thing is, the greater the resistance is.'

The three steps bring us neatly back round to humility and self-awareness because to affect change, you've got to be humble enough to admit your current situation isn't serving you, and curious enough to explore how it could.

***

All of our icebergs are relative.

Jim's iceberg–in 'a job [he] hated so much it made [him] ill'–was losing sight of who he was. The realisation that the job was costing him his health and causing his relationship to suffer prompted him to embark on an incredible journey of self-discovery that has led to him running a successful and thriving business. His conscious exploration of who he was led to him taking destiny into his own hands.

'I like business, entrepreneurship and growth, and I

like travel and adventure. The more I learned about the digital nomad concept, the more it sounded so much better than what I was doing. I could do step one, which was appreciate the situation I was in and quantify the cost easier. That made step two exciting; it was still thriving in chaos and it started to fall into place.'

Jim's resistances 'were overcome bit by bit, kind of chipped away at.' Quitting the job was daunting but taking the plunge and telling his boss that he was leaving 'removed any shred of doubt that it was going to happen.' His partner, now wife, 'could have been a major resistance but she was keen to do the same thing.' He had money in the bank so could start travelling. 'And to be honest, there was also ignorance about the perils of starting my own business and how hard that is but I didn't need much capital to get going and I was going to get to help people. So, on the face of it, it was a huge, risky, life-changing decision but it didn't feel like it was because I had gone through those three stages.'

The good news is that your iceberg isn't melting but you can still be more penguin. Unless you're fleeing Ukraine or Palestine, you don't face a crisis of such unfathomable proportions that your problem is insurmountable. The world's changing and you can change with it, if you're open to it. You can change *your* world if you have a framework around which you can base your intentions.

There are no shortcuts, though. You have to work through all three steps for the change to stick. And you need to start by being more connected. By having the humility to accept that you aren't exactly where you want to be in life and the inclination to do something about it. If you're not entirely happy, do away with the narrative that is stopping you from being everything you want to be, having everything you want to have, and doing everything you want to do. Make–don't try and find–time for yourself to identify your iceberg. Change it.

Oh, and after a while, take a look back and measure how far you've come.

Chapter 22:
And One More Thing

Be interested, selfless, kind, curious, authentic, open to different experiences, etc.
- **My interviewees**

Ok, a few more things actually, because I asked a question to a number of my stellar–if I do say so myself–interviewees over the last few months and was fascinated by the variety of their responses. It was a deliberately open question that I invited my guests, and also my discerning wife, to interpret as they saw fit.

The question: 'What makes you good at what you do?'

Here are their responses in an advicey listicle-type thing, because that seems to be the 'in' format that the BuzzFeeds of the world are going for these days.

Ben Harrison: Be interested

'You need to be genuinely interested in and committed to what you do, with a willingness to keep learning. That requires being true to yourself and your values, while still being able to be collaborative with others and compromise. Hard work is important too.

'Also, for me, I think loyalty and caring about others and wanting them to do the best they can makes me good at what I do.'

Thomas Nabbs: Be open to different experiences

'I focus on my strengths and bring people in to help me with my weaknesses to fill the gaps. How do I build the self-awareness to identify my strengths and weaknesses? That's easy; through many and varied opportunities and experiences, and integrating and connecting with different people from different walks of life. It's not enough to just focus on one thing; you've got to experience different micro-cultures and social norms. When you do that, you start getting feedback on what you're good at, you get it from different perspectives, and you start to build a picture.'

Michael Maisey: Be experienced

'I'd say it's my lived experience. People come to me not because I learned something from a textbook, or have qualifications or accolades. It's because I've been to hell and found a way home.'

Esmée Gummer: Be selfless

'I have a genuine passion for wanting other people to feel good and don't believe anything I do in my work is for myself. Everything I do, talk about and preach about, is done in the hope that at least one person can take something from it. I care about what others are getting out of it, rather than what I'm getting out of it. If at the end of the day, all I get is people telling me, "Well done, you", I haven't done my job.'

Caroline Outterside: Be kind and be curious

'I'd qualify this by saying that I help unhappy people and I want to help them feel better. In order to do this I have specialist knowledge and training but also some personal qualities that are essential to this role.

'The therapy concept that I identify with most is from the great Carl Rogers (the father of the humanistic psychology movement), which is to have "unconditional positive regard" for every client. That encompasses and facilitates kindness, curiosity and empathy and these help me be the best I can be for each client, increasing their self-awareness and facilitating their self-expression in order to understand themselves.

'For me, kindness has to be at the heart of helping people as a good therapist, strongly followed by being curious about what makes people tick and having a fascination with the uniqueness of each person you meet. What has shaped this person to be who they are and how they respond in life? What is their story so far? I always back up kindness and curiosity with genuine empathy, a willingness to stand in their shoes and an understanding of their situations, feelings, thoughts and experiences, whether it is a temporary or unexpected period in their life, or something that has been holding them back and impacted their life. I am fascinated by how complex we are and how we function, and that curiosity extends to a love of continually learning.

'I also need to be able to share, in the most appropriate way for the person sat in front of me, some knowledge of the psychology of the human mind and body, to help them understand what the natural and inevitable psychological and biological responses to difficult life situations are. Boundaries are important too, clear but kindly stated, with compassion. Many people in therapy have lost their ability to be self-compassionate, they are harsh on themselves, and so, compassion in the therapeutic relationship is the best platform for someone to build this important self-talk and self-soothing skill.'

Henry Cookson: Be authentic and be empathetic

'I put the fact that we could do the Pole of Inaccessibility down to a lack of originality on humanity's part. Everyone is just following the crowd. How many thousands of people try to climb Everest every year and most of them are paying a hundred grand to get pushed to the top? There are beautiful untouched peaks out there that you could have to yourself; isn't that beauty part of the challenge? And social media allows you to fake it until you make it. Everyone wants to go from zero to hero straight away. No one wants to learn their discipline or become an apprentice and really understand their craft any-more. So, I struggle with the world at the moment where authenticity is taking a battering because, if there was one word I think which would encompass everything that I stand for, it's 'authenticity'.

'Otherwise, it took me a very long time to work out my talents; I have a weird lack of self-awareness in some respects. I'm pretty logical when I need to be but I've also got a creative side, which don't often come hand in hand. And I can make people comfortable. When I started guiding people, I didn't have years of experience behind me but I had this intuition on how to nudge, encourage and push people.

'Guiding comes down to not cutting corners, not being unsafe, and risk management, that goes without saying. But it's also the psychology of it. It's how to read people, nudge them, get their confidence up. And because I came from civvie street, I could translate that. If you are some Norwegian fucking polar god who's been born attached to a pair of skis and all you know is hardcore shit and age six you're sleeping in snow holes, how are you going to empathise with a hedge fund trader who wants to do something amazing but all they know is business suits and St Tropez?

'The more alpha someone is, the less likely they're going to confide in someone about their weaknesses. But having this depression, the gift of it is you have empathy, you understand people, you can relate to that weakness and you're not just in your own fucking bubble of chest beating glory. Therefore, when it came to the decision of how do I make this my career, and do I go down the polar explorer route or do I become the humble guide, the humble guide was the only way.'

Matt Fynn: Be relentless

'The first thing I think is, "Who said I was good?" Is that negative or is that a good thing? Very rarely would I say I'm good at anything really, but I don't see that in a negative way because that's what makes me good at things. Bringing it back to the running, I came third in my first ultra, out of 2,000 people. Logically I should think, "That's bloody amazing, I'm great." But could I have done better? It's the same for all my races. It's great to come on the podium or fourth in a 200-miler, but why didn't I come third or why did the guy in front of me finish before I did? So, I'm always striving for more. It's not resting on my laurels and always having a high standard that I expect from myself.

'But I'm also very aware that I don't give myself enough slack, for example my internal voice is harsh to myself when I miss a run. Although being aware of it and actually giving myself slack are two different things. I often wonder at what point in life I'll be able to comfortably relax without thinking, "I should be doing something right now." Maybe having children will allow me to sit back–as you have done–slow down, take stock, and simply be present. Although I fear I'll go the other way: "Now's the time to show these kids that anything can be achieved." It'll be interesting how that stage of my life plays out.

'Ultimately, I try not to overthink it; I just get on with the grind. I think there is peace to be found in just getting on with things.'

Sonja Jenkins: Be empathetic

'I had some personal trauma early on in my marriage and as a parent, and was certainly ill-equipped to deal with any of it. I did not have any counselling; it wasn't even thought about. But, when a local judge, who was seeing a lot of families go through divorce and the repercussions on their children, started a free counselling service called Parenthood, I thought I could help and offer some support.

'I think having my own experiences of trauma helps to see a problem in a nonjudgmental way and help the person I am working with to make decisions for themselves. I hope I bring empathy, compassion and common sense to the situation.

'To unpack a problem gives me great satisfaction and I have always considered it a great privilege for people to allow me into their lives at a very difficult time for them.'

Chris Baugh: Be unflinchingly and brutally honest

'What I do, first of all, is give people permission, encourage, and in some cases even oblige people to be brutally honest with themselves about what they think and feel, about the world and about what they're doing in it. That is an important part of the process that I take people through in coaching because, without what I consider to be that brutal self-appraisal, we can't be sure that the goals that we're setting, or that we're working towards, are going to make a significant impact in that person's life. And why do I think that I'm good at that process? Well, I think that I am unflinchingly and brutally honest with myself. More specifically I would say I am and always have been willing to at least consider the worst possible explanation for why I do something or behave in a certain way. That means that when it's probably more popular to assume there's a perfectly reasonable and justifiable reason that I might be saying or doing something, which would get me off the hook and not make me look bad, I will always dig deeper in myself and explore if there's a more sinister reason. If that's the case, why is it? And because I do that for myself, I think it allows me to do it for other people.'

Rich Sheppard: Be yourself and be caring

'There are two things that I always try to do that I learned quite early on in teaching jiu jitsu. One is I always try to be myself and represent myself honestly. That way you live and die by who you really are. Then, if someone doesn't like who you are, at least you've given the best possible account of yourself. I made the mistake, when I first started, of trying to be someone different; more serious, more strict, even, but it was inauthentic and I didn't enjoy it. If I'd been successful like that, I'd have had to carry on with something that was making me unhappy. So, I realised quite quickly that being authentic is really important.

'The other thing is that I genuinely care for my students. Their safety is important, their enjoyment and development are important; I want the best for them.

'Of course, you also have to enjoy what you do too. So, I suppose that's three things! Making sure you're genuine, making sure you really do care, and enjoying it.'

Ollie Phillips: Be authentic

'Because it's me and no-one is better at being me than me. It's authentic and it's heartfelt. It might not always be the finished and polished article but it comes with great intention and with a personal signature rubber stamp of being genuine Ollie Phillips.'

Jim Hughes: Be intuitive

'I'd say there are two things that allow me to do what I do effectively, the first of which is having my own self-awareness; being able to connect with what's going on for me, in terms of my fears, my beliefs, my narrative, my inner monologue. Because I believe that you can only connect with other people to the extent that you have connected with yourself. I noticed that my coaching work became much more impactful the deeper I went on my own personal journey.

'The second thing is being able to sit and listen from an unattached perspective to a client and knowing the difference between what is being said and what they mean. That is based on intuition and I think we're all intuitive, much more so than we give ourselves credit for, but we struggle to connect with our intuition in a modern world which is very fast and filled with distractions.

'I think the root of both of those things is trust; trust in myself and trust that by creating the space with an individual, the truth is going to emerge. It's less about learning, knowledge, systems and theory, and more about holding the space and being intuitive.'

Krista: Be positive

'A positive mindset and self-belief. Life is an obstacle course of risks and rewards and you have to keep running the course despite the setbacks if you're going to keep getting rewarded. And I've found that the rewards get better with age as I've learnt more about myself and I've made better use of my time and energy to navigate life. But without that underlying positivity and belief, I think I'd just grind to a halt.'

And if you were to ask me: Enjoy it and be consistent

Picking up on the concept of unconscious competence that we explored in Chapter 20, I'd say that to truly be good at something, you firstly have to enjoy doing it, and then you have to do it consistently to the extent that it becomes second nature. It goes without saying that you will be more inclined to invest time and effort into the things that you enjoy, and keen to continually improve to the extent that you suck less at them and become 'good' at them. This also picks up on Ollie Phillips' point that you should do what you do *for you*. There is little sense in flogging something that you take little or no pleasure from, or doing something for the wrong reasons.

And it may sound obvious, but in order to find what you enjoy, you have to try stuff. Lots of stuff. Rugby, running and BJJ have been my things, but maybe tiddlywinks or fencing are yours. So, put yourself out there. Experience and experiment. And don't be afraid to suck.

***

A couple more things before I wrap up:

Be on the look out

Eight days after Freddie 'arrive[d] on the planet and, blinking, step[ped] into the sun'[124] (final Disney reference, I promise), it was the annual anticlimax known as New Year's Eve. With no plans because we were so tired our eyeballs were aching, Krista and I received a last minute invite to a low-key dinner with friends on the outskirts of Bath. An agreement to 'pop in' turned into us arriving for dinner and having a very relaxed evening chatting, passing Freddie around for cuddles, Krista enjoying a guilt-free couple of drinks for the first time in nine months, and not noticing the time fly by because we were in good company. As the clock struck midnight and the fireworks were set off over London's Embankment, we kissed each other, told each other we loved each other and pondered how our lives would be changing for the better in the years to come. It was a perfect evening.

The point? The best moments are always the unexpected and unplanned ones. Make sure you spot them.

Be polite

'Manners Maketh Man': a quote attributed to William Wykeham, founder of Oxford University's New College and former Chancellor of England, but decidedly cooler when Harry Hart, Colin Firth's suave, slick and stylish spy character in *Kingsman: The Secret Service*, delivers the line before clattering the living shit out of a group of youves. It helps that he's wielding an umbrella-ballistic shield hybrid.

But that's not the point. The point is he's had 'a rather emotional day' and they're very rude, calling him 'granddad' and not leaving him in peace to finish his 'lovely pint of Guinness'. And he teaches them a valuable lesson; mind your manners. Your Ps and Qs.

So, be polite. Especially to people carrying umbrellas. You never know.

Chapter 23:
Ready, Freddie?

If you haven't found it yet, keep looking.
- **Steve Jobs**

By now you may have realised that I love a cultural reference and they're many and varied in this chapter, starting with Jane Austin's *Emma*, which features the line, 'One man's style must not be the rule of another's.'

There's simply no denying they knew their style back in the Regency Era, when Jane Austin was penning her masterpieces. 'Colin Firth looked like a prat dressed in a tailcoat and cravat,' said no-one ever. Nor was there a single woman that didn't go weak at the knees for Regé-Jean Page, the ridiculously handsome half Zimbabwean who plays the Duke in *Bridgerton*. Although don't get me started on the absurdity that half the cast is black. Don't get me wrong, I'm all for a bit of racial diversity and inclusion but I'm also for a bit of historical accuracy, and it gets a bit silly when Queen Charlotte and half of the English pageantry are black. Or of colour. Or whatever the most current way of saying it is.

But I don't want to discuss equality-gone-mad or how our standards have dropped since the reign of the Mad King George. I could sound off about Crocs, obviously, skinny jeans on men, sweaters that come with holes in them as part of the design and what Sam Smith wore to the 2023 Brit Awards for several chapters. Google it if you fancy a laugh. Incidentally, don't get me started on 'they' as a pronoun. How the fuck can a person, as in *one*, individual, solitary person, be plural?

No, it's not the decline of our fashion sense over the course of the centuries—or our butchering of English pronouns—that intrigues me. It's the perils of trying to serve others; of trying to toe society's line, be it through the influence we discussed all the way back in Chapter 1, or just plain stupidity. I think stupidity in Sam Smith's case, given those trousers come with a warning that reads: 'Always use talcum powder inside before use'[125].

But, if you want to wear inflatable trousers that require you to dust yourself with talcum powder, be my guest. Just make sure you're doing it *for you*, and not because a designer thinks they are a symbol of body positivity, or some such bollocks. Do it to make yourself happy, not others.

Doing so requires self-awareness of what makes you tick; your drivers, your motivations, your 'why'. And the inextricable link to mental fitness has been a running theme throughout my interviews with adventurers, endurance athletes, world record holders, coaches, therapists and more.

It's no coincidence that Chris Baugh, Sonja Jenkins

and Jim Hughes all made the connection between mental fitness and self-awareness independently of each other. Ollie Ollerton talked about building a better understanding of how our operating system works to contradict our negative mindsets and rewrite our programming, while Ollie Phillips spoke of 'building the self-awareness to know that you have done everything that you possibly could' in the pursuit of your goals.

Maybe these guys, albeit from wholly different backgrounds and fields of expertise, are onto something. If they're not, this book has been a monumental waste of time, so I'm plumping for the fact that they are.

As I wrote in Chapter 12, I see mental fitness as the ability to, well, survive life and all the shit that it throws at us on a daily basis. But that's the cynical, ranty, negative spin which I've advocated against, so, perhaps more importantly, it's also the ability to recognise the gold in life that Michael Maisey talked about.

Because 'Dee human world, it's a mess,' but there's also a lot of good in it if you look for it.

For example, the lady who approached me on a dog walk to offer me a tube of used tennis balls for our fox red labrador, Harvey, that she was otherwise going to drop at the local charity shop. Or the young boy, also on a dog walk, who turned to his father to innocently ask: 'Why don't dogs don't go to school?' The father, incidentally, quizzed the boy: 'Why do you think dogs don't go to school?' But his attempt to deflect was met with resistance when the boy simply responded, 'I dunno.' In a tone as if to say, 'Don't deflect. And in hindsight, the answer's beneath me, so forget I even asked.'

In the same vein, whilst Krista and I were perusing shop windows on holiday in Fowey, Cornwall, I spotted one of those wooden plaque-things that you hang in your loo, with the caption: 'Today I will be happier than a seagull with a stolen chip.' Typically, for August in Britain, it was drizzling and many would have seen this as a bad situation. Yet Krista and I were blissfully happy on a grey stroll with Harvey. Far from the rain dampening our spirits, it got us thinking about alternative holidays and the scenarios that might have had us ruing the fact that things weren't perfect. 'If we were in Mauritius, who knows, maybe I'd be complaining that my pina colada was taking too long to arrive,' Krista quipped.

Another shop window loo sign read: 'I'd sooner be in my caravan.' Quite why anyone would want a caravan is beyond me, but I suppose that's the point. Each to their own. Happiness is relative and if you're a seagull, or a caravaner, or an owner of a pair of inflatable trousers, there's a branch on the happiness tree for you.

While we're on trees … another example: in response to the vandalism of the Sycamore Gap tree, I posted my thoughts on LinkedIn, which I know makes me one of 'those people' that bores everyone with personal musings and mundane life updates on a platform that's intended for professional connection, but I felt something had to be said. I posted:

> This goes well beyond the boundaries of professional chat, which (I think) is what LinkedIn is for, but it needs saying. Two months ago, Krista and I were stood underneath the Sycamore Gap Tree. After ceremonially watching Robin Hood: Prince of Thieves the night before, the tree – hundreds of

years old, in a dramatic dip in Hadrian's Wall, with the Northumberland countryside stretched out behind it – had an almost mystical beauty to it. So, to say that I am incandescent with rage at the news that the tree was felled overnight in what can only be described as an act of incomprehensible vandalism, would be an understatement. It is senseless sh!t like this that makes me question humanity on a depressingly frequent basis. In a world of mounting problems surrounding our climate, mindless destruction of nature has to be up there amongst the most sordid of crimes. It's not like tearing down statues of historic slave-traders – although I disagree with such actions, but that's probably for another time. No-one has gained anything. We've all lost something.

A response warmed my heart:

> The world is full of absolute ********s. I share your fury, but even though it's hard to see at times, the world is also full of absolute heroes and kindness and love. Better to think on that.

And you know what? I will. Because I'd rather make the best of a bad situation. And I should really stop being so cynical, ranty and negative, and force myself to see some of the good in the world, because in the moment Zoe the midwife handed Freddie to Krista, covered in blood and balling his eyes out–a sound that was initially the most wonderful sound I'd ever heard but now curdles my blood at the thought that he might be in any sort of distress–the mess that the world is in seemed to evaporate.

And it's the world he will grow up in.

As for young Freddie, in Queen's 50s-style rock 'n' roll tribute to Elvis Presley, *Crazy Little Thing Called Love*, written in five minutes by Freddie Mercury and described as 'stunning in its simplicity' by Billboard[126] magazine, Mercury's band mates ask him in their backing vocals, 'Ready, Freddie?'

So, are you? Ready, Freddie?

Of course, when it comes to Freddie, the question I should really be asking is if *I'm* ready? Because, in that same moment, words cannot do justice to the mix of emotions I felt.

Agony, at seeing Krista go through such a painful ordeal, enduring hour after hour of excruciating pain, her entire body sometimes convulsing as a result of the stress it was under, such that no man could ever imagine. Being kicked in the balls every five minutes all day long wouldn't come close.

Pride, at her achievement and her sheer determination to, somehow, despite being delirious with exhaustion, push through almost three hours of active labour, some 12 hours after the contractions had initially started. Any woman–and I must stress *woman*–that goes through childbirth is a hero in my book and deserves a medal. In fact, all the fucking medals.

Helplessness, at my inability to ease her pain and relative insignificance in the process. All I could really do to avoid being a completely useless lemming was hold an electric fan in one hand and her water bottle in the other, whilst also trying to dab her forehead with a cold towel and offer some vague words of encouragement that didn't result in her telling me to fuck off out of the room because 'you did this to me'.

Love, pure as pure can be, at the sight of him. Some babies are ugly. There, I said it. But not Freddie. He was perfect, yet so tiny he didn't seem real. I couldn't help but sob tears of joy at this arrival and simultaneously felt just as vulnerable as he was, understanding in that moment what it means to be completely devoted to something. As for how I'll ever drive faster than 15 mph with him in the car, for fear of an accident, or go longer than three minutes without checking he's breathing, I really don't know.

And that was just the first few seconds. Nor do I know how the hell I'm supposed to cope with the rest of the inevitable ups and downs of parenthood. I mean, what do I do when he brings home his first girlfriend? Clap him on the back and say, 'Atta boy, son', or take him to one side to warn him of the perils of having your heart broken? At least he's not a girl and I don't have to be the father standing in the doorway with a baseball bat, eyeing up some young scrote and asking, 'What do you want with my daughter?'

What I do know is that Krista and I will devote every fibre of our being to guiding him through the tumultuous shit show that we call life—hey, I didn't say *when* I was going to stop being so cynical—and its multitudinous hurdles and pitfalls. I can't protect him from each and every one of them— some he'll have to figure out on his own—but wherever possible I'll endeavour to be a helping hand, a sounding board, a confidant, a coach and a guiding light if it's ever dark.

***

Your next cultural reference comes in the shape of Cat Stevens' *Father and Son*, which was a firm favourite during the summer I was in New Zealand, spent at a friend's bach [beach house] wakeboarding, drinking 'swappa crates' [wooden crates of 745 ml bottles] of Tui and Speights, and sitting around bonfires on Matarangi Beach, on the idyllic Coromandel Peninsula. With Stevens' distinctive vocals gently wafting over a beautifully strummed melody, it is a gorgeous song and has stood the test of time as one of his most enduring. But I didn't appreciate its sad undertone in the context of fatherhood and finding your way in the world until recently.

Its words tell of an exchange between father and son. The father wishes for his son to 'Find a girl, settle down' and attempts to convince him that, while he may want to experience what life has to offer, there's no need to rush around like a headless chicken, trying to find his place in the world:

> You're still young, that's your fault
> There's so much you have to know
> Find a girl, settle down
> If you want you can marry
> Look at me, I am old, but I'm happy
> I was once like you are now, and I know that it's not easy
> To be calm when you've found something going on
> But take your time, think a lot.

The father doesn't like change and, while it's safe advice, it's archaic, unadventurous and contrary to everything we've discussed, particularly mental fitness, self-awareness, experiencing everything there is to experience and pushing our limits. But if I can't get on board with this advice, the next two of the father's lines really grate on me:

> For you will still be here tomorrow,
> But your dreams may not.

Because I sincerely hope that Freddie's dreams—whether they're of playing rugby for England or joining The Royal Ballet … but hopefully playing rugby for England—won't die off overnight, or at the first failed attempt. If he has his heart set on something, provided he's happy in the moment and aspiring to it because *he* wants to aspire to it, I hope he'll have the gumption to go at it until he succeeds. And if he doesn't succeed, but has given it absolutely everything he can, I hope he'll be content in the knowledge that he tried. Krista and I also hope that we have the awareness to recognise what brings him most joy and do our best to encourage him to do his best at it. Like being an England rugby player.

Fortunately, the son agrees with me. He counters; he's anxious to go on a journey of learning right away, even if he might not be able to explain why. Maybe that's following his dream, maybe that's discovering his dream; either way, he knows he has to make his own way.

Shy of tiddlywinks and fencing, I've given most things a go. My only rules are that I'll never ice-skate or ride a horse. Because, in all honesty, they scare the shit out of me. Why would you willingly sit on top of a half-tonne animal that could throw you off and trample you at any point? Otherwise, taking up Brazilian jiu jitsu was a new martial art itch that needed scratching and it's now—outside of the time I spend with my family—what I'm most happy doing.

And Freddie, how will *he* know what he's most happy doing? Well, we'll also do our best to encourage him, à la Steve Jobs' 'keep looking' quote, to experience as broad a range of activities and adventures as possible. As I mentioned in the Introduction, along the way we'll no doubt mess things up constantly, but if we don't scar poor Freddie for life in the process, I reckon we'll have nailed parenthood. Hopefully he'll mess things up constantly too. And I say 'hopefully' because it's only through trying, failing and learning that he'll find his way in the world. Into the England rugby team.

Charlie Sheen's jingle-writing alcoholic, gambling-obsessed, womanising lothario character in *Two and a Half Men* might not be the best role model for Freddie, but this line in Season 2, Episode 15–*Smell the Umbrella Stand*– struck me as interesting: 'There are no bad ideas. There's just a lack of will to execute them.' In other words, give everything a go and give everything the best go you can. Apart from ice-skating or horse-riding.

With that in mind, what about you, dear reader, are *you* ready? To find your way in the world?

If you've done so already, bully for you. Great job. But maybe keep one eye open to the possibility that you could be shutting yourself off to more opportunities around the corner. After all, you've got your whole life ahead of you. I've just turned 40 and, as the saying goes, this is where life begins.

In Chapter 4, Lisa Simpson's advice to Bart was 'To develop a new and better identity'. That's not to say we can't be content with who we are; we also discussed how we can be more present in the moment, and I stand by that.

But the concept of continually seeking to better ourselves is one that I've attempted to broach throughout the book.

Whether you want to be more Meridius, Mallory, Fynn or Phillips is up to you. Whichever path you choose, remember that shit happens. Henry Cookson spoke of ensuring your mind is in the right place. For that to be the case, you have to know where you want your mind to be. When things get hard, your mind will tell you to stop. So, you have to know your 'why'. If you do, the 'how' will be a hell of a lot easier.

'How' Freddie will make his way in the world remains to be seen. I have no doubt he'll be desperate to discover his independence at some point and when that day comes, maybe I'll write another book to discuss the emotions I feel about him flying the nest. For the time being, though, you'll have to excuse me. I've a tiny human to raise.

Now then, Freddie, where's that rugby ball? You need to practise your spin pass.

Acknowledgements

If I'm honest, this book didn't really start life as a book; it started as a vague idea that it might be fun to jot down a few thoughts on the world as Krista and I learned that we were due to be bringing life into it. But after penning a few words, and then a few more, conversations with some of the fascinating people that I've met along my life's path seemed to be a natural progression, to discuss some of the themes raised.

And the kindness of those people—my knowledgeable and inspiring interviewees—in terms of donating their time, and recounting their experiences and expertise, has allowed me to fill in the many blanks of what would otherwise have probably been a structureless stream of drivel. That they all did so without asking for anything in return has restored my faith in humanity; long lost, if that wasn't clear from the Introduction.

So, in order of appearance, my huge thanks go to: Ben Harrison, Thomas Nabbs, Michael Maisey, Esmée Gummer, Ollie Ollerton, Caroline Outterside, Henry Cookson, Matt Fynn, Sonja Jenkins, Chris Baugh, Rich Shepperd, Ollie Phillips and Jim Hughes.

Throughout my life I've been blessed to have a simply wonderful group of people around me. From the 'band of brothers' that I'm lucky to call my closest friends to the lifelong bonds formed on the rugby field, these absolute legends have stuck by me through the rollercoaster that has been large chunks of my life, never failing to lend a supportive ear, console, comfort and encourage. Among them, Ollie and Rich deserve special mention. I think the true mark of a friendship is that you don't feel jealousy; you root for each other. You can also have conversations about complete bollocks and come away thinking it was the best chat you've ever had. You can tell friends anything and everything, and there's no judgement; they won't be thinking 'What a twat.' And if they are, they'll tell you you're being a twat, because they care.

As for my family, my wonderful family, I've always said that my brother Simon is the absolute nicest human being you could ever hope to meet and it fills me with joy that we've never had the type of brotherly rivalry that can cause a rift. He's kind and caring, and has always kept me grounded. Meanwhile, my parents have guided me, supported me, and, more often than not, lovingly mopped up much of the mess that I've left in my wake throughout the years, doing so without their love faltering or wavering. Their unfailing partnership is something Krista and I will aspire to as we bring up Freddie, while we'll also endeavour to teach him the humility and honesty that both our parents have instilled in us along the way.

And Krista. My partner in crime. My best friend. My soul mate. My fairytale ending. The other pea in my slightly crazy pod, as I said; my wife has allowed me to understand the true meaning of love. She fills me with inspiration on a daily basis with her relentless energy and her total devotion to our family and her friends.

In fact, it is her compassion and willingness to put others before herself that has seen her, as she gracefully makes her way through life, collect countless people along the way, in a spider's web of friendships whose size and complexity constantly confuses me.

She has never shirked at the prospect of me going off and doing a crazy challenge, rather she has been the one either running alongside me, feeding me ice lollies, or scraping me off the floor.

And she is an amazing mother, sensible and sensitive, and her attention to detail is impeccable. In that way, we complement each other perfectly. When we're presented with a problem, Krista will research everything to the hilt and I'll fly by the seat of my pants, but between us, we'll always come up with a pretty solid solution. Ours is a relationship based on mutual respect and complete equality. We laugh every day, we don't have secrets. It might be a cliché, but I am the luckiest guy in the world.

Lastly, Freddie, for being the light in my life that I didn't even know I needed; for filling a space in my heart that I didn't know was there. Words cannot do justice to how much I love you.

Thank you.

References

Introduction

[1] https://www.dailystar.co.uk/real-life/woman-who-identifies-dog-sleeps-32352929
[2] *Dummy*, by Matt Coyne, p.334
[3] *Fight Club*, by Chuck Palahnuik, p.134

Chapter 1

[4] *Fight Club*, by Chuck Palahnuik, p.168
[5] *Fight Club*, by Chuck Palahnuik, p.174
[6] *Fight Club*, by Chuck Palahnuik, p.46
[7] *Sapiens: A Brief History of Humankind*, by Yuval Noah Harari, p.4
[8] https://www.independent.co.uk/news/science/apollo-11-moon-landing-mobile-phones-smartphone-iphone-a8988351.html
[9] *World Obesity Atlas 2023*: https://s3-eu-west-1.amazonaws.com/wof-files/World_Obesity_Atlas_2023_Report.pdf
[10] https://www.who.int/health-topics/mental-health#tab=tab_2
[11] https://yougov.co.uk/topics/politics/survey-results/daily/2024/01/08/6a2ad/1
[12] *Fight Club*, by Chuck Palahnuik, p.166

[13] Various sources, e.g. The Times: https://www.thetimes.co.uk/article/the-ultimate-influencer-pad-inside-lorna-luxes-ghost-house-5hxwst6pm

[14] Forbes: https://www.forbes.com/advisor/business/social-media-statistics/

[15] https://www.insiderintelligence.com/content/digital-trust-benchmark-2022

[16] https://www.cambridge.org/core/services/aop-cambridge-core/content/view/5A04D331090B1CFB889ECDA8B8250D51/S0007125020001592a.pdf/trends_in_generalised_anxiety_disorders_and_symptoms_in_primary_care_uk_populationbased_cohort_study.pdf

[17] https://www.statista.com/outlook/dmo/digital-advertising/social-media-advertising/worldwide

[18] https://influencermarketinghub.com/influencer-marketing-benchmark-report/

[19] https://www.uhhospitals.org/blog/articles/2018/02/90-percent-of-brain-development-occurs-in-first-2000-days

[20] *Invisible Influence: The Hidden Forces that Shape Behavior*, by Jonah Berger, p.2

[21] *Invisible Influence: The Hidden Forces that Shape Behavior*, by Jonah Berger, p.11

[22] *Sapiens: A Brief History of Humankind*, by Yuval Noah Harari, p.45-46

[23] *Sapiens: A Brief History of Humankind*, by Yuval Noah Harari, p.110

[24] *Fight Club*, by Chuck Palahnuik, p.44-45

[25] Intro to all the Asterix books

[26] *Monty Python's The Meaning of Life* (1983), directed by Terry Jones

[27] *Friends: The One with the Birth Mother* (S10, E9)

Chapter 2

[28] *Legacy*, by James Kerr, p.17

[29] *The Matrix* (1999), directed by the Wachowskis, and *John Wick: Chapter 3 - Parabellum* (2019), directed by Chad Stahelski, either way, Keanu Reeves said it in both

[30] *Liddell and Scott's Greek–English Lexicon*
[31] *Nicomachean Ethics*, by Aristotle, Book 1, Chapter 7 https://classics.mit.edu/Aristotle/nicomachaen.1.i.html
[32] *Meditations*, by Marcus Aurelius, 1.9 (Martin Hammond translation, Penguin Classics)
[33] *The Life of Cato Younger*, by Plutarch, 70.5-6
[34] *Gladiator* (2000), directed by Ridley Scott
[35] *Gladiator* (2000), directed by Ridley Scott
[36] *Meditations*, by Marcus Aurelius, 1.15 (Martin Hammond translation, Penguin Classics)
[37] *Meditations*, by Marcus Aurelius, 1.16 (Martin Hammond translation, Penguin Classics)
[38] *Meditations*, by Marcus Aurelius, 2.10 (Martin Hammond translation, Penguin Classics)
[39] *Meditations*, by Marcus Aurelius, 1.16 (Martin Hammond translation, Penguin Classics)
[40] *Meditations*, by Marcus Aurelius, 1.16 (Martin Hammond translation, Penguin Classics)
[41] *Meditations*, by Marcus Aurelius, 2.17 (Martin Hammond translation, Penguin Classics)
[42] *Gladiator* (2000), directed by Ridley Scott
[43] *Meditations*, by Marcus Aurelius, 3.11 (Martin Hammond translation, Penguin Classics)
[44] *Gladiator* (2000), directed by Ridley Scott
[45] *Meditations*, by Marcus Aurelius, 2.11 (Martin Hammond translation, Penguin Classics)
[46] *De Vita Beata*, by Seneca, VII: https://standardebooks.org/ebooks/seneca/dialogues/aubrey-stewart/text/on-a-happy-life
[47] *De Vita Beata*, by Seneca, VII: https://standardebooks.org/ebooks/seneca/dialogues/aubrey-stewart/text/on-a-happy-life
[48] *Meditations*, by Marcus Aurelius, 3.10 (Martin Hammond translation, Penguin Classics)
[49] *Stoicism and the Art of Happiness*, by Donald Robertson, p.xv

Chapter 3

[50] https://www.sfo.gov.uk/2020/02/28/former-barclays-executives-acquitted-of-conspiracy-to-commit-fraud/
[51] *Phaedrus*, translated by Benjamin Jowett: https://classics.mit.edu/Plato/phaedrus.html
[52] Liddell and Scott's *Greek–English Lexicon*
[53] 'Little by Little', from Oasis's *Heathen Chemistry*, released 2002

Chapter 4

[54] https://bmjopensem.bmj.com/content/bmjosem/4/1/e000459.full.pdf
[55] *Nicomachean Ethics*, Book 1, Chapter 7
[56] https://futureforum.com/wp-content/uploads/2023/02/Future-Forum-Pulse-Report-Winter-2022-2023.pdf

Chapter 5

[57] Jenny Was A Friend Of Mine, by the Killers
[58] Disney's *The Lion King*
[59] *Mind Matters*, By Richard Olley, P.238

Chapter 7

[60] https://www.sciencedirect.com/science/article/abs/pii/S0306453021000470
[61] *Shoe Dog*, by Phil Knight, p.55-56
[62] *The Matrix* (1999), directed by the Wachowskis
[63] *3:59.4: The Quest to Break the 4 Minute Mile*, by John Bryant, p.142
[64] *American Psycho*, by Bret Easton Ellis, p.25

Chapter 8

[65] https://www.rei.com/blog/climb/fun-scale
[66] *The First Four Minutes*, 50th Anniversary edition, by Roger Bannister, p.157
[67] *The First Four Minutes*, 50th Anniversary edition, by Roger Bannister, p.161
[68] *The First Four Minutes*, 50th Anniversary edition, by Roger Bannister, p.161
[69] *The First Four Minutes*, 50th Anniversary edition, by Roger Bannister, p.162
[70] *3:59.4: The Quest to Break the 4 Minute Mile*, by John Bryant, p.103
[71] *3:59.4: The Quest to Break the 4 Minute Mile*, by John Bryant, p.6
[72] *The First Four Minutes*, 50th Anniversary edition, by Roger Bannister, p.167
[73] https://hbr.org/2018/03/what-breaking-the-4-minute-mile-taught-us-about-the-limits-of-conventional-thinking
[74] https://www.history.com/news/the-first-4-minute-mile-60-years-ago
[75] https://www.nuts.org.uk/sub-4/Sub-4%20register%206%20June%202022.pdf
[76] https://www.history.com/news/the-first-4-minute-mile-60-years-ago
[77] *Dracula*, by Bram Stoker, Chapter 10
[78] https://www.bbc.co.uk/tyne/have_your_say/bigg_market.shtml
[79] *The First Four Minutes*, 50th Anniversary edition, by Roger Bannister, p.161
[80] *3:59.4: The Quest to Break the 4 Minute Mile*, by John Bryant, p.3

Chapter 9

[81] *Pirates of the Caribbean: The Curse of the Black Pearl* (2003), directed by Gore Verbinski
[82] https://en.wikipedia.org/wiki/El_Yeso_Dam

[83] *Divine Comedy*, by Dante Alighieri, Inferno, Canto XXIV, line 43
[84] *Divine Comedy*, by Dante Alighieri, Inferno, Canto XXIV, lines 47-48
[85] *Divine Comedy*, by Dante Alighieri, Inferno, Canto XXIV, lines 58-60

Chapter 10

[86] *3:59.4: The Quest to Break the 4 Minute Mile*, by John Bryant, p.93

Chapter 11

[87] *Born to Run: A Hidden Tribe, Superathletes, and the Greatest Race the World Has Never Seen*, by Christopher McDougall, p.220
[88] *Endurance running and the evolution of* Homo (2004), by Dennis M. Bramble & Daniel E. Lieberman: https://scholar.harvard.edu/sites/scholar.harvard.edu/files/dlieberman/files/2004e.pdf
[89] Lieberman, Daniel E., and Dennis M. Bramble. 2007. The Evolution of Marathon Running: Capabilities in Humans. Sports Medicine 37(4-5): 288-290.
[90] *Born to Run: A Hidden Tribe, Superathletes, and the Greatest Race the World Has Never Seen*, by Christopher McDougall, p.220
[91] Sjodin, B., Svedenhag, J. Applied Physiology of Marathon Running. *Sports Medicine* 2, 83–99 (1985). https://doi.org/10.2165/00007256-198502020-00002
[92] *The Big Bang Theory: The Contractual Obligation Implementation* (S6, E18)
[93] *Life at the Extremes: The Science of Survival*, by Frances Ashcroft, p.205
[94] TABATA, IZUMI; NISHIMURA, KOUJI; KOUZAKI, MOTOKI; HIRAI, YUUSUKE; OGITA, FUTOSHI; MIYACHI, MOTOHIKO; YAMAMOTO, KAORU. Effects of moderate-

intensity endurance and high-intensity intermittent training on anaerobic capacity and ˙VO2max. Medicine & Science in Sports & Exercise 28(10):p 1327-1330, October 1996.

[95] The Beach Boys, *I Get Around*

[96] *3:59.4: The Quest to Break the 4 Minute Mile*, by John Bryant, p.4

Chapter 12

[97] https://www.forbes.com/profile/michael-jordan/

[98] *Shoe Dog*, by Phil Knight, p.5

[99] *Shoe Dog*, by Phil Knight, p.308

[100] https://www.theguardian.com/society/2023/aug/15/number-children-mental-health-crisis-record-high-england

[101] *Break Point*, by Ollie Ollerton, p.191

[102] Blanchfield AW, Hardy J, De Morree HM, Staiano W, Marcora SM. Talking yourself out of exhaustion: the effects of self-talk on endurance performance. Med Sci Sports Exerc. 2014;46(5):998-1007. doi: 10.1249/MSS.0000000000000184. PMID: 24121242.

Chapter 13

[103] Good Riddance, by Green Day

[104] *Hamlet*, Act 2, Scene 2

[105] *Pulp Fiction* (1994), directed by Quentin Tarantino

[106] https://www.theguardian.com/technology/2015/aug/16/tinder-app-creating-dating-apocalypse-twitter-storm

Chapter 14

[107] https://www.guinnessworldrecords.com/world-records/first-expedition-to-the-southern-pole-of-inaccessibility-on-foot

[108] https://www.polarconsultants.com/meet-the-explorer

Chapter 15

[109] https://www.telegraph.co.uk/news/2024/05/18/instagram-generation-confuse-normal-stress-anxiety-mental/
[110] *Great Expectations*, by Charles Dickens, Volume 1 Chapter xix
[111] *Shoe Dog*, by Phil Knight, p.61

Chapter 16

[112] *Wayne's World* (1992), directed by Penelope Spheeris
[113] https://www.rouleur.cc/blogs/the-rouleur-journal/the-toughest-climbs-of-the-2023-tour-de-france

Chapter 19

[114] Apology, by Plato, 22d: https://classics.mit.edu/Plato/apology.html
[115] https://doi.org/10.1037/0022-3514.77.6.1121
[116] https://www.sciencedirect.com/science/article/abs/pii/B9780123855220000056?via%3Dihub
[117] 'Cannonball', by Damien Rice

Chapter 20

[118] https://woodenspoon.org.uk/events/arctic-rugby-challenge-2015/
[119] https://www.thetimes.co.uk/article/adam-peaty-ive-been-on-a-self-destructive-spiral-nkt2rxwq5

Chapter 21

[120] *Our Iceberg Is Melting*, by John Kotter, P.4-5
[121] *Our Iceberg Is Melting*, by John Kotter, P.8
[122] *Our Iceberg Is Melting*, by John Kotter, P.113
[123] https://onlinelibrary.wiley.com/doi/10.1111/jasp.12506

Chapter 23

[124] 'Circle of Life', from Disney's *The Lion King*
[125] https://apoc-store.com/products/double-handled-vase-trousers
[126] https://www.worldradiohistory.com/Archive-All-Music/Billboard/70s/1979/Billboard%201979-12-22.pdf

Printed in Great Britain
by Amazon

5713d8e8-1f57-4742-a4c3-d7096bafa610R01